The Jossey-Bass Nonprofit & Public Management Series also includes:

The Five Strategies for Fundraising Success

The Five Strategies for Fundraising Success

A Mission-Based Guide to Achieving Your Goals

Mal Warwick

Jossey-Bass Publishers • San Francisco

Jossey-Bass books and products are available through most bookstores. To contact Jossey-Bass directly, call (888) 378–2537, fax to (800) 605–2665, or visit our website at www.josseybass.com.

Substantial discounts on bulk quantities of Jossey-Bass books are available to corporations, professional associations, and other organizations. For details and discount information, contact the special sales department at Jossey-Bass.

 Manufactured in the United States of America on Lyons Falls Turin Book. This paper is acid-free and 100 percent totally chlorine-free.

Library of Congress Cataloging-in-Publication Data

Warwick, Mal.
  The five strategies for fundraising success: a mission-based guide to achieving your goals/Mal Warwick.—1st ed.
      p. cm.—(The Jossey-Bass nonprofit & public management series)
  Includes bibliographical references and index.
  ISBN 0-7879-4994-9 (alk. paper)
    1. Fund raising.   2. Nonprofit organizations—Finance.   I. Title.
II. Series: Jossey-Bass nonprofit and public management series.
HV41.2.W355   1999
361.7'068'1—dc21

99-40772
CIP

FIRST EDITION
HB Printing   10 9 8 7 6 5 4 3 2 1

Contents

This book is dedicated to the youngest generation, especially Andy, Ben, Dayna, Gwen, Iain, Julie, Kaili, and Matt— in hopes that in their own unique ways they will enrich the future through philanthropy.

Introduction

How the Way You Raise Money
Can Help You Achieve Your Mission

Here's the central message of *The Five Strategies for Fundraising Success:*

> Fundraising can do far more than provide the money to
> achieve your organization's mission. The ways in which
> you raise that money can themselves directly help you
> fulfill your mission.

I've written the next 280 pages or so to explain exactly what I mean by that—and more importantly, to outline how you can put this insight to work for the benefit of your organization. This book will acquaint you with the GIVES System, a comprehensive and easy-to-remember method for analyzing, planning, and evaluating your organization's fundraising strategy.

Who Should Read This Book

If you are involved in the leadership of a nonprofit cause or institution—as an executive, a trustee, or a donor—or if you're engaged in the day-to-day work of resource development in a nonprofit, this book is for you. It is my attempt to make sense of all I have learned about fundraising in two decades as a full-time practitioner in the field. I stubbornly believe that you will benefit from reading this book regardless of the breadth or depth of your fund-raising experience.

If you're a novice, this book will supply a comprehensible and easily remembered framework for all the detailed lessons you've learned from other books, in courses, workshops, or on the job. It will illuminate the range of options open to you. As you will see—if you don't already—the craft of fundraising is surprisingly diverse. There is an almost endless variety of methods, techniques, and specialties in resource development. Through this book I will help you put them into perspective.

If you're an old hand at fundraising, this book will show you a new way to interpret the dynamics of development. If you're one of many who have labored in this field far longer than I have, you may know a lot more about fundraising than I do. But I'm sure that the lessons we've learned about fundraising are, inevitably, different. In all humility, then, I'm hoping that this book will be of use to you, too. The enthusiastic reception these ideas have gotten from beginners and pros alike in workshops and seminars all over the continent for the past five years persuades me that you will find this book helpful. It may be of special value as a new template for evaluating your fundraising operations—a fresh perspective, if you will, or a second opinion.

Above all, in writing this book I have aspired to be of help to the tens of thousands of people who work, often deep in the shadows of the nonprofit world, to make the world a better place for our children. I want to share with you some of what I have learned about fundraising over the years, in hopes of helping you raise more money for your organization.

Trade-Offs and Opportunity Costs

One way to view fundraising's "Big Picture" is in terms of trade-offs and opportunity costs. After spending very little time working in the field, fundraisers learn that it's important to *integrate* an institution's fundraising efforts. Each thing we do to raise money must be viewed in terms of its effect on the organization as a whole and on our other fundraising programs. A development department that is organized (or rather, disorganized) into autonomous little fundraising fiefdoms pursuing their own independent goals will eventually encounter trouble—maybe big trouble.

What's lost if you don't integrate your fundraising operations? Opportunity costs—the gains you would have made if only you'd done things right. For example, cause-related marketing is popular these days in nonprofit circles, and that's no wonder. The lure of unearned income or free advertising is powerful indeed. For some organizations, such benefits may be very good—but maybe they aren't good for others. Perhaps cause-related marketing efforts undermine other, more important elements in the fundraising program. For instance, when we offer credit cards or long-distance telephone service, are we letting donors off the hook too easily? Do these choices provide great benefit to the for-profit partner at the expense of philanthropic contributions and potential upgrades? And what about comarketing programs with corporate partners? By entering into these agreements, are we selling our credibility too cheaply?

Success with fundraising in most organizations is tied to short-term, fiscal-year goals. These goals often require fundraisers to "get the money in the door now" rather than permitting them the time required to cultivate donors for the maximum gifts. In the long run, that can be a very expensive proposition. It's another example of opportunity costs at work—in this case, the difference between what you get and what you might have gotten.

Research and development (R&D) is a hard sell in nonprofit organizations. The most successful businesspeople are constantly telling us how important it is to invest in developing new products or programs and in building the infrastructure to support growing programs—upgrades to the database management system, for example, or research into new fundraising methods. Yet in nonprofits, all too often investment in R&D gives way to the need to increase revenue from year to year. Here come those opportunity costs again: the money an organization won't be raising tomorrow because it isn't acting wisely today.

By understanding the five strategies for successful fundraising, you'll gain a vantage point on your development program that will allow you to see the trade-offs more clearly and make choices that are just right for your organization. The book will help you gain perspective on the efforts you are pursuing to raise money for your organization, on how those efforts interact with one another, and on how they may affect your mission. In a thoughtful, systematic way, you'll take a step back from your day-to-day fundraising operations and reevaluate what you're doing—in the context of your organization's mission and the long-term considerations that guide its strategy.

The five strategies for successful fundraising do not provide a formula for success; they are merely procedures for guiding your thinking. The book contains a list of ingredients, not a recipe; it offers guidelines, not instructions. The not-too-subtle differences will become increasingly apparent as you make your way through these pages. You will see that the GIVES System is a method to help you think clearly about the choices you face in launching and sustaining a fundraising program.

Contents of the Book

The book is organized into four parts. Part One (Chapters One through Six) explains the basic terms and arguments advanced in the book. Its objective is to help you answer the question, What's the right fundraising strategy for my organization? You will become acquainted with each of the five fundamental fundraising strategies—Growth, Involvement, Visibility, Efficiency, and Stability—and with how each can be viewed in terms of your organization's special needs. You will learn which of the five strategies guides your development program at this stage in its history. You will also learn whether your organization is ripe for a change in strategy.

Part Two (Chapters Seven through Nine) will help you develop your own unique fundraising strategy. You will explore a strategic planning process through which you can gain clarity about your organization's vision. Then you will translate that vision into overarching (strategic) goals and match them with an appropriate fundraising strategy. Finally, you'll set achievable objectives to bring your vision, goals, and strategy into the practical, workaday world. At each stage along the way you will be provided with a form you may use as a model to put this rigorous planning process to work for your organization.

Part Three (Chapters Ten through Fourteen) will help you choose from among the many versatile tools in the fundraiser's toolbox that you will use to put into practice the strategic and tactical choices you have made in the course of the strategic planning process. For example, should you launch a direct-mail program or a capital campaign? Do special events make sense for you? Part Three includes a number of self-assessments you can use to determine whether some of the most commonly used fundraising techniques would be useful for your organization at this point in its history.

Part Four (Chapters Fifteen through Seventeen) introduces my ten benchmarks for successful fundraising, a method of evaluation that will cast a bright light on the performance of your development program. Using this unique, systematic approach— developed in the course of a decade of hands-on workshops with nonprofit organizations of all types throughout North America—you will craft a simple set of evaluation criteria uniquely suited to your organization and its mission. With this dynamic, numbers-driven system in place, you will be able to track your progress toward the objectives and goals you have adopted, and make any necessary adjustments along the way.

A resource section follows Part Four. Resource A addresses the pesky question, How much should fundraising cost? which crops up at every turn in designing and evaluating fundraising programs. An understanding of the ins and outs of fundraising costs will be immensely helpful as you examine the fundraising methods your organization has chosen to employ. Resource B discusses the "cost" of fundraising ethics. Resource C is a list of recommended Web sites, e-mail discussion lists, libraries, periodicals, books, and consultants.

In short, *The Five Strategies for Fundraising Success* provides an analytical framework that will help you and your colleagues see your organization in a fresh, new light. It will help you reexamine the assumptions that underlie the development program you have put in place.

If you want to understand better why your organization raises money the way it does, if you want to take a fresh look at your assumptions and consider whether another approach using new techniques might be more advantageous, this book will help you.

Where This Book Comes From

The analysis in this book is the fruit of two decades' work as a fundraising consultant serving hundreds of nonprofit organizations throughout North America—organizations large and small; old and new; national, regional, and local; and in almost every conceivable field of nonprofit endeavor, from health care and education to the arts, the environment, and public policy. During most of these twenty years I have specialized in "direct response" fundraising, chiefly by direct mail, by telephone, and over the Internet. My nine previous books deal primarily with these specific topics. For two reasons, however, I feel confident tackling the broader, strategic issues I address in this book.

First, throughout my career I have sought to gain my footing by understanding the reasons behind the use of any fundraising technique. I've never seen direct mail—or any other fundraising subspecialty—as necessary or justifiable for its own sake. The methods fundraisers use are means to an end. Those ends vary from organization to organization and from time to time. So must our fundraising techniques.

My twenty years as a fundraising consultant are part of a much longer career of involvement in organizational development, chiefly in the nonprofit sector. I have been working with private, voluntary organizations since 1961. I have held executive positions, served on countless boards of directors, and founded and nurtured my share—maybe more than my share—of not-for-profit enterprises. During these nearly four decades in the nonprofit sector I have been intimately involved in every stage of the fundraising process, using almost every commonly employed fundraising technique, from special events to direct solicitation to capital campaigns to planned giving to—you name it. This book represents a distillation of all that practical experience.

The Language of Fundraising

Fundraising is a practical craft, grounded in common sense. In recent decades, however, much of that common sense has been obscured by an ever thicker layer of jargon. We have almost reached a point at which a well-educated, level-headed person understands progressively less about fundraising with every passing year. The accumulation of fundraising jargon is largely the outcome of several trends fostered by intelligent, well-meaning people:

• *Professionalization.* Through the efforts of the National Society of Fund Raising Executives (NSFRE), the Association for Healthcare Philanthropy, and like-minded organizations, fundraising practitioners are becoming increasingly adept at our craft. Training sessions at steadily better-attended conferences and popular certification programs are helping us to codify and standardize the techniques we use—in short, to develop our own formal language.

• *Academic research.* The Center for Philanthropy at Indiana University, the Bernard Baruch School for Nonprofit Management at the City University of New York, The Drucker Foundation for Nonprofit Management, and an increasing number of other institutions around the country are introducing academic rigor and precision into nonprofits' pursuit of resource development. (I favor the practitioners' perspective, but there's no denying the growing influence of the academics.)

- *Specialization.* The growth of the fundraising field and the increasing competition for financial resources among the nation's more than one million tax-exempt, nonprofit organizations have spurred the creation of ever more arcane fundraising subspecialties. (For example, who ever dreamed twenty years ago that hundreds of people would find challenging, remunerative, full-time work as specialists in planned giving for health care institutions?) Once upon a time, a fundraiser was a fundraiser. No more.

These powerful trends hint at but do not fully explain, much less justify, the way in which the field of fundraising has become encrusted by jargon. There is one other widespread and very disturbing reason: the all-too-natural tendency for some practitioners—and authors of books and articles—to hide their imperfect understanding of the craft under a veneer of important-sounding (but highly imprecise) language. The result is that the work we do increasingly takes on a mystical, almost priestly character, ever more distant from the real world.

Jargon obscures muddled thinking in almost every profession. I understand just enough of medical and legal jargon to know that when I hear two doctors or two lawyers speaking together in their private argot, I know I might as well be listening to a conversation in Hindi or Aramaic. However, when my family doctor talks to me about medical questions, he speaks English, clearly. That's one of the reasons he's my doctor.

Over the two decades in which I have worked as a development consultant, I have come to appreciate that one of the greatest services I can provide my clients is to translate fundraising jargon into plain, understandable English. In this book I have striven to explain every point in clear, simple language and to illustrate every argument with abundant examples, most of them drawn from personal experience.

These examples, by the way, will all appear to be hypothetical. Many are. Many others, however, represent real-world nonprofits whose identities I have obscured to protect both the innocent and the guilty (as well as myself). I hope the specificity of the examples will convince you that they're real, regardless of the disguises in which I have clothed them.

I'm profoundly committed to philanthropy. I conduct my life and manage my business accordingly. This book is just one more exertion in an ongoing effort to share the knowledge and insights I have gained over the years, in hopes of advancing the cause of philanthropy.

August 1999   Mal Warwick
                                                         Berkeley, California

Acknowledgments

One name appears on the title page, but a cast of thousands took part in producing the book you hold in your hands. It was adapted from material that previously appeared in a limited run of *The Hands-On Guide to Fundraising Strategy and Evaluation*, which was copublished in 1995 by Aspen Publishers and Strathmoor Press. My collaborators in assembling that guidebook were Stephen Hitchcock, Joan Flanagan, and Robert H. Frank. All three made substantial contributions, and the imprint of their knowledge and insight remains in these pages.

Others whose fundraising expertise contributed to the development of that guidebook include Sandra Adams, Virgil Ecton, Kay Sprinkel Beaumont, Evan Grossman, Kim Klein, Donald Kuhn, Patricia F. Lewis, Jerry W. Mapp, Steven Mourning, Jerold Panas, the late Henry W. Rosso, and Joseph H. White Jr.

I'm also deeply grateful to the following organizations for the assistance they generously furnished in compiling the original manual: American Association of Fund Raising Counsel (AAFRC) Trust for Philanthropy, American Telephone Fundraising Association, Association of Direct Response Fundraising Counsel (ADRFCO), Association of Governing Boards, Association for Healthcare Philanthropy, California Association of Nonprofits, *Chronicle of Philanthropy*, Council for Advancement and Support to Education (CASE), The Development Exchange, The Drucker Foundation for Nonprofit Management, The Foundation Center, *Fund Raising Management,* INDEPENDENT SECTOR, National Center for Nonprofit Boards, National Charities Information Bureau, National Council on Planned Giving, National Federation of Nonprofits, National Society of Fund Raising Executives, Philanthropic Advisory Service of the Council of Better Business Bureaus of America, and The Amherst Wilder Foundation. Additionally, public radio stations KHCC (Kansas), KPFA (Berkeley), KUHF (Houston), KUOW (Seattle), and WXPN (Philadelphia) kindly granted permission to include descriptions of their award-winning fundraising programs.

For their contributions to producing this book, which consists of portions of the material that appeared in *The Hands-On Guide*, greatly revised and expanded, I'm especially indebted to James M. Greenfield, whose painstaking review of the manuscript saved me from embarrassment. (Any remaining gaffes are my responsibility alone.) I would also like to thank several individuals who made contributions above and beyond the call of duty: Joan Flanagan and my colleagues Stephen Hitchcock, Bill Rehm, and John Genette, for the wisdom of their insights into many of the case studies related in these pages; Nick Allen and Lissa Rosenbloom, for their perceptive critiques of the draft manuscript; my assistant Bobbye Dones, for her tireless and unfailingly accurate work converting a rough, annotated typescript into a publishable document; and my perspicacious editor at Jossey-Bass, Dorothy Hearst. Dorothy's clear thinking was crucial. She helped me extract just the right pieces from the hodgepodge of a 450-page workbook and flesh them out into the book you now hold in your hands.

—M.W.

The Author

Thousands of nonprofit organizations have learned from Mal Warwick how to raise more money. Through his many previous books, his newsletter (*Successful Direct Mail & Telephone Fundraising*™), and his popular workshops and lectures throughout North America, Warwick has built a worldwide reputation as an authority in the field.

Clients of his consulting firm, Mal Warwick & Associates (Berkeley, California), and of the telemarketing firm he cofounded, Share Group (Somerville, Massachusetts), collectively number nearly a thousand over two decades. These organizations have raised hundreds of millions of dollars with assistance from Warwick and his colleagues.

Warwick's clients have included many of America's largest and best-loved nonprofits, and hundreds of other nationwide and regional public interest organizations and charities, as well as six Democratic presidential candidates.

Warwick is the author of the best-selling *How to Write Successful Fundraising Letters* (1994) and coauthor of *Fundraising on the Internet* (1996). His first book, *Revolution in the Mailbox*, originally published in 1990 and later reissued under the title *Raising Money by Mail*, is regarded as a standard in the field. It is used as a textbook in both undergraduate and graduate courses.

For ten years Warwick served on the board of directors of the Association of Direct Response Fundraising Counsel (ADRFCO) in Washington, D.C. For two of those years he was its president. He led ADRFCO's efforts to promote its Code of Business Ethics and Practices.

Through the National Society of Fund Raising Executives (NSFRE), Warwick has played a leading role in familiarizing the mainstream fundraising community with direct mail, telemarketing, and on-line communications techniques. On behalf of ADRFCO, he organized and led the first educational track in direct response at NSFRE's 1990 International Conference on Fund Raising. Warwick continues to lead overflowing workshops at these important annual conferences.

Warwick has spoken frequently in many other forums as well, including the Direct Marketing Association Non-Profit Council, the Direct Mail Fundraisers Association, the Canadian Congress on Philanthropy, and Fund Raising Days in Washington, New York, San Francisco, and other cities across America.

A graduate of the University of Michigan and a former Peace Corps volunteer, Warwick has been a resident of Berkeley, California, since 1969. He cofounded the Community Bank of the Bay (Oakland, California) and the Berkeley Community Fund, and he has served as vice president of the Berkeley Symphony Orchestra since 1991. He is also a cofounder and charter board member of the national organization Business for Social Responsibility.

The Five Strategies for Fundraising Success

The Five Strategies
for Fundraising Success
spell **GIVES**

Growth

    Involvement

        Visibility

           Efficiency

                Stability

PART ONE

Understanding the Five Strategies for Fundraising Success

1

Getting Acquainted with the Five Strategies

Why do you do what you do?

The answer seems obvious: you're raising money—as an executive, volunteer, or consultant; as a member of the board or staff—to help achieve what is typically called your organization's "mission." Fundraising provides the means: money. But you know it's not as simple as that:

• You know it's important not only how much money you raise but also when you raise it. A gift pledged for next year's campaign won't help pay this month's rent!

• You know it will make a big difference if you have to raise more money next year than you do this year—and even more the following year. Securing enough support to fill a hole in the budget is one thing. It's something quite different if the organization is growing and so is the hole!

• You know it matters a lot what you're raising the money for. It's not just whether your organization is a hospital, a school, or a human services agency. It's not just what your mission is. Whether your school needs the money to build classrooms, provide scholarships to deserving students, or pay the janitor matters, too.

Wait. You say you know all this—after all, it's obvious, right?—but it's tough to explain it to your staff or trustees (or whoever)?

You say your organization can't be doing a good job of fundraising because you're always short of money?

Well, not so fast! The answer may not be so simple.

The starting point is to make sure you're absolutely clear about your fundraising goals. I don't mean just how much money you want to raise. I also mean when and how and from whom you want to raise that money, and what else you might want to accomplish along the way. There are many different ways to travel the fundraising road, and the route you choose will have enormous impact on your organization's future.

Not convinced? Look at it this way.

Most people seem to think a fundraising program should achieve several different goals simultaneously:

- Bring in enough money to guarantee the organization's financial stability

- Continue its budgetary growth

- Build the community's awareness of the organization's good works

- Attract large numbers of volunteers, patrons, or other active supporters

- Take back as little money as possible to pay for the fundraising program itself

Unfortunately, *your fundraising program cannot achieve all of these goals in equal measure*. There are five distinct strategies lurking in the background of these goals. To a considerable degree, these strategies are mutually exclusive. In the next five chapters of this book I make the case for each strategy, one at a time. Along the way, you'll learn some of the reasons why you may trip over your own feet if you try to accomplish all five at once.

I'm well aware that the words *mutually exclusive* raise hackles in some people. I understand why. Almost all of us would like to be able to achieve all five fundraising goals simultaneously.

In fact, in a mature organization a fundraising program may indeed achieve all five, to some degree. But a strategist in any field (military matters, board games, sports, business, you name it) will tell you that a successful strategy is always clear, focused, and directed.

Setting a strategy requires *making choices*. At any time, some things are more important than others.

I hope it's clear that I'm using the term *strategy* in the classic sense derived from military theory—that is, strategy as distinct from tactics. Big Picture stuff, not the details. Strategy means win the war, don't sweat the battle.

For a nation at war, strategic concerns include such matters as the size, morale, and educational level of its population, the availability of essential natural resources, the support of its allies, and the state of world opinion.

For a profit-making corporation, strategy is concerned with such overarching concerns as market share, competitive positioning, growth in productivity, stability of the workforce, security of patents and trademarks, and profit margin.

A nonprofit organization's strategy depends on its age, reputation, and accomplishments; the breadth and depth of its financial resources; the quality and spirit of its staff; and most of all, its mission. A nonprofit's strategy is also likely to involve such corporate considerations as market share and competitive positioning.

A for-profit company's strategy has little to do with this quarter's profits. For a nonprofit, too, factors such as the results of last month's fundraising mailing or a favorable story in a major newspaper are unlikely to be strategically significant.

Strategy is writ large.

Strategy is the province of generals and admirals, not lieutenants and sergeants and such. The latter—noncommissioned officers and enlisted personnel—are involved in carrying out an army's tactics, not its strategy. Tactics are the activities that flesh out a strategy. That's true not just in the armed forces or in business but in the social sector as well. From the perspective of the board of trustees and the chief executive officer, the behavior of the receptionist at a museum, hospital, or social service agency is obviously a tactical consideration, not strategic. In both cases, the scope of impact is limited. As an executive, a trustee, or a consultant, it's your responsibility to take a bigger view, to understand your organization's strategy.

Some tactics may indeed have broad implications. When a nonprofit enlists thousands of new members or successfully introduces a top-priority program, that's important. Even though they are legitimate concerns of an institution's top leadership, questions such as these are secondary to the core issues. They're tactical matters—*means to an end*.

Yes, tactical achievements may have strategic implications. In fact, tactics are (or should be) pursued precisely because—ultimately—they do affect strategy. But the question is, Which consideration is paramount—the tactic or the strategy? There must be no confusion: strategy takes precedence.

When we boil down the things we fundraisers do and scrutinize what's left, what we find, I believe, is that financial development activities foster five different processes—Growth, Involvement, Visibility, Efficiency, and Stability—each to a varying degree. I call these the five strategies for fundraising success. The next five chapters examine these strategies one at a time. The rest of the book explains how to choose and use them.

Bon appetit! I hope you find this food for thought a very tasty dish.

2

Going for Growth

If your organization is new or is supported by too few donors—or if you've bitten off more than your current base of donors can chew—the question you're most likely asking is, How can we get more donors? You're preoccupied by the idea that's at the heart of growth.

For an organization to achieve growth, as I'm using the term, means that its donor base will broaden. If a Growth Strategy works, you'll have a lot more donors next year than this year—and still more the year after that.

Growth doesn't necessarily mean "raising more money" (that is, more net, spendable money). But in the vast majority of cases, that's what a Growth Strategy is supposed to accomplish, later if not sooner.

For centuries, growth has been a fact of life in North America and Western Europe, and increasingly in the rest of the world as well. Growth, as we most commonly interpret it, is central to the mind-set that drove state socialism during the decades of its heyday. The concept of growth drives today's dominant market economies as well.

Usually growth is equated with progress. "Bigger is better." I question that proposition, but I won't argue the point in these pages. The fact is, for most nonprofit organizations as well as the overwhelming majority of businesses, next year's budget is likely to be bigger than this year's. There are multiple reasons:

- Government services and funding shrink while demand from the public continues to swell. Private human service agencies bear the brunt of that trend. Their need for private funding rises all the while.
- Arts organizations, also experiencing a decline in federal tax-funded support, face ever-rising costs at the same time. They must also expand their audiences to keep pace with population growth, demographic shifts, and changing tastes, which requires even more money.
- In education, health care, and virtually every other field where nonprofits operate today, costs are rising—and so is demand.

Is it any wonder that so many of us are obsessed with growth?

Growth is generally characterized by dynamism and thus holds a special attraction for the Western mind. A Growth Strategy commonly entails ambitious goals and bold leadership. The organization's mission requires broad *impact*. In fundraising, Growth Strategies are frequently associated with large numbers of small donors and a businesslike perspective on the investment and patience needed to recruit them.

Why large numbers of donors? Because the mission requires broad public outreach in order to come to grips with a problem that's bigger than the organization's founders and their handful of supporters can tackle, and because big numbers afford a broad pool of qualified prospects for such lucrative fundraising operations as major gifts, capital campaigns, and planned giving. In turn, acquiring these large numbers of donors typically requires a substantial investment. Donor acquisition is rarely profitable and usually requires sustained effort over several years to achieve meaningful growth in numbers.

More often than not, a fundraising program guided by a Growth Strategy will employ techniques for acquiring donors by direct mail (because that's normally the most cost-effective way for a nonprofit to recruit large numbers of new donors or members). In small communities or in narrowly based constituencies, volunteer outreach may make more sense. In specialized cases, charities may employ other means to reach a broad universe of prospects—TV, for example, or ads in wide-circulation magazines or extensive door-to-door canvassing. These specialized techniques work well for few organizations. These days, direct mail—and increasingly the Internet—are the donor acquisition methods of choice for most nonprofit organizations determined to grow.

Almost any kind of nonprofit can utilize a Growth Strategy. But it's most often seen in organizations working on broadly popular issues. Obvious examples include nationwide environmental organizations, groups addressing highly emotional issues such as abortion or tax reform, and organizations promoting medical research into the leading causes of disability and death.

Often, however, an organization that addresses a much lower-profile issue may employ a Growth Strategy in its early years—to broaden its base from one or a handful of initial donors to a larger number of sources of financial support. To some degree, this is true of almost any nonprofit that's just starting out. Every organization must invest in fundraising, and that investment may take considerable time to pay off. This is, of course, why fundraising costs typically represent a higher proportion of revenue in younger nonprofits than in older ones.

The characteristics of typical Growth Strategies are summed up in Table 2.1.

TABLE 2.1 Signs of a Growth Strategy.

Core attribute	Dynamic
Characteristics	Audacious goals, bold leadership, low entry-level gifts
Representative tactics	Direct-mail acquisition
Typical examples	Environmental groups, animal rights organizations, anything new
Mission requirements	Broad reach, substantial impact

There are many yardsticks by which to measure growth. Among these are revenue, impact, effectiveness, and public recognition. In these pages, however, I refer to growth strictly in terms of the *expansion of the donor base*. A Growth Strategy may lead to growth in other dimensions of an organization's character. Certainly it is typically assumed that *revenue growth* will follow as the donor base grows. An executive or the members of a board of trustees might also reasonably expect that growth in the number of donors will result in greater organizational impact as well. But these assumptions are not necessarily valid. Understanding why this is so is central to mastering the concept of growth and its implications for your organization.

The Pros and Cons of Growth

Let's take a look at three real-world examples of Growth Strategies in practice: one that worked well, one that required midcourse correction, and a third that proved catastrophic.

People for the Environment

Here's one that worked like a charm.

In the early 1980s, a far-sighted board of directors surveyed the landscape of U.S. organizations in the environmental and wildlife fields. It didn't take long for the leadership of People for the Environment (PFE) to conclude that its membership of approximately 65,000 was a small fraction of the number of Americans who might reasonably be expected to support PFE's popular and effective conservation programs, then under way all around the world.

One director, a principal in a major advertising agency, volunteered to conduct an extensive series of focus groups to explore the dimensions of PFE's appeal, at cost. Ultimately, more than one hundred focus groups were conducted in the mid-1980s at the total bargain-basement cost of about $100,000. (Focus groups typically cost $3,000 to $5,000 each.) The insights gained through this intensive marketing research led to the design of a new logo, now widely recognized, and the selection of familiar "signature species" to represent the broad array of endangered species that PFE sought to protect. These concepts were incorporated, in turn, into a series of direct-mail donor acquisition tests, in which hundreds of thousands of letters were mailed nationwide to a broad range of donor, subscriber, and consumer lists.

At length these tests identified the most cost-effective combination of the *offer* (the amounts of money requested and the promises made to those who would send it) and the highest-impact text, graphic design, and package contents. This process led to a so-called control package. With very few changes, this classic direct-mail package was sent in prodigious quantities to every conceivable list of high-potential prospective PFE members in the years that followed.

Fortunately, PFE's Growth Strategy included not only extensive acquisition (or prospecting) activities but also careful attention to the "back-end" operations occasioned by the influx of hundreds of thousands of new members. These operations included donor acknowledgments, membership newsletters, and other frequent communications with supporters, all designed to make new members feel welcome, and to induce them to stick around long enough to become more involved and committed to PFE's mission.

The upshot: by the end of the 1980s, PFE's membership topped one million. Now, that's growth!

Along the way, the group's annual revenue more than quintupled, permitting PFE to increase spending on wildlife conservation programs by more than 300 percent. Expenditures on fundraising mushroomed, of course—especially those on the direct-mail program. But these additional expenditures—the *investment*—clearly paid off handsomely, and in just a few years.

To this day, PFE is one of the nation's largest and best-funded environmental organizations. The base built in the 1980s has sustained PFE in all the years since and has laid the foundation for continuing prosperity in the twenty-first century. For PFE, the strategy of Growth worked.

We Care

By 1994, a special event–oriented fundraising program and a combination of increasing costs and competition in the mail had induced We Care to call a halt to its direct-mail donor acquisition program, the engine of its growth for a number of years previously. An aggressive direct-mail consulting agency hired to resuscitate We Care's prospecting efforts counseled the group to institute a large-scale program. We Care, the agency argued, was one of the country's largest, best-known, and most effective AIDS service organizations. An intensive effort to recruit new supporters would be fruitful.

The new program quickly got under way. In 1995, We Care mailed a total of 1.6 million letters. Response fell a bit short of projections, but the donor base grew nonetheless. The agency proposed to mail three million packages in 1996 and initially We Care staff consented. However, the second year's initial mailings proved even less productive than those in 1995. Once again, We Care called a halt to the program and hired a different agency to assist in maximizing the organization's direct-mail potential.

The new consultants' first conclusion upon analyzing the complex picture they encountered at We Care and upon conducting initial tests was that a Growth Strategy appeared feasible though it needed to be less ambitious. This came as a pleasant surprise because of the widespread (but mistaken) belief among donors that advances in AIDS treatment therapies made the need for services for people with AIDS less urgent. (In fact, up to a point, the need had grown *because* of new therapies, which extended lives and thus increased the demands for assistance.) The program employed by the previous agency had been well conducted. It was simply too ambitious.

In 1997 and 1998, then, We Care mailed about 1.2 million donor acquisition packages per year. The donor base grew by some ten to twelve thousand persons per year— enough to exceed the natural attrition of previous donors who moved without leaving forwarding addresses, died, or drifted away.

To optimize the value of We Care's existing donors as well as that of the new recruits required even greater attention to the agency's relationships with its supporters. Donors, both old and new, were carefully cultivated, educated, culled, and classified—all with a view toward conducting the most productive and cost-effective fundraising donor development program We Care could devise.

We Care continues on this course of moderate growth, progressively increasing the efficiency of its fundraising operations as time goes on.

The International Institute for Justice

Early in the 1980s, this nonprofit organization was founded to lobby against U.S. foreign policies that jeopardized human rights abroad. This mission limited its reach, and thus its donor base, to a small circle of "progressive" foundations and major donors. However, in 1983, when I began work as a consultant to the institute, a new program offered promise of much broader appeal: an effort to mobilize domestic opposition to the Reagan administration's policy of military intervention in Central America. The increasing visibility of this policy, its constantly growing unpopularity, and the charismatic appeal of the man enlisted to head the institute's mobilization effort held out hope that the donor base could be dramatically enlarged.

With the approval of the board of directors, and generous support from a handful of major donors who provided seed money, the institute set out on an ambitious Growth Strategy based on direct mail. For several years, the strategy worked flawlessly. The institute's donor base quickly grew from fewer than two thousand donors to ten thousand, then to twenty thousand, thirty thousand, forty thousand, and more, and revenue grew proportionately. During most of this time, response to the donor acquisition mailings was so enthusiastic that the direct mail program as a whole was generating substantial *net revenue*. (Usually, significant net revenue follows only after several years of growth.)

Then, in 1986, the institute made a fateful decision. Refusing to accept results indicating that in the future direct-mail donor acquisition would no longer be profitable, it plunged ahead with ever-larger donor acquisition mailings. The goal was 100,000 donors. But the institute never got there. It didn't even get close.

Instead, the earlier indications that further growth would not be cost-effective proved all too true. By 1987, the institute was a quarter-million dollars in debt, and its donor base was not appreciably larger. A year later, the base—now stagnant because the institute could no longer secure capital to invest in acquisition—began to show distinct signs of wear and tear. By the end of the decade, there were once again fewer than ten thousand active donors. Most of the donors who had been recruited in the salad days of the mid-1980s had proved to be inconstant. Since the wars in Central America were winding down and the institute had begun addressing other, less clear-cut international human rights issues, many of those who had been enlisted during the crisis turned their attention to other issues as well.

Growth Isn't Always What It's Cracked Up to Be

As you can see, a fundraising strategy designed to encourage growth may be financially inefficient in the short run because of the substantial investment that must be made to acquire new donors. Growth might also undermine the relationships between an organization and its donors by spreading staff too thinly to attend to donors' needs. And if it fails—or if it simply proves to be overly ambitious—a fundraising Growth Strategy might sabotage the organization's long-term financial stability.

Growth, then—seen as meaningful increase in the number of donors—is not necessarily good. It's a strategy that entails significant costs as well as benefits.

Growth is not the right strategy for every organization. It may not even be the right strategy for every organization that aspires to broaden its financial base.

For many an organization, the character of its relationships with its donors or members is far more important than sheer numbers. The extent to which individual supporters become involved in the work of the organization may be just as meaningful, perhaps even more so. Let's turn, then, to the second of the five strategies: Involvement.

3

Enhancing Involvement

Surveys and focus groups repeatedly demonstrate that many of the people who send money to support nonprofit organizations aren't conscious of being donors to these groups. Frequently a large proportion of the donors or members to a nonprofit can't remember the group's name. Sometimes they don't even recognize the name when they see it.

Involvement is the fundraising strategy that wise organizations may adopt to cure that malady and narrow the distance between cause and supporter. Involvement means building stronger relationships with your donors.

Unfortunately, most nonprofits *discourage* donor involvement, consciously or not. After all, what executive director or board of trustees wants the United Way or the local community foundation to meddle with their independence? What trustee in her right mind prefers gifts with strings attached?

In the real world, however, the strings are usually present, even if in a subtle form. Every donor—whether an individual or an institution—has some expectations about the use to which donated money will be put. These expectations set up a relationship between the giver and the recipient of every philanthropic gift.

Accountability

One current buzzword describing the two-way relationship between donor and donee is *accountability*. It's no accident that this word is coming to seem a cliché through overuse. Research consistently shows that nowadays donors truly demand accountability. They want more financial information. They want a clear statement of the organization's purpose. They want to know what it has accomplished.

To me, accountability is merely one aspect of involvement. Today's donors aren't inclined to give and forget. They want to know how their gifts are used. They want some measure of control over those uses. Unlike their parents, today's emerging donors don't see themselves as passive participants. As donors, they often feel entitled to an active role.

Many nonprofit executives and trustees resist these demands (though usually in a passive way, encouraging donors to believe that they really retain more influence than they do). There are legitimate reasons for nonprofits' reticence to accept donor direction. After all, an organization's *mission*—not the whims or prejudices of its donors or volunteers—must guide its activities. However, some organizations carry their resistance to donor direction much too far, treating donors' expectations cavalierly—and occasionally even using funds for purposes for which they were never intended.

The picture is complicated, as it is in any field of human endeavor. When it comes to accountability, some nonprofits are good, others are bad, and most lie somewhere in between. However, the trend is clear. In mounting numbers, donors are demanding accountability.

Most organizations raise far more money when their supporters are active and committed, so there are inherent advantages in promoting donor involvement:

• The most standoffish private foundation almost always appreciates an occasional gesture of accountability: an annual report, for example, or a face-to-face meeting with key staff, or perhaps just a letter spelling out the impact of a project it supported. Most individual donors, regardless of how modest their gifts are, think that something's gone awry unless they receive periodic updates on the progress of an organization they have supported.

• Over time, individual donors are likely to become progressively more generous if they are kept steadily informed and offered opportunities to learn firsthand about the organization's work. Open houses, periodic donor briefings, and such can provide the means, or at least convey the impression that the opportunities are there for the taking, if donors wish.

• In a benefit event for a large organization, large numbers of volunteers may raise money effectively and have lots of fun in the process. The goodwill this experience creates can bring multiple benefits.

The most dramatic and most common form of involvement are volunteer opportunities. Study after study shows that volunteers give at three times the rate of nonvolunteers. They give more often and more generously.

Question: Which comes first, the volunteer involvement or the generous donations?

Answer: What difference does it make? The relationship works both ways. Volunteers may also be good donor prospects.

In fact, some nonprofits have trouble raising any money at all unless their donors are involved. Take, for instance, a lobbying organization that seeks to change legislation on overseas trade policy. The lobby is likely to see the response from its donors shoot sharply upward once they're offered the chance to play an effective personal role in the lobbying effort—even if they don't all take advantage of that chance. Why? Because people who can be induced to contribute money to a lobbying group are people who care about the issues the lobby addresses. They may also be engaged, even professionally, in work that relates to those issues.

A fundraising strategy built around donor involvement may help an organization increase the number of its donors, gain greater visibility, build a volunteer base, and even, over the long haul, help ensure its financial stability. More importantly, an Involvement Strategy may strengthen the organization's pursuit of its mission—because the mission requires more than just staff work. Others must participate, too. But chances are that *the extra cost attached to donor involvement efforts will limit the program's short-term financial efficiency, and the greater demands placed on donors could even limit the organization's growth in numbers.* An unencumbered relationship may be more attractive to many donors.

The attribute most commonly associated with an Involvement Strategy is that donors *get a lot out of giving.* In that way, you could think of this strategy as *democratic,* with a small *d.* Whether volunteer work, voting for members of the board of directors, helping set institutional priorities through membership surveys, or signing a postcard to the president of the United States, there's some form of *participation* in any fundraising program geared to involvement.

Participation takes many forms. Involved members or donors are ordinarily active, not passive. The organization's mission requires that large numbers of people participate—as activists, patrons, or volunteers.

In addition to volunteer programs, techniques frequently employed in pursuing an Involvement Strategy include special events such as meetings, briefings, or tours; membership development programs; telephone fundraising efforts that entail direct, personal contact with donors; and frequent communications with members or donors through such devices as newsletters, fax alerts, or e-mail bulletins. Involvement devices may be as varied as the imagination will permit.

Some of the most obvious examples of Involvement Strategies occur at museums, performing arts organizations, and grassroots lobbying groups. These are all organizations that virtually require donors to participate.

The characteristics of typical Involvement Strategies are portrayed in Table 3.1, and Sidebar 3.1 (on pages 22 and 23) illustrates one organization's successful Involvement Strategy.

Donor Involvement and Its Rewards

An Involvement Strategy might grow from a variety of contrasting needs and entail a wide range of techniques. Here are three real-life examples.

People Against Rip-Offs

In the mid-1980s, People Against Rip-Offs (PAR), a consumer protection group, was almost exclusively dependent upon direct mail (a worrisome state under any circumstances). The emphasis in PAR's direct-mail packages at that point was on emotionally charged, snappily written, and methodically oversimplified presentations of complex consumer issues. No matter what the issue, however, the point tended to be, "The corporations are ripping you off."

With skillful application, this flamboyant approach had succeeded in attracting a sizable number of donors. Unfortunately, however, the donors were renewing their support in only modest numbers. Follow-up letters brought only limited response—and

TABLE 3.1 Signs of an Involvement Strategy.

Core attribute	Rewarding
Characteristics	Volunteer programs, grassroots lobbying
Representative tactics	Direct-mail membership, telephone fundraising, donor newsletters, welcome packages
Typical examples	Museums, performing arts organizations, public policy groups
Mission requirements	Public participation

there was, of course, a limit to the degree of hysteria any honest, sensible person could introduce into a fundraising letter. Something more than colorful and emotional language was needed to motivate donors to continue their support for PAR.

Something else was lacking, too. Although PAR depended on its direct-mail donors to underwrite a very large share of its operating budget, there was virtually no other connection between the donor base and the organization's work. Here was a lobbying group whose purpose was to bring popular pressure to bear on government and corporations—and the group's biggest asset, a base of more than 25,000 donors, was lying fallow!

Here, then, was a classic opportunity for an Involvement Strategy—a redirection of PAR's fundraising program to involve its donors in the day-to-day work of supporting the organization's mission. In practice, this required a number of new elements in the fundraising program. These included the following:

• *Use of "involvement devices" in donor acquisition.* Successive tests over several years ultimately led to the development of a consumer satisfaction survey, which proved to be the most cost-effective vehicle for recruiting new donors and for introducing them to the active, hands-on role that donors could play in PAR's work.

• *Membership development.* To strengthen the relationship that donors had with the organization and its board of directors, PAR introduced a structured annual membership program. This formalized the link between the individual and the organization with a membership card, a regularly scheduled newsletter, and an annual series of membership notices to maximize the rate at which members renewed. In other words, all these techniques tended to increase donors' involvement in PAR.

• *Continuing use of involvement devices in member communications.* Both PAR's newsletter and its frequent fundraising appeals afforded new opportunities for PAR members to make their views felt, not just to increase their financial support. These involvement devices prominently included petitions and postcards to decision makers addressing the most pressing issues of the day.

In the decade that followed the introduction of these new fundraising techniques, PAR's membership grew substantially to more than forty thousand. More importantly, however, revenue rose by an even greater proportion—and PAR's lobbyists gained the advantage of tens of thousands of cards, letters, postcards, and petitions from the membership. PAR members became more loyal and more generous because they were involved—squarely confronting PAR's mission.

Body & Spirit

The continuing success of Body & Spirit, a faith-based nationwide organization that advocates on behalf of poor and hungry people, rests

---

SIDEBAR 3.1   INVOLVEMENT: NOT YOUR ORDINARY CUP OF TEA

Radio Kansas–KHCC-FM (Hutchison, Kansas) received a national award for the innovative direct-mail campaign described here. This is a simple, hands-on example of donor involvement, as explained by the station's development staff. Radio Kansas did more than gain the donor's attention with this involvement device. The station also gave her something to do with her hands.

We wanted to put the theme "Radio Kansas is important to you" into a pleasant package, while at the same time encouraging people to give. "Radio Kansas Is Your Cup of Tea" was born out of this urge.

We thought if there was something special tucked into the envelope it would encourage more giving—so we approached tea companies about providing tea.

R.C. Bigelow and Stash Tea provided tea bags to go into nine thousand mail pieces. We asked for foil-wrapped packets, thinking they would hold up much better to the rigors of the mail service. Volunteers worked to get them organized, labeled, and out the door. We used information provided by National Public Radio (NPR) about the correlation between NPR news listeners and hot tea drinkers in our approach to the companies.

Promotion director Patsy Terrell came up with the concept, approached the tea companies, and designed the piece. It was intended on the participation of its members. Increasing the number of members seemed necessary, not just desirable, if the group were to make any headway in unsympathetic times. However, after six years of intensive and largely frustrating efforts to double its membership, Body & Spirit chose a new course in 1992 under a dynamic new chief executive.

Growth in numbers was still possible, but at a heavy price. Ever larger acquisition mailings sent out to less responsive lists were necessary to support membership growth, and relatively few of the new members recruited in this fashion showed a willingness to be active citizen advocates for poor and hungry people. While the number of members in the organization was growing slightly, the impact of its work was not increasing, and net revenue was climbing far too

---

to work with existing membership cards and return envelopes. Membership director Teresa Short drew the artwork for the envelope and saw it off to the printer. We're fortunate to have the talent and cooperation in-house to do projects like this.

We had the printer print a credit line on two thousand of the packages for Stash Tea, and on the other seven thousand packages for Bigelow. (Anyone considering doing this should be aware that individual packets of tea do not all weigh the same—different flavors weigh different amounts—a big potential problem for bulk mail. Fortunately, we discovered it in time.)

Compared to the mail piece that went out the previous year at the same place in the fundraising cycle, this package boosted revenue by 126 percent—and increased the number of people giving by 97 percent.

Of course, donor involvement goes much further than gimmicks like this. Volunteer service is the ultimate donor involvement. But such devices as questionnaires, postcards to decision makers, and yes, indirectly, even teabags can help signal an organization's interest in the opinions and efforts of its donors. If nothing else, Radio Kansas made clear that it wasn't just taking its donors for granted by mailing them the same old appeal time after time. Involving donors means firming up your relationships with them.

---

slowly because of the rising cost of acquiring new donors from increasingly marginal sources.

Instead of continuing to emphasize growth, the new president decided that he would seek to increase *net income*. Involvement would be the vehicle for this revenue growth.

The new Involvement Strategy entailed several new initiatives, including the following:

• The president himself, along with several members of the development department, some of them newly hired, would undertake intensive new efforts to contact and establish closer relationships with major donors. The president would personally meet regularly with and seek advice from key donors. Through these more intimate contacts, staff could seek larger gifts from existing donors because the donors would learn more about Body & Spirit's work and have more direct opportunities to participate.

• A set of high-dollar annual giving societies (at $1,000, $2,500, $5,000, and $10,000), each with its own distinctive name and benefits, would open up new roles for donors to play in the affairs of Body & Spirit. These giving clubs would also, not incidentally, increase the organization's revenue from its existing donor base.

The strategy worked. In the course of a decade—a period during which antihunger and antipoverty agencies often experienced great difficulties raising funds—Body & Spirit's revenue doubled, from $2.5 million to $5.5 million, while the number of members remained virtually constant.

Central City YMCA

The Central City YMCA had labored for years over a capital campaign to refurbish and expand its downtown facility. The campaign was well along the road to exceeding its $3 million goal long before reaching the "public phase," during which members of the community at large were to be invited to contribute smaller gifts to put the campaign over the top. Those gifts no longer seemed essential. The

Y could easily secure the remaining funds in some other way, with less effort and less expense.

Wisely, however, the Y's leadership chose to proceed with a direct-mail-based public campaign. Why? To involve the community!

There were several ways in which the Y would benefit from an active, high-profile fundraising campaign despite the lack of urgency to raise additional funds:

• The Y's primary revenue-generating activity was its health and fitness facilities. An aggressive direct-mail campaign would raise awareness in the community about the attractive new amenities of the renovated and expanded building—awareness that would, in short order, bear fruit in the form of additional memberships.

• As a private social service agency—the largest in Central City, in fact—the Y required high visibility. Support from members of the community helped underwrite many of its services to the disadvantaged. In all likelihood, some, perhaps even many, of those recruited as donors to the capital campaign would be much more inclined to respond favorably to appeals for support of the Y's charitable activities.

Ironically, the direct-mail campaign, though budgeted as a break-even proposition, netted a modest amount of money while attracting a significant number of new donors to the Y. In any event, the extra funds were put to very good use!

This effort at the Central City Y helps illuminate a subtle difference between two of the five strategies: Involvement and Visibility. In this case, the Y's objective was not just to raise community awareness of its new facility but also to establish relationships with large numbers of community members. As donors to the capital campaign, they became involved in the Y in a hands-on fashion, thus increasing the likelihood that they would play an even more active role as participating members who took advantage of (and paid for) the use of the health and fitness center.

The next chapter looks closely at Visibility Strategies, in which raising public awareness may be a sufficient end in itself.

4

Increasing Visibility

Museums, symphony orchestras, and other performing arts groups gain more than money by hosting large and splashy fundraising events. They also receive attention from the public and broaden their donor base. They attract patrons as well as contributors. Similarly, advocacy and lobbying groups may enlist thousands of citizens in efforts to sway votes in a state or provincial legislature, the U.S. Congress, or Parliament; or a special event may put the spotlight on a human service agency that depends on funding from local government.

All of these examples illustrate what I mean by visibility.

Just about any nonprofit that receives a significant share of its funds from the United Way is in a stronger position the better known it is, especially in these days when "donor choice" is taking hold in workplace campaigns. Increasingly, donors are choosing individual charities to support through their workplace gifts. If they've never heard of your organization, will they pick you?

Often a high public profile isn't just desirable, it's necessary. But there are exceptions, and there are both appropriate and inappropriate ways for a nonprofit organization to gain public attention. For example, an aggressive, door-to-door canvassing effort is probably not a good idea for a civil liberties organization dedicated to prisoners' rights. Such a controversial issue is unlikely to generate much support. And a university's long-range stability isn't likely to be enhanced by a raging media controversy stoked by disagreement among its faculty. Nor is that university in a position to attract large numbers of new donors from its alumni—not this year, anyway.

Visibility, then, isn't always good. But most of us think it is. After all, we're children of a society in which each of us is promised fifteen minutes of fame.

What's Visibility Good For?

There's no mistaking what a Visibility Strategy is all about. The object is often merely to gain name recognition—to make an organization a household word (even if within just a single community). *Visibility is about becoming familiar to the people who matter most.*

Organizations devoted to a Visibility Strategy are involved in issues that lots of people care about. The public feels they have a big stake in these organizations' success or failure. These organizations tend to be, or to become, name-brand charities. Public opinion is crucial. Brand identification is a central preoccupation of the organizations' leadership.

Competition with mature, well-established charities is uppermost among the considerations that lead many nonprofits to elect a Visibility Strategy. The public is already familiar with the Red Cross, the Salvation Army, and the American Cancer Society. A more recently established charity that seeks to highlight some less familiar issue or activity may have to go to great lengths to claim what advertisers sometimes refer to as "share of mind." (Don't we all have quite enough things on our minds already?) Because even the most capacious of our brains has limited capacity, and because the instinct to resist change is deep-seated and widespread, it's often difficult for a new idea, a new issue, or a new organization to become established in the public consciousness. This is doubly true if that new organization seeks to enter the same turf as a revered charity that is widely known to address the same issue.

Visibility, then, is more often a strategic consideration when a nonprofit organization is young. In fact, the opportunity to pursue other strategies, such as Growth or Involvement, may depend in the first instance on familiarizing the public with the organization's unique qualities.

Organizations seeking visibility tend to use electronic media and big, splashy public events. They're also most likely to seek (or be sought after for) cause-related marketing programs. A corporation with a large advertising and marketing budget may well find that it can multiply the impact of its expenditures by associating the company or one of its products with a popular nonprofit cause—or even by investing enough to help that cause gain the visibility it needs to grab public attention. Similarly, a nonprofit organization that springs into existence to address an important emerging issue may well discover that the news media are eager to highlight its work because the issue is of obvious concern to the public at large—and there's no better publicity than the free kind.

The typical attributes and techniques of organizations pursuing Visibility Strategies are summed up in Table 4.1, and Sidebar 4.1 provides an example of one organization's successful Visibility Strategy.

Think, for example, of Mothers Against Drunk Driving (MADD), or the American Foundation for AIDS Research (AMFAR) (at least in its early years), or the March of Dimes back in its heyday, when polio was America's public enemy number one. In all these

TABLE 4.1 Signs of a Visibility Strategy.

Core attribute	Familiar
Characteristics	Broad public interest, public opinion is key, many stakeholders, brand identification
Representative tactics	TV/radio, special events, cause-related marketing, publications
Typical examples	Medical research organizations, emergency relief charities
Mission requirements	Broad public awareness and understanding, name recognition, action

SIDEBAR 4.1 VISIBILITY: RAISING THE FLAG PAYS OFF

Public radio station KUHF-FM (Houston, Texas) learned, from pleasant experience, that raising its visibility in the community can bring big dividends—in other words, that fundraising involves more than just hauling in money. The station's outstanding overall development program was recognized at a national Public Radio Development Conference. The story follows. It's a great example of the virtues of a Visibility Strategy.

KUHF's programming hasn't seen any major changes in quite some time, but the Arbitron numbers keep rising. Why? We feel it's due in large part to KUHF's increased visibility in the Houston community.

KUHF is the media sponsor for several events each month. At least once a month KUHF hosts a free movie screening at a local theater. Employees staff booths at area festivals, such as downtown's huge International Festival. At each event we hand out KUHF buttons, magnets, and window decals, and network with the community.

Two years ago, crowds wore blank looks at the call letters KUHF. Now they cheer! We brought Garrison Keillor to Houston in June. At the Keillor Phone-a-Thon ticket sale, KUHF members overloaded the Southwestern Bell trunk lines demanding tickets! Both newspapers gave us wonderful coverage for this event.

For our six-week children's series, "Classical Kids," KUHF worked with area schools. We developed special stickers, giveaways, and weekly on-air questions. We received hundreds of responses to these questions. KUHF also aired a public service announcement on commercial television stations for this series.

Two years ago, KUHF had reached a plateau. It is now seventeenth in the Houston radio market, out of forty-plus stations.

Source: Copyright © 1995 by KUHF-FM, Houston, Tex. Reprinted with permission.

cases, a nonprofit organization set out to make the public aware of a dramatic new issue. Usually, the initial effort involved high-profile celebrities: Elizabeth Taylor for AMFAR, President Franklin D. Roosevelt for the March of Dimes, and even Candy Lightner, who attained virtual celebrity status, for MADD. Each of these organizations seeks to advance a momentous cause: eliminating death and injury from drunk driving, funding medical research on AIDS, and when polio was still a threat, finding a cure for it. Each contributes to its cause in substantive ways. But the first, key step along the way was to make its issue visible.

Two Dimensions of Visibility

Let's look briefly at two more modest and more recent examples that reflect my personal experience.

Community Hospital Foundation

The Community Hospital Foundation, a large community hospital system and nonprofit organization headquartered in a medium-sized city, encompassed a hodgepodge of hospitals and clinics that had been cobbled together in a rapid-fire series of mergers. The component units, located in nearby towns and suburban communities in several adjacent counties as well as in the central city, had banded together to compete more effectively with a for-profit system managed by one of the nation's most aggressive marketing-minded hospital-management companies. Though the Community Hospital itself was well known both locally and in health care circles, the residents of the region were often unaware of the recent mergers through which the Community Hospital had absorbed more than a dozen other local health care facilities. Many of these facilities were well-established within their local communities under their original names. The Community Hospital was almost universally regarded as serving "the city."

The challenge for the Community Hospital's management was obvious: in marketing terms, to reposition the Community Hospital as a regional health care *system* serving nearly a million people throughout a broad area, and to establish brand-name recognition for the system throughout the area. The fledgling Community Hospital Foundation faced an even more daunting task: to communicate the same metamessage to potential donors and at the same time to make the case for giving.

In short order, it became apparent that the foundation rarely had the chance to communicate with prospects in any substantive way. Prospective donors were preoccupied by the larger question: What does the Community Hospital have to do with us? Obviously this didn't create a climate conducive to giving. It was no surprise, then, that the Community Hospital Foundation was raising only a fraction of the revenue that could reasonably be expected from such a large and prosperous region.

Here was a clear-cut case for a Visibility Strategy. Public awareness had to precede any fundraising efforts. In turn, then, the foundation's fundraising efforts needed to contribute substantially to the hospital's broader marketing and public relations program—to establish visibility—and a base of donors loyal to the merged institution needed to be built from scratch.

Techniques employed by the Community Hospital Foundation included dinners headlined by world-famous entertainers, celebrity-studded athletic events, cooperative marketing efforts with a local professional sports franchise and the region's largest business, and for a time, an extensive direct-mail donor acquisition program targeting the more affluent and more mail-responsive residents of the region. In each case, the foundation piggybacked its publicity efforts on those of the hospital, reflecting the same look and feel, the same symbols and slogans as those in the hospital's extensive billboard, TV, newspaper, and magazine advertisements. Together these activities attracted large numbers of prospective donors—"qualified prospects" familiar to some degree with the hospital—and thus the raw material of a donor base for the newly expanded foundation. Few of these fundraising activities yielded profits commensurate with the investment of time and money that went into them. They weren't expected to. But collectively, over a period of several years, these highly visible efforts paved the way for more cost-effective fundraising efforts.

Excelsior State University–Central City

Like the Community Hospital Foundation, Excelsior State University–Central City, a large urban campus of a far-flung Midwestern state university, faced a special challenge in seeking to raise more money from its alumni. Traditionally, the Central City campus had served commuters, who often attended classes in the evening. Many of them were older than the typical university student. Frequently they were enrolled part-time. There was little school spirit, either on campus or among alumni, and communications with alumni had been spotty and usually drab. Sporadic alumni fundraising efforts had typically yielded slim margins.

However, a few years ago, Central City's fortunes changed abruptly. In an extensive building program financed by the state, the campus was dramatically expanded. New classroom and laboratory buildings were erected, new professional schools and academic departments were added, and dormitories were built for full-time students, many of whom were from out of state.

But there was still little school spirit. The commuter-campus mind-set held sway.

Under these circumstances, how could the staff of the Central City campus's Annual Fund hope to raise substantial amounts of money? The campus's older alumni rarely identified closely with the school. Truth to tell, many alumni harbored less than fond memories of their time at Central City, and the younger alumni, who were leaving with more generous feelings about their experience, were for the most part too young to contribute significant sums. Clearly the Annual Fund was unlikely to be a lucrative proposition.

The answer to this challenge was a Visibility Strategy. Resources available to the Annual Fund were turned to the tasks of "branding" the campus in a favorable light and building school spirit. A new look and powerful, evocative new themes dominated communications with alumni, parents, and students—not just in the new alumni magazine and in letters and bulletins addressed to students and parents by campus administrators, but also in every fundraising appeal or special-event invitation from the development department, the alumni office, and the Annual Fund. The Annual Fund also launched an intensive effort to recruit undergraduate seniors with modest, initial gifts.

At the outset, this Visibility Strategy did not lead to increased net revenue for the Annual Fund. Chances are the Central City Annual Fund will not grow substantially for several years (unless some individual alumnus unexpectedly bestows a major gift). Clearly, however, if the Annual Fund staff resists the temptation to waver from its strategy and persists for a few more years, the fruits of the investment will come in time.

As a Visibility Strategy pays off, with fundraising efforts becoming more cost-effective over time, a point is eventually reached when a change of strategy is in order. In many circumstances, the institution's leadership will be greatly attracted to a strategy based on efficiency. That's the subject of Chapter Five.

5

Fine-Tuning for Efficiency

Are you raising money at the lowest possible cost per dollar raised?

That's the question most people have in mind when they talk about a "good" fundraising program. The cost per dollar raised is the most common and most important measure of fundraising efficiency.

Efficiency means raising money by spending as little as possible in the process. It's that simple—and that complicated.

Nonprofits that pursue an Efficiency Strategy typically seek, above all, to come across to the public as trustworthy. Ethics have special meaning to an organization following this strategy, if only because efficiency requires that money be raised with the least possible muss and fuss. Controversy and efficiency don't mix well. Efficiency-driven organizations are cost-conscious, sometimes obsessively so. They literally can't afford trouble.

Of course, the most efficient way to raise money is to secure just a handful of very large gifts. These *major gifts* are sought through planned giving, institutional fundraising (from foundations, corporations, and government agencies), and monthly sustainer programs involving small donors or members.

Table 5.1 lists some of the emblematic attributes of and fundraising methods employed by organizations seeking efficiency as their overarching goal, and Sidebar 5.1 (on page 36) provides an example of one organization's successful Efficiency Strategy.

TABLE 5.1 Signs of an Efficiency Strategy.

Core attribute	Resourceful
Characteristics	Cost-conscious, well-established
Representative tactics	Planned giving, major gifts, foundations, corporations, monthly giving, workplace giving, government grants
Typical examples	Social service agencies, hospitals
Mission requirements	Frugal management

Efficiency, Like It or Not

Some organizations have little choice but to pursue an Efficiency Strategy. Public pressure—from government regulators, self-appointed charitable watchdog agencies, or the public at large—may force an Efficiency Strategy on such organizations, like it or not.

However, it is sometimes not wise to raise funds at very low cost, and it is frequently not possible to do so. Spending little money on fundraising will probably mean you have to depend on the same old tried-and-true fundraising methods and programs, even when the old ways aren't working so well anymore.

Be careful: achieving the most favorable fundraising ratio (cost per dollar raised) may not be the most profitable course to pursue. Take, for example, a long-time client of mine, a large nationwide environmental organization. Let's call the group EarthPeople. Simple arithmetic analysis indicated that it was both inefficient and improvident for EarthPeople to include all of its many members in every special appeal mailing, regardless of how recently, frequently, or generously they had given. It was inefficient because the cost per dollar raised was higher for those members who had contributed the fewest, smallest, and least recent gifts. It was improvident because research showed that "overmailing" undermined membership loyalty *over the long run*, reducing the rate at which members renewed. Still, overmailing was more profitable because it enabled Earth-People to raise more net revenue *in the short run*. Unfortunately,

SIDEBAR 5.1 EFFICIENCY: MAKING THE MOST OF
              A GOOD THING

*Public radio station KUOW-FM (Seattle, Washington) received plaudits
from its peers at other public radio stations for its efforts to boost membership
support. KUOW's experience—described here in its own words—is a case
history in the successful pursuit of an Efficiency Strategy.*

Direct Mail
KUOW's direct-mail program has become more consistent and refined
over the past year. We went from sending three similar-looking renewal
notices per renewal month and sporadic lapsed mailings to four distinct
renewal notices per renewal month followed by two lapsed-donor mailings. By personalizing the upgrade request, our average gift through
direct mail increased from $58 in 1993 to $63 in 1994. [Note: A rising
average gift obviously reflects increased efficiency.]

   We have also increased the average gift by promoting our Day
Sponsorship program and adding $250 and $500 membership levels.
Day Sponsors are at the $180 level. For that amount, a contributor
receives four on-air messages on the day of his or her choice to cele-
brate a birthday or anniversary. [Note: The use of higher-dollar membership levels increases efficiency, too, because it raises donors'
average gifts.]

Major Donors
Once a potential major donor is flagged, our cultivation begins. This
year we implemented two successful evenings called "Behind the
Scenes at KUOW." We invited current donors of $180 or more, poten-
tial large donors, and other influential friends of KUOW to attend a
tour, meet station staff and board, and schmooze over wine and cheese.
These evenings were well received by the attendees. Several told our
general manager they would happily increase their contributions.

   We are also cultivating large donors by noting their interest and
inviting them to cosponsored events that they may find of interest.
This year we also began listing donors of $250 or more in our news-
letter that prompted many lower-level donors to move up to the
$250 level.

that was the course doggedly pursued by EarthPeople. (See Sidebar 5.2 [on pages 38 and 39] for a dramatization of these circumstances.)

On the other hand, maximizing your fundraising efficiency could make it impossible for your organization to gain public visibility or to grow, and it could easily threaten your long-term financial stability. Popular convictions notwithstanding, efficiency isn't the be-all and end-all of fundraising!

To a great degree, you cannot control the efficiency of your fundraising program. Efficiency is a function of the size of an organization and its donor base, the popularity of its cause or timeliness of its issue, the length of time it has been in existence, the extent of its public name-recognition, and other factors. But there are many things you can do to raise money either more or less efficiently, and choosing among them calls for judgment.

Efficiency for Results, Not for Its Own Sake

Some of the considerations involved in making these often-difficult choices come to light in the following two examples—one in which an Efficiency Strategy was clearly indicated and proved successful, and another (typical of a great many others) in which a slavish devotion to efficiency sabotaged an otherwise promising fundraising strategy that pursued a different goal.

Young Entrepreneurs

Fundraising for Young Entrepreneurs' nearly two hundred chapters was conducted largely at ground level, by the chapters themselves. The organization's national development staff was convinced that costs could be cut and net income raised if the organization made two deceptively small but clearly strategic changes:

• For years, Young Entrepreneurs had invested heavily in mailing and phoning the alumni of its experience-based business training programs. This effort proved to be only marginally productive—and was therefore eliminated.

SIDEBAR 5.2 TRADE-OFFS AND OPPORTUNITY COSTS FOR EARTHPEOPLE

This chart depicts a stylized and simplified but typical *segmentation model*, a direct-mail donor solicitation conducted by EarthPeople, an aggressive nonprofit organization. In practice, the three segments, or categories, of donors would be broken down much more finely, classified by the recency, frequency, and dollar amount of the donors' previous gifts (and probably by other criteria as well). In the following table, the second column from the right portrays the cost per dollar raised (C/$) for each of the three segments. The rightmost column shows that cost ratio as a cumulative figure; there the number corresponds to the C/$ if one, two, or all three segments are included in the appeal. The obvious conclusion: C/$ is lowest and efficiency is highest if the appeal is mailed more selectively. By contrast, total profit (net revenue, or net) is highest when all three segments are included, but efficiency is lower.

Segment	Quantity	Revenue	Cost	Net	C/$	Cum C/$
Top Donors	5,000	$100,000	$5,000	$95,000	$0.05	$0.05
Average Donors	60,000	180,000	60,000	120,000	0.33	0.23
Inactive Donors	35,000	50,000	35,000	15,000	0.70	.30
Total	100,000	$330,000	$100,000	$230,000	$0.30	$0.30

Now carry the logic of this example one step further. Assume, for example, that investing an extra $5,000 in the process of soliciting EarthPeople's top donors will yield an additional $5 per donor, or $25,000. In that case, the net revenue from that donor segment increases by $20,000—from $95,000 to $115,000. At the same time, this additional investment will raise the fundraising cost from $0.05 to $0.08, thus significantly reducing efficiency (for that particular segment alone). But it becomes easy to make the case that the additional $5,000 spent on the top donors was far better spent than the $35,000 spent on the inactive donors. Play with the numbers a little and the trade-offs will become crystal clear.

As you'll see, Efficiency is not the strategy for raising the most money—even the most net income.

Economists and business analysts talk about *marginal costs* and *marginal gains* when they confront such situations: the added $5,000 invested in the top donors brings substantially greater net revenue than would an equal sum invested in the inactive donors. This is the logic that escaped the staff of People for the Environment (see Chapter Two).

By extension, it will quickly become clear that up to a point a marginal (additional) investment in your best donors will very likely boost your net revenue significantly more than an equal investment in your more marginal donors. This underlines the importance of segmenting your donor file.

I don't mean to suggest that you should lavish warmth and affection on big donors and cold-shoulder those who give less. Every person must be treated with equal respect! Everyone deserves a gracious acknowledgment. That's not only the right thing to do—it's also common sense. A $20 gift may someday be a $20 million bequest. However, it's almost always appropriate to invest more time and money in building relationships with generous donors than with those whose support is marginal. For example, you might make a practice of arranging for the executive director to call every donor who sends you a gift of $500 or more (or $100, or $10,000, depending on the scale of your operation). You might also use first-class postage on all correspondence with big donors and favor third-class postage with most others, or you might confer special benefits on those who contribute larger sums.

• To supplement the chapters' fundraising efforts, national development staff had devoted considerable time to making personal contact with almost all of Young Entrepreneurs' many corporate donors. This program, too, was using more resources than could be justified by the returns. Instead, under a new Efficiency Strategy, staff concentrated their time and efforts on making personal contacts and establishing close relationships with only the top corporate donors (those who contributed $50,000 or more per year). Instead of personal calls to the other donors, Young Entrepreneurs used direct mail, a much less costly method of contact, yet a little less effective.

As a result of these changes, Young Entrepreneurs' fundraising costs dropped dramatically in just three years, and its net revenue rose sharply. Here a strategy based on efficiency quickly bore fruit. As long as this strategy does not cause the membership rolls to shrink, it will serve the organization well for a long time to come.

Law for the People

My experience with Law for the People, a pseudonymous legal-assistance organization, represents what has happened to me in dozens of other cases.

Over many years, this small nationwide organization had built an admirable reputation for effectiveness in defending the rights of minority citizens. Throughout this time, Law for the People had survived—sometimes just barely—because of generous foundation grants and an occasional large court award. There were few individual donors. Law for the People had made only sporadic attempts to recruit individuals. That became my job—to design and launch a direct-mail donor acquisition program that would enlist tens of thousands of individual supporters who might, over time, become generous donors.

The project started well. An initial test mailing performed better than expected, revealing that Law for the People had a powerful and effective message to deliver to its admittedly limited constituency. Surprisingly, revenue from the test mailing nearly matched its costs (which are usually amortized over a longer period that includes many subsequent mailings). It was clear that the donor acquisition package my colleagues and I had developed was likely to perform well if mailed in larger quantities to many of the lists we tested. Securing tens of thousands of individual donors seemed feasible. We were, of course, eager to proceed.

The bucks stopped there, however—all the bucks.

Members of the board of directors—perhaps not adequately consulted by staff before the test mailing was launched—objected (understandably) that the project had not made money. It was grossly inefficient, in other words. Not so understandably, however, the board members could not be persuaded that efficiency was the wrong yardstick to use in evaluating a donor acquisition program.

"Why," they complained, "even if this program continues as projected for three or four years, we'll still be making only forty or fifty cents on the dollar from direct mail. We'll do much better if we invest in other kinds of fundraising, such as getting big gifts."

Here was efficiency run amok. The directors were right, of course, that major donor fundraising would be much more efficient than a start-up direct-mail donor acquisition program. But from whom did they plan to raise those big gifts? Law for the People had only a handful of individual donors, almost none of whom were financially able to contribute large sums. Major contributions can sometimes be obtained cold from outsiders, but that's a hit-and-miss process and inefficient in its own right. There would never be a sufficient number of qualified prospects for major gifts unless Law for the People built and cultivated a sizable base of individual donors. This reality clearly indicated the need for a sizable investment (and considerable patience) to conduct, and sustain, a donor acquisition program, which in turn meant growth.

Some day—if Law for the People pursues a methodical course of development—an Efficiency Strategy might make eminently good sense. However, when the board of directors pulled the plug on the Growth Strategy that its staff had elected to test, that day was far off—and the chances are strong that if the organization's leadership persists in this strategic misconception, that day will never come. Law for the People will then remain forever a small, underfunded organization.

As you can see, then, selecting a strategy must take into account the life cycle of a development program or the age of the organization, or both. The experience of Law for the People clearly illustrates that principle.

Willpower and arbitrary goal setting alone are no substitute for a careful analysis of a nonprofit's strategic choices. Nor is a single strategy likely to remain appropriate for all time for any given organization. Many organizations that for years have pursued Efficiency Strategies have learned that lesson—sometimes at great cost. Often, even in a long-lived and mature organization, a strategy centered on stability may be the wisest course, despite the fact that pursuing stability may (at least temporarily) reduce the organization's fundraising efficiency. Chapter Six looks at some of these trade-offs.

6

Ensuring Stability

Board members, bankers, accountants, and others consigned by fate to be professional worrywarts are often most concerned about the long-term stability of a nonprofit's finances. Well, they should be! Proper stewardship of donors' gifts—and of the taxes forgone by nonprofit organizations—cry out for a long-term perspective on an organization's prospects. Few nonprofits fulfill their missions within a finite period. For nearly all nonprofits, financial stability—the ability of an organization to foresee how its bills will be paid next year, in five years, in a decade, or a century from now—is a legitimate and often urgent concern.

How you raise money has a lot to do with your organization's stability. For example:

- Can you reasonably expect to continue receiving as much income in future years if you stick with the same fundraising methods and programs you have in place now? For instance, if you're flush with grants from the United Way or the Rockefeller Foundation this year, can you expect the same level of support next year, and the year after that? If not, where will the money come from?

- Is your fundraising program diversified so that you're not overly dependent on one or very few sources of funds?

- Even if your program is adequately diversified, are you paying enough attention to the differing needs and desires of the donors who support each of your fundraising programs to ensure that their support will continue?

So, here's where we really get down to business.

An organization devoted to stability must seek to convey an image of permanence, of solidity. A stable organization is one that endures.

Normally, organizations that employ a Stability Strategy seem, or try to seem, as though they've always been around—and always will be. Their missions are rooted in unchanging values. Their programs respond to unending needs. They require, and typically attain, a broad financial base.

The most characteristic fundraising technique of a nonprofit guided by the principle of stability is to build an endowment fund that generates investment income. A Stability Strategy may also entail broadly diversified development efforts so that all of the organization's eggs aren't in that one proverbial basket.

More often than not, colleges, universities, and private preparatory schools pursue stability. So do residential care facilities such as nursing homes.

Inevitably, *it costs money to achieve stability*, at least in the short run. That cost may be well worth paying. For some organizations, stability must be the overriding goal—at any near-term cost to the efficiency or visibility of your fundraising program.

Table 6.1 summarizes the typical attributes and techniques of organizations employing Stability Strategies, and Sidebars 6.1 (on page 46) and 6.2 (on pages 48 and 49) provide examples of two organizations' successful Stability Strategies.

Two Roads to Stability

To gain perspective on the costs and consequences of stability, let's review recent experiences by two dissimilar nonprofit organizations.

Save the Trees

Save the Trees, a scrappy little environmental advocacy organization, was dedicated to saving the unique, unearthly beauty of a remote redwood forest from the ever-growing demand for lumber. With a fundraising campaign conducted by direct mail and little else, Save the Trees waged its fight in the news media and the state legislature for years. Lo and behold, in significant part because of the group's ceaseless efforts, there came a time when the metropolitan newspaper serving the entire region headlined, "The trees are saved!"

Unfortunately, this was not true. An agreement had been reached in the legislature to refer the issue to the Commission on the Environment, an agency known to be sympathetic to environmental causes. The commission was charged with negotiating with the land development and forest products companies that dominated the area, and with developing a twenty-year restoration plan. This agreement did not guarantee that the trees would be saved.

The newspaper was so widely read in the region, however, that the public soon came to believe that, yes, indeed, the trees had been saved. Obviously this did not bode well for Save the Trees' fundraising program. In fact, response to the organization's occasional special appeals plunged soon after the editorial appeared.

Clearly a strategic reassessment was in order. A new strategy was crafted around the theme "It's not over." Save the Trees' programmatic emphasis shifted from an action-oriented, short-term perspective to a twenty-year restoration plan that would at length,

TABLE 6.1 Signs of a Stability Strategy.

Core attribute	Enduring
Characteristics	Unchanging values, unending needs, broad financial base
Representative tactics	Endowment, planned giving, diversified fundraising, electronic funds transfer
Typical examples	Universities and colleges, residential care facilities
Mission requirements	Sound finances, cash reserves, long-term perspective

SIDEBAR 6.1   STABILITY: LITTLE CHANGES MAY HAVE BIG IMPACT

The challenge for public radio station WXPN (Philadelphia, Pennsylvania) was to adjust to changing public attitudes and market conditions, which had undermined the effectiveness of the station's traditional fundraising efforts. WXPN was lauded at a Public Radio Development Conference for its successful pursuit of stability. Here are excerpts from the WXPN story.

Philadelphia radio has become much more competitive. To meet the challenge, WXPN made a number of adjustments over the last few years designed to increase listener loyalty. Because long on-air membership drives tend to have a negative effect—by encouraging listeners to try other stations—we decided that our primary objective for 1994 would be to shorten significantly the time we spent on air in membership drives, while maintaining overall levels of listener support.

Among the key steps we took were improvements in our direct-mail and telemarketing efforts:

• With professional advice, we revised our direct-mail materials and stepped up our mailing schedule. Expiring members now receive four notices, beginning two months before expiration. At the end of this cycle, two months after expiration, we refer nonresponding donors to telemarketing. These changes doubled our direct-mail response in a single year.

• We evaluated several different telemarketing firms and solicitation styles. We found that energetically offering premiums improved pledge results and dramatically improved the fulfillment rate. We also revised our office procedures to reduce our response time to pledges. These changes generated a 247 percent increase in telemarketing revenue in a single year.

The proof of our success lies in the numbers: we cut on-air fund drives by 40 percent—with no loss of revenue. In fact, member support rose 9 percent!

Source: Copyright © 1995 by WXPN Radio, Philadelphia, Pa.
Reprinted with permission.

it was hoped, ensure the permanence of this natural treasure. At the same time, the group's approach to fundraising was transformed as well.

With a twenty-year plan on the books, the future of Save the Trees (and of the forest itself) rested in the staying power—the stability—of the group's finances. For years Save the Trees had funded its efforts on the basis of a decidedly unstable direct-mail program—unstable because it was prey to unfavorable headline news (such as actually happened) and because resource development was not diversified. Virtually all the organization's operating funds came from direct mail—a precarious situation for nearly any organization. Under its new Stability Strategy, Save the Trees set out to change this picture in dramatic ways:

• Plans were laid for a capital campaign to capitalize some of the group's operating expenses (by erecting a new headquarters building) and to launch an endowment fund that would further reduce the need for day-to-day fundraising.

• New development staff set out—with early success—to secure grants from foundations and government agencies. These institutional gifts came to represent nearly 40 percent of Save the Trees' budget within three years, reducing direct mail's share to just over half.

• The direct-mail program itself, driven largely by revenue from episodic special-appeal mailings, was broadened with the introduction of a monthly sustainer program. This effort required some up-front investment in marketing but soon paid off when hundreds of Save the Trees donors began converting to the monthly plan. (Once monthly sustainers are recruited, the cost of raising a dollar from them is remarkably low—often only two or three cents on the dollar.)

The organization's quest for a sound, diversified fundraising program continues. A radical transformation such as this may require significant capital—to construct a building and hire new development staff—and years to effectuate. The end product, however, is stability.

Meals for the Hungry

For years, Meals for the Hungry had operated under another, more bureaucratic-sounding name, raising money through special events and recruiting volunteers to deliver free hot meals to people stricken with grave illness and to staff other human service programs. Meals for the Hungry proved to be the most popular of the several projects, so in a strategic repositioning of the agency, the board adopted that name for the organization as a whole.

But the name change was only one cosmetic aspect of Meals for

---

SIDEBAR 6.2   STABILITY: ELECTRONIC FUNDS TRANSFER

The development staff of public radio station KPFA-FM (Berkeley, California), affiliated with the Pacifica Radio network, describes its early experience with electronic funds transfer (EFT). This pilot program was recognized for innovation by the station's peers in public radio.

This is a good example of a nonprofit's success in pursuing the goal of financial stability. The station's EFT initiative diversified its funding base and assured a steady, predictable source of revenue that defrays many unglamorous, hard-to-finance, fixed expenses.

In spring 1992, KPFA initiated a pilot EFT program. In fiscal year 1993, we raised $141,984.85 from EFT. By the close of fiscal year 1994, KPFA received $173,058 from EFT.

EFT is a system by which KPFA withdraws donations directly from a subscriber's checking or savings account. The subscriber's bank information is sent to our EFT processing company. They in turn withdraw a set amount on a monthly basis from that subscriber's account. Donations continue until we are notified by the subscriber to revoke authorization. Each month the EFT management firm sends us a disk full of subscriber donation data that we are able to import directly into each subscriber's account in our database management system.

This fundraising technique offers an easy and affordable way for subscribers to make larger donations or any donations at all and receive higher-ticket premiums, a sustaining support option that enables long-term subscriptions at minimal cost, and an automatic source of renewals.

Each year, KPFA conducts three on-air marathons, offering listeners the Hungry's realignment. Much more significantly, staff launched an intensive effort to convert the group's almost exclusively event-driven donors into direct-mail contributors, and to recruit additional supporters by mail. A precarious strategy wholly dependent on occasional events would clearly gain stability if direct mail could be used to renew existing donors—more easily and reliably than at events and more inexpensively—and if the donor base could be expanded. This broader base would in turn enable Meals for the Hungry to undertake a major gifts program, planned giving, and other more efficient fundraising efforts.

---

payment through credit cards and EFT. During marathon plugs, EFT is explained. Everyone who makes a non-credit-card pledge will receive a brochure and may choose to pay off their pledge in that manner, at a minimum of $5 per month. In addition, renewal bills and occasional mailings include EFT brochures.

The pledger returns the brochure to us via our service center or general mail. We ask for a completed brochure, an initial payment (to cover the first month until the EFT plan kicks in), and a voided check that the EFT company will use for bank data. We create an installment plan, post the first payments to it, and start the program guide subscription. We enter or change the donor's member type in our database. We process and approve any premiums covered by the pledge. We bundle EFT pledges and forward them to the EFT agency.

Withdrawals from then on will be automatic. Three months before their anniversary due date, EFT subscribers are offered the opportunity to cancel. If they do not respond, EFT is continued, uninterrupted, for another year.

By the close of fiscal year 1994, 2,300 listeners had paid their pledges through EFT for total revenue of $173,058. The average annual giving of EFT subscribers is $27 to $76 higher than that of regular subscribers. The fulfillment rate for EFT subscribers is 95 percent—versus 65 percent for regular subscribers.

Additional support for KPFA comes from direct mail, telemarketing, foundations, major gifts, and planned giving solicitation. Total revenue for fiscal year 1994 was $2.5 million.

Source: Copyright © 1995 by KPFA-FM, Berkeley, Calif. Reprinted with permission.

The strategy worked. In just a few years, revenue rose sharply and the number of donors more than doubled. Meals for the Hungry was well on its way to stability.

What Does Growth Have to Do With Stability?

In the case of Meals for the Hungry, a new Stability Strategy entailed significant *growth* in the donor base as well as diversification. For Save the Trees, the Stability Strategy produced substantially greater *efficiency*.

What gives? How can two strategic concepts be merged in a single fundraising program? When is a strategy not a strategy? That's the question taken up in Chapter Seven.

PART TWO

Choosing Your Fundraising Strategy

7

Sorting Through the Contradictions and Subtleties of the Five Strategies

By now you have completed the first lap of your journey toward a sound, productive fundraising strategy for your organization. In Part One you became acquainted in broad terms with each of the five distinctive fundraising strategies (see Sidebar 7.1 [on page 54] for an overview). But you're not quite ready yet to choose an ideal strategy. In Part Two, which includes this and the following two chapters, you'll come to grips with the subtleties and apparent contradictions of the five strategies, and you'll learn a little about some of the common obstacles to implementing them. By the end of Part Two you'll be ready to pick the strategy that's right for your organization.

This chapter talks about three crucial topics: understanding how two organizations' Involvement (or Growth or Efficiency) Strategies may be very different from each other, the importance of sticking to a strategy despite setbacks, and when to move on to a new strategy.

Strategy Reflects Circumstances and Aspirations

Clearly, each of the five strategies encompasses a wide range of circumstances and fundraising options. In fact, this analysis—this five-strategy typology, if you will—could hardly work if that were not the case, given the enormous differences between any one nonprofit

SIDEBAR 7.1 OVERVIEW OF THE FIVE STRATEGIES

What GIVES?

The easy way to remember the five strategies is with the nifty little mnemonic device GIVES: Growth, Involvement, Visibility, Efficiency, Stability.

The characteristics of the five strategies are summed up in the following table. Please note that the attributes and examples cited illustrate only the broad-brush characteristics of the strategies. It would be a serious error to assume that every organization of a given type named in the table should pursue the corresponding strategy. Each organization is unique and every organization's fundraising needs change over time. Also, much better examples may be available—perhaps even your own organization!

Strategy	**G** Growth	**I** Involvement	**V** Visibility	**E** Efficiency	**S** Stability
Core attribute	Dynamic	Rewarding	Familiar	Resourceful	Enduring
Characteristics	Audacious goals, bold leadership, low entry-level gift	Volunteer programs, grassroots lobbying	Broad public interest, public opinion is key, many stakeholders, brand identification	Cost-conscious, well-established	Unchanging values, unending needs, broad financial base
Representative tactics	Direct mail acquisition	Direct mail membership, telephone fundraising, donor newsletters, welcome packages	TV/radio, special events, cause-related marketing, publications	Planned giving, major gifts, foundations, corporations, monthly giving, workplace giving, government grants	Endowment, diversified fundraising, EFT
Typical examples	Environmental groups animal rights organizations, anything new	Museums, performing arts organizations, public policy groups	Medical research organizations, emergency-relief charities	Social service agencies, hospitals	Universities and colleges, residential care facilities
Mission requirements	Broad reach, substantial impact	Public participation	Broad public awareness and understanding, name recognition, action	Frugal management	Sound finances, cash reserves, long-term perspective

organization and almost any other. Consider, for example, the two stories I related in the preceding chapter:

- In the case of Meals for the Hungry, a new Stability Strategy entailed significant *growth* in the donor base as well as diversification in the fundraising methods and programs employed.

- For Save the Trees, a Stability Strategy produced substantially greater *efficiency*, introducing new initiatives that were more cost-effective than the organization's traditional direct-mail fundraising efforts.

Here, two very different nonprofit organizations, with missions nearly poles apart, both sought stability, but in very different ways.

Similarly, the examples of Efficiency Strategies in Chapter Five hinted at institutional stories that contrasted sharply with one another:

- Young Entrepreneurs elected an Efficiency Strategy that they accomplished in large part through the development staff's deeper *involvement* with donors. Intensified, personal attention to the organization's biggest donors proved to be the key to attaining the efficiency that was the hallmark of the organization's strategy.

- By contrast, Law for the People, in spurning a Growth Strategy to follow the banner of efficiency, neglected to consider that efficiency was not really feasible for them at that stage in their development. While Young Entrepreneurs' Efficiency Strategy truly reflected the organization's unique circumstances, that was not the case for Law for the People. There the Board of Directors misread the signals that reality was sending. Law for the People's single-minded emphasis on efficiency was an obsession rather than a well-considered strategy.

The cases noted in Chapter Four, depicting two versions of Visibility Strategies, illustrated two equally dissimilar approaches:

- For the Community Hospital Foundation, *growth* was a secondary goal—and a result—of a Visibility Strategy. Splashy special events and direct mail primarily designed to heighten the hospital's visibility also built a base of qualified fundraising prospects. There's no question which came first: visibility was a *prerequisite* for growth.

• At Excelsior State University–Central City, the secondary consideration was *involvement*. Here, too, visibility was a necessary precondition before involvement became feasible. Central City had its eyes on the future, understanding that its current students and recent alumni were the best long-term prospects for fundraising success, and that the campus's future prosperity lay in building solid relationships with those young people by involving them heavily at the earliest possible time. But the first step in approaching those young people was to heighten their awareness, and that was best accomplished by involving them more deeply in the university's affairs.

In Chapter Three I cited three examples of Involvement Strategies. Each illustrated a distinctive set of strategic considerations:

• For People Against Rip-Offs (PAR), the consumers' group, the path through the forest of involvement led in a straight line toward increased *stability*. That course was not necessarily more efficient. Nor did it lead to growth or heighten PAR's visibility. The diversification of the fundraising program and the strengthening of relationships between PAR and its donors simply helped ensure the organization's future by *stabilizing* its base. Involvement was the primary instrument used in this process. Stabilization came later.

• In electing an Involvement Strategy, Body & Spirit sought over time to increase the *efficiency* of its fundraising operations. Involvement came first and for a long time was paramount. Greater efficiencies resulted from the accumulated impact of Involvement Strategy activities. Had Body & Spirit reversed the process—basing its current fundraising efforts on efficiency in the short run—the extra time and effort invested in the Involvement Strategy would have been seen as inefficient. Thus, in the long run the fundraising program would in fact have been much *less efficient* than it ultimately came to be.

• The Central City YMCA's Involvement Strategy entailed *growth* as well. The Y chose direct mail as the centerpiece of the public phase of its capital campaign. Targeted in large part at the community in general and not just at the Y's previous donors, direct mail yielded a significant number of new donors. The overriding consideration, however, was to involve the community in the completion of the new facility. The Y's long-term best interest lay in pursuing an Involvement Strategy abetted by growth in the donor base.

The three Growth Strategies cited in Chapter Two portray an equally broad variety:

• People for the Environment's (PFE) dramatic years-long growth trajectory was accompanied by intensive efforts to *involve* new members, offering them a wide range of options for more meaningful participation in PFE's work. (These options included, for example, a monthly sustainer program and a high-dollar annual giving society.) The overriding consideration was membership growth, but the key to sustaining that growth—by maximizing renewal rates—was to involve new members as quickly and as deeply as possible.

• At We Care, modest, continuing growth was a primary means to achieve increased *efficiency* in the fundraising program. Once enlisted as donors, We Care's supporters became prospects for more generous gifts and were treated to a series of donor-upgrade activities, including special direct-mail appeals, telemarketing, and in appropriate selected cases, direct solicitation. Efficiency was both a major consideration and a result of the process—but growth was the mechanism that made it possible.

• The International Institute for Justice was a case of growth run amok. Too little consideration was paid to the costs and consequences of growth. The organization's efforts to maximize support from both new and old donors were limited by the cash-flow strictures imposed by an expanding and increasingly less productive direct-mail donor acquisition program. The institute might have elected *involvement* as a secondary emphasis, as PFE did; or it could have based its back-end operations on *efficiency*, like We Care did. It did neither. There wasn't enough time or money to do so.

For the most part, the examples I've cited involve large-scale nonprofits. The communications techniques they employed might be out of the reach of many small and local nonprofit organizations. In many such circumstances, however, volunteers can do the heavy lifting that a better-heeled organization might relegate to subordinate staff, a fundraising counsel, an event planner, or a direct-mail or telemarketing agency. Significant volunteer participation in fundraising may make all the difference (and not only at small nonprofits). Here are just a few of the many examples that come to mind:

• Using volunteers to raise money by phone is often ineffective, but a volunteer thank-a-thon to acknowledge donors' gifts may be an ideal way to encourage donor goodwill, and a volunteer phone tree to invite or confirm attendance at a fundraising event may be just the ticket!

• Every development director knows that his or her job will be a lot easier if all members of the board give annual gifts (even if those gifts are small). Board members can multiply their effectiveness in fundraising by supplying names and details of prospective donors, and ideally by making face-to-face contact with them, either alone or in the company of another board member or a development staffer.

• A planned giving program is likely to be much better received if members of the board or other volunteers have themselves made commitments for legacy gifts.

• Active volunteer participation in planning and staging special events may slash costs and increase revenue. For a small or local organization, there's no more effective way to promote an event than through word-of-mouth.

With such a broad array of choices available within any given strategy, what gives meaning to each of the five? How can we know whether We Care's strategy was really built on growth rather than efficiency? What leads me to state that PFE's strategic emphasis was on growth, not involvement? In both cases, elements of each of these strategies were present. In other words, which end is up?

Now the plot thickens. Hold onto your seat!

Sticking to Your Strategy

To realize its full potential, every nonprofit organization must concentrate its resource development activities on one of the five strategies at any given point in its history.

If you skipped the preceding sentence, please read it now, slowly.

Effective fundraising requires setting a strategy that's exactly right for your organization, then doggedly following that strategy month after month or year after year, using the optimal mix of techniques and approaches best calculated to help your organization get where it wants to go.

Put another way, you pay a price—often a high price—for setting priorities and sticking to them. You will have to give up attractive opportunities or ignore interesting options. (Yes, every strategy entails opportunity costs.) But making those sacrifices is the only way you'll get where you want to go as quickly as you need to.

For example, if your organization is now overly dependent on one or two sources of financial support, you'll probably devise a strategy in which stability is a central consideration. If virtually all your money now comes from foundation grants, for instance, you might well decide to launch a major gifts program, a direct-mail campaign, or a corporate giving initiative—or all three.

In the first year or two—maybe even for several years—none of these new efforts is likely to pay off in a big way. At first they could all lose money. You may even lose some foundation funding because your attention has been focused elsewhere. Naturally, your overall fundraising ratio (your cost per dollar raised) will go up. The ratio may even stay up for a long time to come. But that's okay. In a strategy based on stability—on the need to ensure an organization's *long-term* survival—any measure of short-term fundraising efficiency is secondary.

Remember, strategic thinking requires that you single out *one overarching goal*: "Win the war," for example (better yet, "Win the peace") or "Conquer cancer."

But there also comes a time when you may need to shift your primary strategy. Even a strategy that has worked well for thirty years may suddenly prove impractical as circumstances change.

Changing Strategies Over Time

A large, unexpected bequest, a dramatic breakthrough in research, or any number of gradual changes—such as the aging of the donor base or changing public perceptions about the issue you address— might rearrange the fundraising landscape for your organization. Here's where insightful leadership becomes essential.

Failure to adjust your organization's activities to dramatically changed circumstances can be harmful to its financial health. Don't get caught in this potentially fatal bind if conditions cry out for a fresh approach. *Evaluate your fundraising program at least once every three years!* Indeed, many organizational development specialists recommend that you reevaluate your organization's strategic plan every three to five years.

Evolution and change are the natural order of things. Like any organic entity, a nonprofit organization will experience a sequence of phases in its historical development, and the circumstances that prevail in each phase will likely call for unique responses from the development department. Consider, for example, the course of events that dictated changes in fundraising strategy for some of the organizations already cited:

• At PFE, growth was clearly indicated for a period of six or seven years. Had that Growth Strategy been launched earlier, before PFE had established a visible nationwide presence and built a meaningful base of support, it might have foundered. Similarly, had PFE sought to continue pursuing growth beyond the point of saturation revealed by real-world results, the organization would have been equally ill served. At each of these stages, a strategic change was called for. PFE's leadership had the wisdom and the flexibility to adjust to these changing conditions.

• Similarly, Body & Spirit was continually frustrated during several years of attempts late in the 1980s to achieve dramatic growth in its membership. A new Involvement Strategy was clearly the right direction for the organization to go at that stage in its history. At some point, stability—or efficiency—may well become the overarching concern. But conditions are sure to change in some fashion.

• The need for visibility was unmistakable at the Community Hospital Foundation. Circumstances—chiefly the merger and shifting public attitudes toward health care institutions—dictated that course at that particular time in the hospital's development. After a time, however—perhaps a short time, given the huge investment in visibility—the hospital will achieve an adequate measure of public awareness. Then the foundation's strategy will need to change again. Either stability or efficiency may become the touchstone of its fundraising activities.

• For Young Entrepreneurs, efficiency was both necessary and possible. In the preceding years, however, an Efficiency Strategy might well not have been attainable or even desirable. A time may well come, too, when a single-minded emphasis on efficiency will appear counterproductive. For example, new organizational priorities, a restructuring of the relationship between Young Entrepreneurs' chapters and the national office, or new opportunities brought about by a striking upsurge in interest in business among young people might occasion the need for a fundraising strategy based on growth. Or over time the strictures imposed by an Efficiency Strategy might prove too confining. A somewhat less efficient strategy centered on stability may be indicated.

• One day the earth shifted underneath Save the Trees and a long-time Growth Strategy became obsolete virtually overnight. The organization's own success, and the overexuberant reporting of a major newspaper, made it virtually impossible to continue on the same course. Resourceful and thoughtful leadership saved the day by shifting the emphasis of the group's fundraising activities from growth to stability. Perhaps at some point in the not-too-distant future, Save the Trees will have ensured its stability and can shift to a more efficient fundraising program. Time will tell.

These examples demonstrate the virtues of strategic change. Refusal to change in the face of new circumstances poses serious risks. But it's just as important to steer clear of the inverse problem: avoid making changes too often, or for the wrong reasons. Donors as well as volunteers may become confused, disenchanted, or just plain pooped (as they do after any major campaign). Boredom is not a sufficient justification to shift your organization's fundraising strategy. Make sure that any new strategy reflects reality, not wishful thinking!

For instance, let's assume that a nonprofit symphony orchestra has set a strategic goal along the following lines: *to construct a magnificent new hall that will establish the orchestra as the city's premier performing arts group and spark new interest in traditional music throughout the region.* A moment's thought makes clear to the orchestra's leadership that a new hall, magnificent or not, will never be built without an ambitious capital campaign—and this orchestra doesn't have a big enough donor base to support a capital campaign. True enough, one or two megagifts might supply most of the needed funds, but that appears highly unlikely. And the community will have to be involved—and feel involved—in building the new hall if the facility is to be looked upon as an arts magnet for the entire region.

So the orchestra's goal requires a Growth Strategy for a long enough period to build an ample donor base.

The board, the executive director, and the trustees of the foundations that support the organization may all want the orchestra to keep its fundraising costs consistently low. But the need to recruit thousands of new donors—with all the costs that entails—rules out efficiency as a guiding principle *at that stage* in the orchestra's development.

The orchestra's strategy must be driven by growth, above all. Under the circumstances, there's no way around that.

But the world being the way it is—complex and diverse—there's room to question that single-minded focus on growth. A lot of room.

Interestingly, there is a rough correlation between the GIVES hierarchy of fundraising strategies and the traditional "ladder of involvement" or "pyramid of giving." Just as an individual donor climbs up the ladder or scales the pyramid, a not-for-profit may cycle through a sequence of organization-building experiences: building a donor base through growth increases opportunities for involvement and at length improves visibility, too—all of which in turn lends greater efficiency to the organization's fundraising program and ultimately stabilizes its performance. It's a bit of a stretch but it works, after a fashion.

Now it's time to get to the bottom of this confusion. The following chapter explores how real-world conditions require any fundraising strategy to be designed to suit the unique circumstances and needs of a particular organization. It shows what other dimensions a real-world strategy entails.

8

Adapting the Strategies to Work in the Real World

In reality, as we have learned, it's unusual for an organization's fundraising efforts to be driven *exclusively* by a single strategic concept. In other words, our practical choices will be much more complex than the simple strategic analysis outlined in Chapters Two through Six. We've already seen that the organizations used as illustrations in those chapters employed similar strategies that in many ways were very different from one another. We've seen, too, that over time strategy may change.

So, fundraising in the real world is a lot more complicated than any mere theory. (What else is new?)

A mixture of elements and motives dominates any real-world strategic planning process—if only because fundraising strategy is driven by donors' needs and characteristics, which may vary widely, and because human beings, with all our fallibilities, are inevitably in charge of the process. People don't always agree with one another. In fact, agreement may be rarer than disagreement, when you get down to cases. And it's all too easy to get tangled up in the conflicting circumstances of reality and the contrasting views of different people involved in the planning process. Unfortunately, the result is frequently a muddle—no strategy at all. Decision makers often choose to avoid the tough choices involved. In truth, a great many nonprofits—maybe most—muddle along throughout their lives, making do through pluck or luck. By shying away from a rigorous strategic planning process, they may pay a very big price. That process is fundamentally simple, however, once the facts are laid bare. The basic ingredients are clear, careful thinking and a willingness to make difficult decisions.

Here's the key point:

Most organizations will flourish only if their fundraising plans are based principally *on one strategic course and* secondarily *on another.*

Let's call a fundraising strategy with a primary and a secondary focus a *real-world strategy*—as opposed to the simpler textbook strategies spelled out in Chapters Two through Six—and instead of busting a gut to produce a definition of real-world strategy, let's look at two hypothetical examples. In the process, we'll gain a clearer understanding of the difference between primary and secondary strategies, and how to decide which is which.

The Institute for Research in Organic Farming: STABILITY + visibility

The Institute for Research in Organic Farming is the nonprofit arm of the Organic Farmers of America (OFA), a trade association. As OFA's think tank, the institute is charged with research and public education in a field of growing interest nationwide. Lacking an explosive issue to spark public excitement, the institute has been largely dependent on assessments and contributions from organic food producers. But times are changing in the world of organic farming. Wholesale food distributors and retail outlets alike in many key markets across the country are seeking more organic products. Television, radio, magazines, and newspapers are treating the topic with increasing seriousness. All this rising interest is generating new pressure for scientific proof of the virtues of organic food, placing an ever-weightier burden on the institute. Viewing the changed circumstances, OFA has decreed that the institute must broaden its financial base. Its fundraising strategy has to change—fast.

Previously, the guiding principle was efficiency. After all, what could be more efficient than walking across the hall to collect a check? But now circumstances require a strategy driven primarily by stability: the overarching concern is to diversify the institute's funding base and relieve pressure on the food producers for ever-rising subsidies. The institute must seek funding from institutions and people who may not have much, if any, previous knowledge of organic farming.

Likely candidates include the food distributors, who may chip in corporate contributions. Consumers who wish to receive sound, unbiased information about organic farming directly from a respectable institution might be willing to pay a modest annual fee for its newsletter or other publications. Some foundations may be induced to think of the issues raised by the institute as grounds for possible grants in the field of health and nutrition. And professional groups with a stake in good nutrition—health care providers, for example, or nutritionists—might find common cause with the institute.

Obviously there's substantial potential for new revenue—but a "cold" fundraising campaign addressed to these new markets may fall flat. Food distributors may argue that public awareness of organic food is growing too slowly. Consumers may look the other way when receiving an appeal for help. Foundations and allied professional associations may think that the constituency for organic farming is too small and that the chances of organic farming's survival are too slim.

What's needed is a degree of visibility—to demonstrate the value of the institute's work to the broader public. If the food distributors, the general public, the foundations oriented toward health and nutrition, and the allied professionals all detect a broad surge in media attention that suggests a coming shift in public attitudes, the job of selling them on the value of support for the institute will become meaningfully easier.

Thus the institute, in seeking stability, must make use of the techniques of Visibility Strategies as well. In shorthand, the institute's strategy might be written as STABILITY + visibility.

Why not VISIBILITY + stability instead? Two reasons:

• *Visibility is necessary to make a strategy based on stability feasible, but visibility in itself is not the principal end desired.* What's most important to the institute is to broaden the financial base. Visibility is only a means to that end (although a significant one). Strategy must be based on the organization's most important goal.

• *Achieving visibility costs money, but the institute's problem is that funding for its activities is already outstripping the funds available from organic farmers.* In other words, even if it were desirable to focus primarily on establishing a larger public presence, the institute couldn't afford to do so. The means for conducting a high-priced media and public relations campaign are simply not at hand. Unlike milk producers or raisin farmers, the organic crowd can't afford the likes of a thirty-second spot during the Super Bowl. The institute must settle for visibility efforts that are much more modest. Strategy must reflect the resources available. You can't sidestep reality, however harsh it may be.

But even a modest visibility campaign will be expensive. Can't the institute seek stability *without* visibility?

Not likely. Almost any scheme to gain funding from sources outside the closed community of organic food producers and consumers will require making the institute's work better known. That necessary investment in new activities rules out efficiency as a unifying concept, and an Involvement Strategy seems clearly off the mark.

Well, you might say, what about growth? Isn't the institute actually setting out to grow its donor base?

Not necessarily. A successful reorientation of the institute's fundraising strategy might involve acquiring very few new sources of funding.

For the institute, one way to achieve diversification might be to undertake a cause-related marketing initiative with a large food-distribution company. (For most nonprofits, cause-related marketing poses obvious risks, but to the institute the risks may seem small, given the "green" image of organic food producers.) Instead of acquiring more donors, the institute could seek common cause with other industries. Health professionals, in conjunction with a far-sighted public foundation, might find it in their long-term self-interest to fund and help spread the word about the nutritional value and other advantages of organic foods. Also, institute staff may choose to put their own considerable knowledge on the market. They are, after all, world-class experts in the chemistry of food. They might gain a lot of income for the institute through consulting contracts, exclusive business conferences, or technical publications sold to the pharmaceutical industry, for example. None of these approaches would constitute growth.

So, it's clear: the institute's fundraising strategy is best described as STABILITY + visibility. Now let's look at a strikingly different institution with a different set of challenges.

Northern College: GROWTH + involvement

You'd think that Northern College would be sitting pretty. Ever since Erasmus Milton, a long-forgotten alumnus with a gift for picking stocks, gave them that $12 million last month, everybody's been assuming that the college is all set. Now they can afford to plug those holes in the faculty, resume long-neglected maintenance of the buildings and grounds, and maybe even double the size of the scholarship program.

Not so.

Turns out that Milton's gift was a challenge grant. Northern College won't get a nickel of that money unless it can match the entire sum, dollar for dollar, and the matching money can't come from just any source: the donors must be alumni of Northern College. Not only that, the college has to raise the entire $12 million match within five years or it will lose every cent of the grant!

Northern's president has been led to believe that Milton won't insist on their raising the full sum. The president suspects, too, that if the college shows steady, year-to-year progress, the donor may even be willing to release funds much sooner than in five years. But at a minimum Milton will clearly expect a large proportion of the alumni to step forward and share the load. Milton does not want to go it alone.

Now, you might think, what's so tough about all that? Simply launch a five-year, $25 million capital campaign. Should be a piece of cake, with all those Northern alumni! After all, the college is almost a century old.

Not so fast. Northern College alumni have been downright miserly. Only about one out of every twenty Northern alums have contributed to the annual fund during the last two years—a pathetic rate of participation compared to similar liberal arts institutions.

What to do? The alumni office staff, who after all must answer for that low alumni-participation rate, have gotten a $12 million wake-up call. And with a little unwelcome attention from Northern's president, the development people have come up with exactly the right strategy: GROWTH + involvement.

Northern College will undertake that $25 million capital campaign, but not along classic lines. The principal goal is to persuade a much larger percentage of the alumni to become donors, because it's the best way to identify those alumni who may be good prospects for major gifts to the capital campaign, and because the participation rate in itself will be one of the major benchmarks of success. But to boost the rate will require that numbers of alumni first become a lot more deeply *involved* in campus affairs. The capital campaign, then, will have to spend an unusually large amount on high-profile reunions, campus tours, and presidential briefings, and on impressive new alumni publications and other efforts to spark pride—and action—among the grads. This will be especially true in the campaign's first year or two.

Why is this precisely the right course to follow? Why isn't the strategy described instead as INVOLVEMENT + growth, for example? Here's why:

- The most important goal is to broaden the financial base among Northern College alumni—in other words, to increase the number of donors in the first place and ultimately to generate far more in gifts than ever before received from graduates of the college. Those are the elements of a classic growth strategy.

- Involvement is a means to growth in this case—essential but secondary. Northern College gains little from alumni involvement in and of itself. The strategic advantage lies in what (presumably) happens later—after the alumni become involved.

With such sharply different paths beckoning to the fundraiser, it's no wonder some fundraisers go astray. The potential for conflict and confusion is enormous. For instance, it may be difficult to grasp the difference between a Visibility Strategy and a Growth Strategy. Both require large investments in extensive public outreach efforts, but they are undertaken for very different reasons. They may employ different means (such as billboard advertising for visibility as opposed to door-to-door canvassing for growth) and they call for different perspectives on the financial results. In a Visibility Strategy, for example, the true test of cost-effectiveness may be to measure gains in market penetration (and thus in building awareness). In a Growth Strategy, by contrast, expenditures might be measured in terms of dollars spent per new member recruited.

Real-World Strategies and the Test of Time

A wealthy software engineer, Myron Goldberg, has pledged a staggering $30 million to establish the Goldberg Institute of Interactive Technology on the site of your city's antiquated science museum. As vice president for development of the museum, you've long favored resorting to the wrecking ball, wanting to start over from scratch. But that would cost $60 million, so Mr. Goldberg's gift is a godsend. Now it's fallen to you to help build the institute and convert the initial megagift into a successful fundraising program.

You're already firmly committed to building a membership base for the new institute. You clearly understand the benefits of securing a large and growing membership. Obviously members pay dues, which will help cover the institute's ongoing expenses, and members will take greater interest in the institute than nonmembers. Besides, every self-respecting institution open to the public has members, right?

There are also many ancillary benefits of the membership development process—positive outcomes of the marketing and promotional efforts you'll undertake to attract members and sustain their interest. These ancillary benefits are integral to the institute's financial development strategy, and indeed to accomplishing its larger mission.

Such ancillary benefits include the following:

- *Visibility.* The membership development campaign will dramatically increase the institute's visibility in advance of its opening and help maintain a high public profile in the years ahead. Membership recruitment efforts conducted by direct mail, by telemarketing, on TV and radio, through the institute's Web site, and by other means will reinforce (and in turn be reinforced by) other media, public relations, and promotional efforts undertaken by the institute.

- *Fundraising.* Some members will become generous donors. Eventually some will make significant bequests to help build the institute's endowment. In fact, in the long run, bequests and major gifts from highly committed and deeply involved members may constitute the principal financial advantage of the membership program.

- *Public education.* Newsletters and other materials produced for members will advance the institute's work to promote science literacy. Direct mail, in particular, is an ideal medium for public education, because it allows for detailed information to be widely disseminated.

- *Merchandising.* Members are likely to buy branded merchandise. Even some prospective members who may not choose to join will buy science kits, books, or branded jackets. Recruitment materials will afford opportunities to market merchandise.

- *Outreach.* Members will help recruit other members, through casual word-of-mouth exchanges or even through active friend-get-a-friend campaigns. Many members will become active ambassadors, promoting attendance at institute activities and showing off institute merchandise.

- *Volunteer recruitment.* Some members may become involved in the institute as volunteers or board members. To the extent that they do, the likelihood will increase that they will give additional gifts.

- *Influence.* Membership will constitute a broader web of influence that will help marshal public support for the institute. This network of connections will operate informally, but it may also be formally activated from time to time, as necessary—for example, if renewed public funding is ever in question.

In other words, viewing the institute's financial development in a larger context, the membership development program you want to launch will have multiple purposes and consequences. Clearly, however, *some of these ancillary benefits will be far more important than others, and their relative importance will shift over time.* In fact, the membership development activities you undertake can best be viewed in phases.

Phase 1: Launching the Institute (Year 1)

Your long-term financial goal remains to secure the additional $30 million needed to build the new institute. Initially, though, you'll need to place the greatest emphasis on visibility and focus secondarily on involvement. Clearly the greatest task at the outset is to establish a large public presence for the institute. If this Visibility Strategy is to succeed, large numbers of patrons must be attracted (that is, involved) and word-of-mouth must spread the good news about the institute's opening. This indicates a strategy of VISIBILITY + involvement.

At this early stage—when you'll be financing an effort to launch and position the institute—it's unreasonable to expect your fundraising operations to be highly efficient. Nor can the financial development program in its early years be characterized as stable. Efficiency and stability must wait. The institute must first invest heavily in establishing itself through a Visibility Strategy.

Until the end of the first year, membership development activities must be planned, and subsidized, with these considerations in mind.

Phase 2: Building the Base (Years 2 to 4?)

The need for growth—and the possibility of attaining it—will immediately follow the initial launch stage. Growth will become the centerpiece of your financial development strategy, and it will stay there for at least a couple of years. But the need for substantial involvement—by the public as well as by institute members—will continue to loom large as growth dominates the picture. In other words, the institute's strategy in phase 2 must be GROWTH + involvement.

To expand the membership base, the institute will invest continuously in membership acquisition mailings and in collateral activities that support them. The money raised in the form of first-year dues from new members will very likely fall short of covering the cost of these mailings.

In other words, you'll invest heavily in acquiring new members during this phase. For the institute to grow its membership to five thousand by the end of the first year (and to ten thousand after three years), that investment might average anywhere from $15 to $35 per new member. (The amount can be determined only by experience, and it can be fairly evaluated only in comparison with the long-term financial benefits that these new members bring to the institute.)

Meanwhile, of course, you'll undertake a wide range of activities conceived to recoup some of that investment, such as the following:

- Occasional lucrative "special appeals" to selected members for additional support for special programs or at special times

- Major-gift fundraising activities that zero in on appropriate individual members

- A monthly sustainer program that enables small donors to contribute significant amounts a little bit at a time

- At the appropriate time, cost-efficient annual membership-renewal notices to keep members coming back for more

All of these back-end fundraising and membership development activities will, in fact, generate net revenue from dues and donations that will help defray the investment in acquiring new members. There will be indirect revenue as well, in the form of admission fees and merchandise sales. But even combined, all that revenue will still fall short of covering the full membership acquisition costs for at least a year or two (and possibly for as many as four years all told).

Thus, during this second, growth-oriented phase of the institute's membership development program, efficiency and stability will remain elusive. You will have to continue to invest substantial amounts of money to build the membership base and to provide benefits, services, and involvement opportunities to members.

Phase 3: Securing the Future (Year 5 to ?)

At some point, the institute's membership acquisition activities are likely to reach a plateau. It will then become apparent that further expansion of the membership rolls will exact too high a price. For instance, you might find that the institute can sustain a membership of ten thousand, paying only a modest acquisition cost for new members recruited to replace those lost to attrition (nonrenewal, illness, death). To increase the membership to, say, fifteen thousand would require investing a prohibitively large sum, and by then the institute's board (and perhaps the public) may not be prepared to sacrifice fundraising efficiency any longer.

Only at this stage will the goals of efficiency and stability appear within reach. Indeed, the institute's leadership will now need to choose which of these two goals is paramount, or whether greater visibility, increased involvement, or continued growth constitute more desirable goals. Any one of the following scenarios (and many others besides) might look attractive as this phase begins to unfold:

- *EFFICIENCY + stability*. Membership acquisition would be restricted to the minimum necessary to replenish members lost to attrition. The institute would devote special attention to major-donor fundraising activities. The development staff would look for ways to cut costs on membership services without jeopardizing the membership renewal rate. An ambitious capital campaign would be launched to secure a sizable endowment.

- *STABILITY + efficiency*. This scenario is similar to the foregoing, but the institute's leadership is preoccupied by thoughts of the future and inclined to invest even more heavily in building an endowment. (For instance, you might hire a larger capital campaign staff and launch an initially costly bequest-marketing program.) This stepped-up investment will result in lowered fundraising efficiency, but efficiency will by no means be ignored.

- *INVOLVEMENT + efficiency*. The board may conclude that the more heavily involved institute members become, the more benefits they will bring to the institution, and the more responsive they will be to fundraising appeals. For example, experience may show that a bequest-promotion program conducted among active members is unusually productive. Paying close attention to membership involvement, both in acquisition activities and in subsequent services to members, may appear to be the best possible way to ensure the institute's continuing success. Even though this Involvement Strategy undermines the short-term efficiency of the development program, it's clear that the institute's long-term interest requires its leadership to err on the side of involvement.

- *STABILITY + growth*. Perhaps the institute's membership may continue to grow without excessive investment in acquisition. (The market may prove to be national rather than local or regional, and the institute's reputation may spread far and wide.) In this case, the board may wish to keep growing the membership indefinitely— as long as the membership acquisition program can be conducted cost-effectively. The goal, however, is more than a larger membership base. Even more important, the institute's bigger membership provides an expanded pool of prospects for major gifts, bequests (as well as other forms of planned gifts), and capital campaigns. These activities become the backbone of the financial development program, together guaranteeing the institute's long-term stability by diversifying its fundraising efforts and enlarging its endowment.

It's far too early to answer any of the questions raised by these scenarios. But when the time comes, you must be prepared to ask them.

In other words, the institute's strategic priorities will indeed shift from time to time. But there always needs to be one clear, overarching, and dominant strategy. Muddled planning leads to mixed results, at best. And frequently shifting priorities—lurching from one campaign or one priority to the next—may leave donors feeling jerked around. This feeling does not foster either trust or enthusiasm.

Doing things right—choosing one paramount goal and a clear direction for getting there—isn't easy. A fundraiser may fall victim to one of six factors that commonly undermine strategy: conflicting demands, indecisiveness, confusing means with goals, mistaking tactics for strategy, giving up too soon, or personal biases. The next chapter looks at each of those pitfalls in turn.

9

Avoiding Common Pitfalls in Developing a Sound and Productive Strategy

Don't think for a minute that I believe the strategic approach I advocate is easy. Any number of obstacles may crop up along the way—often several at once. Among the more obvious of these are fear of accountability, fear of change, the lack of good records to measure success, and instability within the board and senior staff. However, over the years I have observed repeated examples of five pitfalls of the would-be strategist that deserve a little explanation. Any of these five common and all too human conditions may sabotage your organization's path to a strategically clear fundraising plan.

• *Pitfall 1: Conflicting demands.* Circumstances may make it impossible to set a higher priority on one goal than on a second one. For example, restrictions imposed by the United Way or other funders might force you to keep costs way down every year, even though your analysis shows that you should invest large sums for several years to expand your donor base. Because there's no way to have your cake and eat it too, this conflict leads to strategic failure.

Or perhaps no one has full control over the planning and direction of the development program. Any fundraising strategy must incorporate benefits for many different people in the organization— including people with conflicting goals. The capital campaign staff might require a bigger donor base, but the membership department won't invest the necessary sums in donor acquisition because the returns they can reasonably project from their own activities simply aren't high enough to justify the investment. The two departments may both succeed only if they pool their resources.

- *Pitfall 2: Indecisiveness.* A second way to make strategic errors is to be—well, what would you call it? Indecisive?

Indecisiveness is often born of mistrust or fear. ("I don't trust our donors to respond" or "If we choose just this one strategy, we may fail").

At Northern College, for instance (see Chapter Eight), the same sleepyheaded folks who failed to excite the alumni during all those years might lack the resolve to undertake a sustained, effective, alumni involvement campaign. Fussing and fooling around in the face of Erasmus Milton's $12 million challenge, they may not be up to the job of setting a clear goal and zealously pursuing it.

Or perhaps the problem lies with the trustees. The alumni staff might discover that no matter what might make the most sense for the college, the president and the board of trustees just won't go along. The alumni staff thus have to compromise. Instead of a clear strategy of GROWTH + involvement, they're forced to set out in futile pursuit of growth, involvement, and visibility—shackled by unrealistic demands for efficiency in the program. In other words, a muddle.

In a similar fashion, the Institute for Research in Organic Farming (Chapter Eight) could falter if staff fail to persuade the board that they'll have to invest money in the short-term (in a visibility campaign) to serve their chosen goal: diversification to secure the institute's stability. If the board insists instead that the fundraising program must never spend more than, say, ten cents on the dollar, chances are slim that the goal can be reached. A visibility drive will require a larger investment.

Either way, the problem is indecisiveness, and it frequently inflicts mortal wounds on an institution's fundraising program. Strategy requires clear thinking—and a generous measure of willpower.

- *Pitfall 3: Confusing means with goals.* One of the most common problems encountered by the would-be strategist is getting means and goals mixed up. For example, at the Institute for Research in Organic Farming, the staff might get carried away with the visibility campaign. Instead of investing just enough in the effort to serve the strategic purpose of diversifying the funding base, the institute could devote entirely too much time and money in an effort to make *organic food* a household word.

Similarly, at Northern College the development office and the trustees could get carried away with the alumni involvement program. They might decide that the purpose of the five-year campaign is to involve alumni, not to match Milton's $12 million pledge. By devoting too many resources to that task, they could spend the whole $12 million in matching funds on reunions, campus tours, and fancy publications (perhaps only to find out that Milton lost the whole $12 million in the market).

- *Pitfall 4: Mistaking tactics for strategy.* Things might be even worse at Northern College. Instead of overinvesting in an alumni involvement program, the development staff might insist on spending huge sums on donor research before even launching the campaign.

Donor research will be necessary—indispensable, really—at the right time. But the priorities in Northern's strategy of GROWTH + involvement are to recruit donors among the alumni, in large part by involving them in the college's affairs. These are the strategic considerations. Donor research is a tactic.

Once the development staff succeeds in qualifying a significant number of alumni as genuine prospective donors—by securing token gifts, for example, or enlisting them in the alumni association—then donor research becomes timely and important. But it's still only a tactic.

- *Pitfall 5: Giving up too soon.* Fundraising normally takes a long time to bear fruit. North Americans are generous, but just getting their attention or involving them—as volunteers, for example—requires competing with many other activities in their lives. From your point of view, those other activities may be distractions. But your donors are unlikely to view things the same way.

Consider another key factor often overlooked by fundraisers who think single-mindedly of large-scale contributions. Most North Americans aren't rich. We can contribute really substantial sums only by making repeated gifts over the course of several years.

Any fundraising strategy requires a significant amount of time to succeed. Trustees, executive directors, and development staff must be patient and persistent.

I imagine you're familiar with painful examples from your own life of the failure to persist. Like most worthwhile things in life, strategy requires stick-to-itiveness. No more need be said.

However, these five pitfalls are not the only reasons why some people stumble in devising fundraising strategies. Real life abounds with examples of other potential problems that can undermine the execution of any fundraising strategy.

Six Surefire Ways to Bankrupt a Nonprofit

It's all too easy to misinterpret strategic needs, to misunderstand their financial implications, or to go overboard in pursuing a strategy (and risk drowning in the process). Here, for example, are six ways to go off the deep end, leading a nonprofit organization into bankruptcy, irrelevance, or worse.

• *Obsessive devotion to efficiency.* Cut way back on recruiting new donors or members because it's "too expensive." Limit your fundraising programs exclusively to those that yield immediate net returns—the bigger the better. Forget about donor attrition. ("We've got plenty of donors, don't we?")

• *The democratic fallacy.* Treat all your donors exactly the same, whether they give you $1 or $1 million. Send everybody, without exception, a gold-embossed, hand-signed acknowledgment for every gift. And keep them all on the mailing list so they'll continue to receive your newsletter and all your fundraising appeals until the end of time.

• *Unreasoning attention to financial stability.* Stuff every available cent into the endowment fund. Slash the operating budget so you can add even more to the endowment. Turn away donors who want to underwrite current projects unless they're also willing to help endow the organization. Build an unassailable fortress of money that will permit your operations to continue until the fourth millennium. Somebody else can worry about what to do to make all the effort worthwhile!

• *Representation without taxation.* Send your donors lots of information but solicit them only once a year. Keep fundraising costs as low as possible and maintain a low organizational profile. ("It's not polite to bother people.") Leave it to donors to come forward with the help you so richly deserve. ("Besides, if they don't give this year, maybe they'll help again next year.")

• *Making fundraising the end, not the means.* Accept big gifts from donors who want to underwrite new projects that aren't in the organization's plans and that aren't consistent with your priorities. Hang out a for-sale sign on the portals of your institution. Go for the gold. Sacrifice your organization's soul to meet current needs.

• *Following personal preferences, ignoring experience.* Design all your fundraising programs exclusively on the basis of your board chair's opinions about what will work and what won't. Be sure to heed words of wisdom such as these:

> "Our donors don't like to be bothered."
> "Forget our donors—we've got to concentrate on
>   the people in town who've got lots of money."
> "Nobody reads newsletters."
> "Our donors are *different*."
> "People don't read long letters."
> "Everybody hates fundraising calls at home."
> "People are insulted if you ask for too much money."
> "The only thing that motivates people to give is guilt."

The best policy to follow in the face of superstitions such as these is to smile politely and then get on with the business at hand: pursuing your strategy.

A strategy is a road map. It reminds you where you're going and how you'll get there. You've got to be certain that the road you've chosen actually leads in the direction in which you want to go.

Zeroing in on Your Strategy

At last! You're ready to settle on a strategy for your organization— or more likely, on both primary and secondary strategies. To some extent, the overarching considerations will become clear as you dissect the guts of your organization: vision, goals, and objectives. Like any road map, strategy reflects reality. A detailed look at that reality may affect your strategic assumptions. But there's a quick and dirty way to get a fix on your strategy before launching into the minutiae of strategic planning.

Following this chapter is a self-assessment called, "What's the Right Strategy for Your Organization?" This handy worksheet is the easiest and most straightforward way to narrow down your organization's options to one or two paramount strategies. The self-assessment may be completed individually by any trustee, executive, or staff person who wants to get to the bottom of the organization's top-priority fundraising needs. It may be even more productive, however, as a strategic planning tool, used as the basis for group discussion at a board or staff meeting or an organizational retreat. The answers you find through the process of completing the self-assessment may not be definitive, but they'll certainly lend clarity to the additional discussion that's sure to follow before your organization sets out on any bold new course. In short, once you've chosen the proper strategy, you'll be ready to start learning more about where you're going and what you'll find along the way.

That's the next challenge: reviewing your organization's vision and setting goals and objectives for the fundraising program. We'll take up that topic in Part Three.

Self-Assessment 1

What's the Right Strategy for Your Organization?

Fundraising—especially in its broadest sense of "resource development"—covers a lot of territory. Raising money to support the mission of a human service agency in a suburban community is a challenge only superficially similar to that faced by Harvard University or the California Pacific Medical Center. Not only are their techniques and objectives—their tactics—very different, but they also employ different strategies.

Every nonprofit organization must develop a distinctive and internally consistent strategy to meet its own unique fundraising challenge.

Unfortunately, that's far more easily said than done. The following self-assessment proves challenging for many organizations because it requires making many difficult choices. Setting a strategy, however, is a matter of choosing one path rather than another. (Whoever said fundraising would be easy?)

Hint: if you're heavily engaged in doing A in order to achieve B, your strategic goal is B, not A. For instance, a nonprofit organization may decide that it needs to expand its donor base (to grow) in order to diversify its funding sources (perhaps to add new streams of revenue from direct mail and telephone fundraising.) In that case, the organization is pursuing a strategy of stability (diversification), not growth.

In the table that follows, place a check or an X in the column on the right under the letter that matches your choice. Avoid boxes shaded gray. Use only the white boxes.

Question	A	B	C	D	E	Neither	Not sure
(A) Is it more important for your organization to raise money at the lowest possible cost per dollar raised? or (B) Is it more important to ensure the long-term survival of your organization?							
(A) Is it more important for your organization to raise money at the lowest possible cost per dollar raised? or (C) Is it more important for your organization to gain public visibility?							
(A) Is it more important for your organization to raise money at the lowest possible cost per dollar raised? or (D) Is it more important for your organization to involve donors as volunteers, activists, or patrons?							
(A) Is it more important for your organization to raise money at the lowest possible cost per dollar raised? or (E) Is it more important to increase your fundraising revenue to allow for the organization's growth?							

Question	A	B	C	D	E	Neither	Not sure
(B) Is it more important for your organization to ensure its long-term survival? or (C) Is it more important for your organization to gain public visibility?							
(B) Is it more important for your organization to ensure its long-term survival? or (D) Is it more important for your organization to involve donors as volunteers, activists, or patrons?							
(B) Is it more important for your organization to ensure its long-term survival? or (E) Is it more important to increase your fundraising revenue to allow for the organization's growth?							
(C) Is it more important for your organization to gain public visibility? or (D) Is it more important for your organization to involve donors as volunteers, activists, or patrons?							
(C) Is it more important for your organization to gain public visibility? or (E) Is it more important to increase your fundraising revenue to allow for the organization's growth?							

Question	A	B	C	D	E	Neither	Not sure
(D) Is it more important for your organization to involve donors as volunteers, activists, or patrons? or (E) Is it more important to increase your fundraising revenue to allow for the organization's growth?							
TOTAL							

Scoring

1. If you checked "Not sure" at any time, think about the comparison again. Do research if necessary. Talk to staff or trustees. To be clear about your fundraising strategy, you need to be able to answer all ten questions. In setting strategy, clarity is paramount.
2. If you checked "Neither" more than once, you may have a problem making decisions. To establish clear goals, every nonprofit needs to set priorities in all these critical areas. Think it through again!
3. If you answered at least nine of the ten questions, count the number of times you selected each letter (A through E) as more important.

The following table shows how to interpret your score. If you checked two of the five letters twice, your fundraising goals blend two of the descriptions in the table. Most nonprofits pursue such dual fundraising strategies, but the priority must always be clear. It is impossible for any organization to achieve all five goals simultaneously.

Letter Checked 3+ Times	Interpretation
A	The hallmark of your fundraising strategy is efficiency. The preponderance of your fundraising activities need to be focused on raising money at the lowest possible cost per dollar raised.
B	Stability is the key to your development strategy. Most of your effort and creativity ought to zero in on ways to ensure your organization's long-term survival.
C	Your mission requires broad-based public support, which you can achieve only through visibility. Your fundraising program needs to be designed to help you gain public attention and executed in ways that are consistent with the image your work requires.
D	Donor involvement is central to your organization's mission because your work requires broad-based participation in volunteer activities, grassroots lobbying, merchandise sales, or attendance at performances or other events. Your fundraising efforts ought to be reviewed for the contributions they make to involving your donors in the organization's affairs.
E	Your primary goal is growth, whether in revenues or in the number of your donors or members. Your development program will be shaped by the demands (and the costs) of sustaining a high rate of growth.

PART THREE

Developing a Practical Plan to Pursue Your Strategy

10

Getting a Fix on Your Organization's Vision and Goals

If you're with me so far, you've gotten a pretty good idea about the fundraising strategy that's right for your organization. Here's where we start to translate that strategy into an operational reality.

In the Chapters in Part Three I talk about *organizational vision* and fundraising *goals* and *objectives:* what they are, how they're different from one another, why you need all three, and how they all relate to your fundraising strategy. Then I get down to the nitty-gritty of fundraising—the techniques or tactics that fundraisers use to achieve our objectives, approach our goals, and fulfill the vision that animates us. Together we'll explore ten of the most widely used fundraising techniques and examine their various applications in each of the five strategies. At the end of Part Three you'll find five self-assessment exercises that will help you determine your organization's readiness for some of the riskiest and most consequential of these fundraising methods.

But first comes *vision*.

Vision Is Paramount

Fundraising takes guts.

The most successful fundraiser is a clear-headed thinker with sharply defined personal values and an unclouded vision of the potential her work holds to make the world a better place.

But even the most dedicated, visionary, and technically proficient fundraiser will not succeed if her organization isn't "donor ready." For donors to view a nonprofit as seaworthy and climb on board, the organization has to have, at a minimum, certain basic characteristics:

- A vision of a better world
- Focus on a worthy cause
- Strong leadership
- A credible plan of action
- Unquestionable honesty and integrity

No matter how much you might fuss or tinker with your fundraising program, your organization must first be in good overall health. You can't even hope to assess the performance of your fundraising efforts unless you view them in that larger context.

All donors expect, quite rightfully, that their gifts will be put to productive use in pursuit of your organization's mission. Prospective major donors have even higher expectations. They won't even consider supporting you unless you can demonstrate the ability to use large sums productively and administer them wisely. In truth, many nonprofits simply aren't yet ready for major gifts.

For the moment, I'll give you the benefit of the doubt. I'll assume that your organization is in fine shape overall, with good grounds for hope for the future. Your mission is clear and broadly supported. You know who your customers are: they're your students, patients, parents, patrons—fill in the blank—and they *know* they're your customers. The services you provide are of great value to them. Your organization's achievements are dramatic and widely acknowledged, and you have a dynamic, workable plan under way that ensures that your customers will receive even greater value from you in the years ahead.

Taking all that for granted—at least for the sake of argument—let's delve a little more deeply into one point that may already be furrowing your brow: What do I mean by *vision* and *mission?*

Thousands of words have been wasted in what I believe is a futile effort to define *mission*.

The word *mission* is so widely used and abused in the nonprofit world that I prefer the coward's way out of the debate over its meaning. I choose to sidestep the question. I use the word *vision* instead.

Others may prefer to distinguish between vision and mission. An organization's vision explains *why* the organization does what it does. Its mission expresses *what* it does (some say *how* it does it). I've seen organizational mission statements that run for many pages— in small type! If you want to call such a thing a "mission statement," so be it. I won't argue with you. But I care a whole lot more about the *why* behind your organization—and so do your donors! For convenience's sake, I call that *vision*. Refer to it as your mission, if you insist. Just be sure you express it in twenty-five words or less—and be doubly sure that it's *inspiring*.

Here are examples of what I mean by vision from five hypothetical organizations we'll examine in much more depth in the chapters ahead:

Institute for Advanced Cancer Research: *To shine a beacon of hope into the lives of cancer patients everywhere.*

One for All: *To bring closer the day when racism no longer poisons our lives.*

Citywide Community Hospital: *To sustain a state-of-the-art health care facility to heal the sick and injured in the local community, regardless of financial circumstances.*

Potential Plus: *To help developmentally disabled children live full and productive lives.*

Silver City Symphony Orchestra: *To help contemporary music lovers find new meaning in the classical symphonic repertoire.*

Now, before we get lost in the trees of this vast, sprawling forest, let's climb a little higher up that nearby hill to gain perspective on the Big Picture. Please join me now in a look at the widely mis-understood topics of *vision* and *fundraising goals*.

Goal Setting: Reach for the Sky

What are your goals?

Ask that question of your development director, or the presi-dent of the board, or almost anybody else. Chances are the response will be along these lines: balance the budget, avoid layoffs, start a new program, recruit five hundred new members, raise $20 million this year—

Are these goals?

Nope. Not in my book. They're focused on the short term—and that's only the beginning of the problem. They're unambitious. Worse yet, some of them are even negative.

Goals are the concrete expression of an organization's vision. A vision explains *why*. Goals spell out *what* the organization actually proposes to accomplish within a given period (usually expressed in years).

Ask Sam, the guy next door, what his personal vision is. Chances are he'll give you a funny look. But ask what his personal goals are and you're likely to get a different reaction. If Sam is at all typical (and what else can you expect from the guy next door?) he will tell you something like, "Put the kids through college, become president of the company, retire at fifty-five, and buy a Winnebago."

Now, these are *goals!*

Sam probably won't ever achieve all that. But he's got a shot at it, because he knows what he wants and is prepared to work hard to get it. Very likely, the kids will stagger through five or six years of college and graduate by the skin of their teeth. Their father will never become president of the company, but he will receive a long series of promotions and will eventually be entrusted with a respon-sible management position. He'll probably think better of retiring at fifty-five a few years before he reaches that age, but because he's been planning for that day, he and his family will be in strong finan-cial condition. They may even buy *two* Winnebagos!

Now, what chance do you think Sam would have of accom-plishing all that if he hadn't set out with ambitious goals?

Is it likely that he would have risen as high in the company if he hadn't been striving for the presidency?

Could Sam really have managed to put two kids through col-lege if he hadn't begun saving two decades in advance and working his tail off over the years?

If he hadn't been planning to retire at fifty-five, would he have been able to buy that Winnebago?

The answer to all these questions is no. Our individual personal goals govern our actions in the present by endowing the future with meaning. So it is, too, with organizations.

Your organization faces a much greater challenge than the guy next door, however. He's just one person. No matter how much he depends on other people for his survival, his personal goals are ulti-mately his alone. In theory, he can decide all by himself which goals to pick.

Your organization's goals are, by definition, a legitimate con-cern of many people. Setting goals for a group (or worse, for a col-lection of individuals) requires agreement. That means that many individuals must buy into those goals.

Now, there may be some people who would be absolutely over-joyed at the thought of working themselves into a frazzle to achieve goals such as balancing the budget, avoiding layoffs, starting a new program, recruiting five hundred new members, or raising $20 mil-lion this year.

Not I!

To persuade me to become involved in your organization—whether as a donor, staff person, or board member—you'd better have something more ambitious in mind. You might secure my acquies-cence to a wimpy objective like balancing the budget, but you won't get my agreement. And if I don't really agree, I won't buy in.

To secure my agreement, you'll have to dip into the deepest well of your aspirations and communicate your *vision* to me.

You'll have to make me understand why I should go out of my way to help you attain your goals. Otherwise, they'll never be *my* goals.

Worthy goals are rooted in a vision of a brighter future.

An organization's vision is ideally—well, visionary. Call it starry-eyed. It's necessarily vague.

Regardless of how ambitious they are, organizational goals express vision in concrete terms. Goals may be unattainable, but they fall within the realm of popular imagination.

Translating Vision into Organizational Goals

To gain more perspective on the relationship between vision and goals, let's take a look at how the five hypothetical nonprofit organizations whose visions we examined earlier in this chapter might tackle the goal-setting process.

Institute for Advanced Cancer Research

The organizational vision of the Institute for Advanced Cancer Research has been defined as follows: *To shine a beacon of hope into the lives of cancer patients everywhere.* That lofty vision requires upgrading staff and increasing the number of beds in the facility. The organization's goals, therefore, might be expressed as follows:

- Advance the science of cancer research by attracting and training the world's best-trained and most insightful oncologists.
- Treat more than one thousand of the most challenging cancer cases each year for the next five years.

Both an inspiring vision statement and a short, digestible list of credible, worthy goals are indispensable building blocks as the institute lays the foundation for its future.

One for All

The vision of One for All, a community-based activist organization dedicated to fostering interracial harmony, is *to bring closer the day when racism no longer poisons our lives*. In a time when intercommunity relations are sorely strained, One for All must step up its efforts. Its overarching purpose dictates an unrelenting effort to educate the community—one neighborhood, one classroom, one person at a time. In concrete terms, this means holding more workshops than ever before, producing and distributing more printed materials, and intensifying local lobbying efforts. One for All might spell out these goals in the following way:

- Conduct antiracism workshops for every significant community group within the next three years.

- Distribute "Teach Understanding" kits to every fifth grade teacher in town.

- Secure agreement from the county's board of supervisors to rename a major highway in honor of Dr. Martin Luther King Jr.

Citywide Community Hospital

Like health care facilities all over the nation, the Citywide Community Hospital must respond to dramatic changes in how health services are organized, delivered, and paid for. Its vision, as noted earlier, is *to sustain a state-of-the-art health care facility to heal the sick and injured in the local community, regardless of financial circumstances*. In large part this calls for a merger with two other facilities and coming to terms with the reality of the health maintenance organizations (HMOs) that now dominate the market. Keeping the community informed and favorably disposed to these changes is the key to the hospital's long-term success. The hospital's organizational goals, then, might be described as follows:

- Within five years, merge the community hospital with two specialized clinics.

- Contract with a major HMO to provide inpatient services.

- Upgrade the staff by launching a resident fellows program in cooperation with the nearby medical school.

Potential Plus

The vision of Potential Plus, a residential care facility, is *to help developmentally disabled children live full and productive lives*. For several years, then, the work of this organization will be dominated by one overarching goal: to bring scattered and uncoordinated services for "mentally retarded" children under one roof in a new, $10 million facility largely supported by private gifts.

Silver City Symphony Orchestra

The Silver City Symphony Orchestra wishes *to help contemporary music lovers find new meaning in the classical symphonic repertoire*. The orchestra can attain this vision only by achieving new musical heights and increasing its impact in the region. Its goals, therefore, might be described as follows:

- Expand the orchestra's repertoire.

- Attract world-class guest artists.

- Launch a recording program within two years.

- Double the number of public performances within four years.

Positioning Your Organization for Success

Obviously, the organizational vision and goals described in these five examples encompass far more than fundraising. They're organization-wide and must be reflected in virtually everything the organization does: in all of its marketing and communications, in staff recruitment and training, in its management style—you name it.

This calls for a restatement of the vision and goals in what marketers call a *positioning statement*. This brief document—ideally no longer than a sentence or two—describes your organization's target market, the competitive framework in which your fundraising program operates, and the benefits a member or donor will enjoy. Every marketing and fundraising effort and all new printed materials should be evaluated against this statement.

By putting a positioning statement into practice, the nature, goals, and objectives of your work will immediately become clearer to everyone involved: you and your colleagues, contractors and vendors, and prospective donors or members. That way, you can help your organization stand out in the crowd, and thus obtain higher margins, increase your market share, and attract the most profitable donors.

For example, positioning statements for the five hypothetical nonprofits might be something like the following:

Institute for Advanced Cancer Research: *The nation's oldest and most productive center for new insights into cancer research.*

One for All: *Working toward the day when racism no longer poisons relations among the people of this community.*

Citywide Community Hospital: *For more than one hundred years, the place where the people of this city—all the people—have gone for state-of-the-art health care.*

Potential Plus: *Enriching our community by helping developmentally disabled children live full and productive lives.*

Silver City Symphony Orchestra: *Helping contemporary music lovers throughout the region find new meaning in the classical symphonic repertoire.*

Now let's take one big step further and see how the examples of vision and goals introduced in this chapter relate to fundraising.

11

Translating Vision and Goals into Fundraising Goals

Now let's delve a little more deeply into the aspirations and needs of the five hypothetical nonprofit organizations introduced in the previous chapter.

Institute for Advanced Cancer Research

For the Institute for Advanced Cancer Research, the lofty vision of giving new hope to cancer patients requires upgrading staff and increasing the number of beds in the facility. All this will cost money, of course—a lot of money. This means that the Institute must enlist the support of a much larger number of donors and persuade some of them to give substantially larger sums than they ever have before.

In short, to achieve the ambitious strategic goals its leadership has identified, the institute's board and staff must dramatically broaden the base of financial support. That overarching need points to a Growth Strategy, which in turn requires that the institute's public profile be raised substantially, both in the region it serves and nationally—in our terms: GROWTH + visibility. These organizational goals and this strategy translate into fundraising goals along the following lines:

- Triple the number of donors from the present narrow base (that is, increase their number from less than one thousand to three thousand or more).

- Secure at least ten megagifts ($1 million plus).
- Increase the institute's annual budget from $20 million to $55 million.

The institute's vision, organizational goals, and fundraising goals are summarized in Table 11.1.

Where do goals like this come from? Are they just plucked whole from the air? Of course not—not if the institute has any serious intention of achieving them! The institute's goals—like those of any organization—are a negotiated agreement

- Between the people who will spend the money and the people who will raise it (assuming they're not all the same people)
- Based on rational, measurable needs
- Grounded in a realistic assessment of the institute's history, its capacity for fundraising, and the breadth and strength of its constituency
- Drawn from experience with comparable institutions and similar circumstances

TABLE 11.1 Vision, Organizational Goals, and Fundraising Goals of the Institute for Advance Cancer Research.

Vision	Organizational Goals	Fundraising Goals
To shine a beacon of hope into the lives of cancer patients everywhere.	Advance the science of cancer research by attracting and retaining the world's best-trained and most insightful oncologists and treating more than 1,000 of the most challenging cancer cases each year for the next five years.	Triple the number of donors, secure at least ten megagifts ($1 million plus), and increase the institute's annual budget from $20 million to $55 million.

One for All

From top to bottom, from its vision to its operational plans, One for All reflects its founder's realization that eradicating racism can be achieved only one person at a time. Its vision acknowledges the decades (if not centuries) that will be required. Its strategic goals encompass both educational programs and symbolic measures.

One for All's fundraising goals must mirror the involvement that is central to the way the organization does business. The organizational focus on public education necessitates keeping tabs on public opinion and the media—in short, using all its activities, including fundraising efforts, to maintain a high public profile.

One for All must hold more workshops, produce and distribute more printed materials, and step up local lobbying efforts. To fund this agenda, One for All must pay special attention to institutional fundraising opportunities while continuing to build a broad community base of support. This means a strategy of INVOLVEMENT + visibility.

In quantitative terms, One for All's fundraising goals for the next three years might be as follows:

- Secure grants of at least $10,000 each from three new foundations or corporations.
- Double the number of Penny Potluck fundraising events each year.
- Recruit a group of politically savvy donors (a community advisory council) who will fund the drive to lobby the board of supervisors.
- Raise the yearly budget by $25,000 per year.

One for All's vision, organizational goals, and fundraising goals are summarized in Table 11.2.

TABLE 11.2 Vision, Organizational Goals, and Fundraising Goals of One for All.

Vision	Organizational Goals	Fundraising Goals
To bring closer the day when racism no longer poisons our lives.	Conduct antiracism workshops for every significant community group within the next three years, distribute "Teach Understanding" kits to every fifth-grade teacher in town, and secure agreement from the County Board of Supervisors to rename a major highway in honor of Dr. Martin Luther King, Jr.	Within the next three years, secure grants of at least $10,000 each from three new foundations or corporations, double the number of Penny Potluck fundraising events each year, recruit a group of politically savvy donors (a community advisory council) who will fund the drive to lobby the board of supervisors, and raise the yearly budget by $25,000 per year.

Citywide Community Hospital

Rapid change in the delivery of health care services and the hospital's imminent three-way merger dictate that the hospital devote considerable resources to keeping its profile high in the community. In confusing times, with a set of goals that virtually guarantees continuing confusion in the public mind, the hospital's fundraising efforts aren't likely to succeed if they don't focus on visibility. Also, some of the changes the merger will bring will inevitably be unpopular. That too will require proactive efforts to cultivate broad support. (Call it advertising and public relations, if you will. It's a matter of building goodwill in the community.)

Of course the hospital's institutional interests imply that financial stability must not be sacrificed for the sake of high visibility. The ultimate goal, after all, is to prepare the hospital for an unforeseeable future.

Visibility is the key to the hospital's long-term success. Because the amounts of money involved in executing an effective Visibility Strategy dramatically overshadow the modest philanthropic gifts that seem within reach in the near term, the hospital's fundraising program must in effect play a dual role. This means an intensive effort along the following lines:

- Blanket the community with dual-purpose appeals (playing a public relations function as well as a fundraising role).

- Highlight the hospital's contributions to the community through frequent public events that bring citizens into the facility.

- Secure major gifts from leading citizens to expand women's health programs, especially those related to childbirth, and launch a regional marketing and promotion plan for those services.

The hospital's vision, organizational goals, and fundraising goals are summarized in Table 11.3.

Potential Plus

For Potential Plus, the central preoccupation in operations as well as in its fundraising activities is efficiency—keeping the cost of doing business tightly under control. Achieving the vision of Potential Plus requires a broad base of financial support (growth), but primarily because the agency must increase the efficiency of its fundraising program.

For years to come, the work of Potential Plus will be dominated by a large-scale exercise in bricks and mortar. This of course means a problematic capital campaign. A substantial amount of money must be raised, and apart from limited federal and state funding, there's no source in sight but private funds. This poses a managerial challenge—a complex merger—as well as lots of hard work to broaden the cause's financial base.

TABLE 11.3 Vision, Organizational Goals, and Fundraising Goals of
the Institute for Citywide Community Hospital.

Vision	Organizational Goals	Fundraising Goals
To sustain a state-of-the-art health care facility to heal the sick and injured in the local community, regardless of financial circumstances.	Within five years, merge the community hospital with two specialized clinics, contract with a major HMO to provide inpatient services, and upgrade the staff by launching a resident fellows program in cooperation with the nearby medical school.	Blanket the community with dual-purpose appeals (playing a public relations function as well as a fundraising role), highlight the hospital's contributions to the community through frequent public events that bring citizens into the facility, and secure major gifts from leading citizens to expand women's health programs, especially those related to childbirth, and launch a regional marketing and promotion plan for those services.

The fundraising goals that result from this challenge are as follows:

- Merge the individual agencies' development programs into a united effort, sparked by a $10 million capital campaign.
- Continue donor acquisition designed to enlist support from at least ten thousand new donors.
- Increase aggregate annual income by 10 percent per year.

Potential Plus's vision, organizational goals, and fundraising goals are summarized in Table 11.4 (on page 106).

Silver City Symphony Orchestra

The Silver City Symphony Orchestra can attain its vision only by achieving new musical heights and increasing its impact in the

TABLE 11.4 Vision, Organizational Goals, and Fundraising Goals
of the Institute for Potential Plus.

Vision	Organizational Goals	Fundraising Goals
To help developmentally disabled children live full and productive lives.	Bring scattered and uncoordinated services for "mentally retarded" children under one roof in a new, $10 million facility largely supported by private gifts.	Merge the individual agencies' development programs into a united effort, sparked by a $10 million capital campaign and continuing with a donor-acquisition program designed to enlist support from at least ten thousand new donors, and increase aggregate annual income by 10 percent per year.

region. This requires investing new resources on a significant scale—resources that must come in part from a larger number of donors. Existing donors, however, will clearly have to bear the lion's share of the load. Special efforts to motivate them must obviously be a central concern of the fundraising program. Meanwhile, the orchestra's focus on permanence dictates that stability must be the overriding consideration in conducting the fundraising program. Increasing the orchestra's financial support calls for a measure of growth—but growth that only helps bolster the institution's stability.

In practical terms, the orchestra's fundraising program might be structured along the following lines:

- Launch a $10,000-per-year Conductor's Club that will meet the budget for the recording program and permit paying higher fees to guest artists.
- Double the number of donors, to support additional performances.
- Increase the budget by 10 percent annually.

The orchestra's vision, organizational goals, and fundraising goals are summarized in Table 11.5.

Using This Approach for Your Organization

Now we're getting down to business! Has your strategic reassessment brought you to goals like "attracting and retaining the world's best-trained oncologists" or "featuring world-class guest artists?" Have you really gotten a long, clear look at the Big Picture? Then and only then will you be able to inspire both your colleagues and your donors.

To breathe life into the fundraising process, your goals must be expressed in superlatives, or in big round numbers, or in lofty, unquantifiable terms. That's what it takes.

As Jerold Panas has written so eloquently in *Mega-Gifts*, "There must be dazzling dreams and glorious visions for the future, all wrapped around the mission."

Take care, though: in your zeal to build high expectations, don't overreach. Unmet goals serve no one. When the time comes to

TABLE 11.5 Vision, Organizational Goals, and Fundraising Goals of the Silver City Symphony Orchestra.

Vision	Organizational Goals	Fundraising Goals
To help contemporary music lovers find new meaning in the classical symphonic repertoire.	Expand the orchestra's repertoire, attract world-class guest artists, launch a recording program within two years, and double the number of public performances within four years.	Launch a $10,000-per-year Conductor's Club that will meet the budget for the recording program and permit paying higher fees to guest artists, double the number of donors to support additional performances, and increase the budget by 10 percent annually.

tally the results, high morale swiftly plummets. Also, goals that are looking increasingly out of reach may tempt an organization's leadership to fudge its reports. Honesty and accountability must be the hallmarks of the fundraising process.

Still, your fundraising program needs what Stanford Graduate Business School professor James Collins has called a "Big Hairy Audacious Goal." (Since I've been sensitized by feminists, I'll just call it an Audacious Goal.) And here's what that means:

Be the best.

Do the most.

Get there first.

Make a difference!

Okay, you say, but what if the sky really isn't the limit? What if our organization has much more modest aspirations and capabilities?

That's easy.

Few people will expect you actually to be the best, do the most, or get there first. But everyone you approach for support must be absolutely convinced that what you're doing will truly make a difference! Otherwise, what's the point? Why not just close the agency's doors?

An audacious goal must be unattainable—at least in the short run. To inspire staff, board, and donors alike, your organization has to have high aspirations. There's really no way around that if you want to stay in business for long.

But it's tough to evaluate your progress toward unattainable goals! That's where *objectives* come in. We'll explore that topic in the following chapter.

12

Turning Fundraising Goals into Achievable Objectives

All these highfalutin concepts—vision, strategy, goals—are indispensable. They're the bread and butter of leadership—of generals, presidents, board chairs, and CEOs. As far as most people are concerned, they're the fun stuff. But as any self-respecting fundraiser knows, vision, strategy, and goals alone won't raise a nickel.

There's *work* to do. Somebody's got to convert these million-dollar concepts into saleable, digestible chunks of reality that will enable the likes of you and me to secure the necessary funding. That's where *objectives* come in.

An objective is a concrete, usually quantifiable target that will carry you partway toward a goal—from point A to point B, say, on your way to point Z. Objectives are goals writ small. Like a goal, an objective is

- A negotiated agreement between the people who will spend the money and the people who will raise it (assuming they're not all the same people)
- Based on rational, measurable needs
- Grounded in a realistic assessment of the institution's history, its capacity for fundraising, and the breadth and strength of its constituency

- Drawn from experience with comparable institutions and similar circumstances

Objectives have one attribute, however, that's not necessarily true of goals: they're *achievable*. Goals are meant, in part, to inspire. Objectives serve to encourage, by illustrating that measurable, incremental progress is a practical route toward lofty goals.

Enough abstract concept mongering! Let's get down to cases again. Let's see how the choice of objectives will help each of the five hypothetical nonprofits move steadily closer to its goals.

Institute for Advanced Cancer Research

Assume that you've just been hired by the institute as its new vice president for development. As the CEO and board members made clear in your interviews, your job is to guide the institution through a five-year development program, primarily focusing on growth in the donor base but secondarily ensuring that the growth doesn't destabilize the institution. Your goals are summed up as follows: *triple the number of donors, secure at least ten megagifts ($1 million plus), and increase the institute's annual budget from $20 million to $55 million.*

OK, now what? What do you *do*?

If you're methodical, you take a step-by-step approach:

1. Research any additional information you may need to quantify the goals. For example, find out how much it will cost to build that new research wing.

2. Figure out what has to happen to get you from point A to point Z. For instance, make sure you understand what "tripling the number of donors" means—not just how many donors you'll have to acquire but what level of effort that will entail and what resources it will require.

3. Break the job up into digestible, bite-sized chunks—efforts that will take you from point A to point B, then from B to C and so forth—and space them out over the course of the time available (in this case, five years), such as in the following scheme:

- *Year 1*: Increase active donors from 2,000 to 2,500 and identify and begin cultivating one hundred new megadonor prospects.

- *Year 2*: Increase active donors to 3,500 and identify top fifty prospective megadonors.

- *Year 3*: Increase active donors to 4,500, secure first megagift, and identify top thirty other prospects.

- *Year 4*: Increase active donors to 5,500 and secure two more megagifts.

- *Year 5*: Increase active donors to 6,500 and secure seven more megagifts.

In reality, you'll need to develop plans to a much finer level of detail, with quarterly or even monthly objectives. Naturally, at that level of resolution, details will matter a lot: it won't suffice to divide the numbers into fourths or twelfths. Specific events, fundraising schedules, and seasonal factors will weigh in heavily when you're determining quarterly or monthly objectives. (For example, the lion's share of those new donors may come from a single large event or mailing.)

Table 12.1 (on page 112) gives an overview of the institute's emerging strategic plan.

One for All

One for All's three-year challenge includes expanding one successful ongoing effort (Penny Potlucks) and launching two new initiatives: institutional fundraising (foundations or corporations) and creation of a community advisory council. All three efforts require careful spacing throughout the three years of the plan, as follows:

- *Year 1*: Secure a $10,000 corporate gift for Teach Understanding kits from one of three local companies, increase the number of Penny Potlucks from twelve to sixteen, and recruit the

TABLE 12.1 Emerging Strategic Plan of the Institute for
Advanced Cancer Research.

Vision	Organizational Goals	Fundraising Goals	Fundraising Objectives
To shine a beacon of hope into the lives of cancer patients everywhere.	Advance the science of cancer research by attracting and retaining the world's best-trained and most insightful oncologists and treating more than 1,000 of the most challenging cancer cases each year for the next five years.	Triple the number of donors, secure at least ten mega-gifts ($1 million plus), and increase the institute's annual budget from $20 million to $55 million.	Year 1: Increase active donors from 2,000 to 2,500; identify and begin cultivating 100 new megadonor prospects.

Year 2: Increase active donors to 3,500; identify top 50 prospective megadonors.

Year 3: Increase active donors to 4,500; secure first megagift; identify top 30 other prospects.

Year 4: Increase active donors to 5,500; secure two more megagifts.

Year 5: Increase active donors to 6,500; secure seven more megagifts. |

first three members of the new $500–per-year community
advisory council.

- *Year 2*: Bring in a $10,000 grant from one of five new
  foundations, increase the number of Penny Potlucks from
  sixteen to twenty, and add three members to the community
  advisory council.

- *Year 3*: Bring in a $10,000 grant from another new foundation
  or corporation, increase the number of Penny Potlucks
  from twenty to twenty-four, and add four members to the
  community advisory council.

Table 12.2 (on page 114) gives an overview of One for All's
emerging strategic plan.

Because involvement is the guiding principle in One for All's
fundraising program, as many of its fundraising efforts as possible
must involve donors in the group's educational work. This is certainly the case in its Penny Potluck programs, which offer excellent
opportunities for demonstrations and discussion, and in its community advisory council, which will be directly engaged in representing One for All to the community's political leadership. The
only exception (and not necessarily so) are the new institutional
donors the group wants to recruit. There may well be good reasons,
from One for All's perspective as well as from the perspective of the
donor institutions, for such donors to be involved.

Citywide Community Hospital

Citywide Community Hospital's fundraising objectives are as follows:

- *Year 1*: Mail Community Health Care Surveys to all fifty
  thousand households at six-month intervals, organize the
  first annual $100-minimum gala with a top film star, and
  launch a lecture and workshop series featuring hospital staff.

- *Year 2*: Mail one Community Health Care Survey to each of
  fifty thousand households, launch a community health care

TABLE 12.2 Emerging Strategic Plan of One for All.

Vision	Organizational Goals	Fundraising Goals	Fundraising Objectives
To bring closer the day when racism no longer poisons our lives.	Conduct antiracism workshops for every significant community group within the next three years, distribute "Teach Understanding" kits to every fifth-grade teacher in town, and secure agreement from the County Board of Supervisors to rename a major highway in honor of Dr. Martin Luther King, Jr.	Within the next three years, secure grants of at least $10,000 each from three new foundations or corporations, double the number of Penny Potluck fundraising events each year, recruit a group of politically savvy donors (a community advisory council) who will fund the drive to lobby the board of supervisors, and raise the yearly budget by $25,000 per year.	Year 1: Secure $10,000 corporate gift for Teach Understanding kits from one of three local companies, increase number of Penny Potlucks from 12 to 16, and recruit first three members of new $500–per-year community advisory council. Year 2: Bring in $10,000 grant from one of five new foundations, increase number of Penny Potlucks from 16 to 20, and add three members to the community advisory council. Year 3: Bring in $10,000 grant from another new foundation or corporation, increase number of Penny Potlucks from 20 to 24, and add four members to the community advisory council.

newsletter, hold the second annual gala, continue the lecture and workshop series, and recruit a lead donor for the women's health program.

- *Year 3*: Mail one Community Health Care Survey plus two issues of community newsletter to each of fifty thousand households, hold the third annual gala, continue the lecture and workshop series, and recruit the second lead donor for the women's health program.

Table 12.3 (on page 116) gives an overview of Citywide Community Hospital's emerging strategic plan.

Potential Plus

Following are the fundraising objectives of Potential Plus:

- *Year 1*: Consummate merger, conduct capital campaign feasibility study, and launch sixty-thousand-piece donor acquisition test mailing.
- *Year 2*: Secure $2 to $3 million lead gift for capital campaign and mail 300,000 letters to recruit two thousand new donors.
- *Year 3*: Secure $4 to $6 million in additional leadership gifts and mail 500,000 letters to recruit four thousand new donors.
- *Year 4*: Launch public phase of capital campaign for last $1 to $3 million and mail 1,000,000 letters to recruit six thousand new donors.
- *Year 5*: Reach $10 million campaign goal and mail 600,000 letters to recruit four thousand new donors to replace those lost through attrition.

Table 12.4 (on page 117) gives an overview of Potential Plus's emerging strategic plan.

TABLE 12.3 Emerging Strategic Plan of Citywide Community Hospital.

Vision	Organizational Goals	Fundraising Goals	Fundraising Objectives
To sustain a state-of-the-art health care facility to heal the sick and injured in the local community regardless of financial circumstances.	Within five years, merge the community hospital with two specialized clinics, contract with a major HMO to provide inpatient services, and upgrade the staff by launching a resident fellows program in cooperation with the nearby medical school.	Blanket the community with dual purpose appeals (playing a public relations function as well as a fundraising role), highlight the hospital's contributions to the community through frequent public events that bring citizens into the facility, and secure major gifts from leading citizens to to expand women's health programs, especially those related to childbirth, and launch a regional marketing and promotion plan for those services.	Year 1: Mail community health care surveys to all 50,000 households at six-month intervals, organize first annual $100-minimum gala with top film star, and launch lecture and workshop series featuring hospital staff.

Year 2: Mail one community health care survey to each of 50,000 households, launch community health care newsletter, hold second annual gala, continue lecture and workshop series, and recruit lead donor for women's health program.

Year 3: Mail one community health care survey plus two issues of community newsletter to each of 50,000 households, hold third annual gala, continue lecture and workshop series, and recruit lead donor for women's health program. |

TABLE 12.4 Emerging Strategic Plan of Potential Plus.

Vision	Organizational Goals	Fundraising Goals	Fundraising Objectives
To help developmentally disabled children live full and productive lives.	Bring scattered and uncoordinated services for "mentally retarded" children under one roof in a new, $10 million facility largely supported by private gifts.	Merge the individual agencies' development programs sparked by a $10 million capital campaign and continuing with a donor-acquisition program designed to enlist support from at least ten thousand new donors, and increase aggregate annual income by 10 percent per year.	Year 1. Consummate merger, conduct capital campaign feasibility study, and launch 60,000-piece donor acquisition test mailing. Year 2. Secure $2–3 million lead gift for capital campaign and mail 300,000 letters to recruit 2,000 new donors. Year 3. Secure $4–6 million in additional leadership gifts and mail 500,000 letters to recruit 4,000 new donors. Year 4. Launch public phase of capital campaign for last $1–3 million and mail 1,000,000 letters to recruit 6,000 new donors. Year 5. Reach $10 million campaign goal and mail 600,000 letters to recruit 4,000 new donors to replace those lost through attrition.

Silver City Symphony Orchestra

The Silver City Symphony Orchestra intends to stay around for a very long time. Despite the ups and downs of fundraising results and the twists and turns in musical tastes, the orchestra's leadership—including you as director of development—has resolved to boost the stability of the fundraising program by launching a new major-donor giving society and increasing the number of donors. In other words, the orchestra's strategy can best be described as STABILITY + growth. Its fundraising goals are to launch a $10,000-per-year Conductor's Club that will meet the budget for the recording program and permit paying higher fees to guest artists while doubling the number of donors to support additional performances.

In practice, this strategy requires three years of hard work. As with the other organizations, that work must be broken up into more manageable pieces:

- *Year 1:* Launch Conductor's Club with first three $10,000 gifts and increase active donors from 500 to 650.
- *Year 2:* Recruit five new Conductor's Club members and increase active donors from 650 to 800.
- *Year 3:* Recruit seven new Conductor's Club members and increase active donors from 800 to 1,000.

Table 12.5 gives an overview of the orchestra's emerging strategic plan.

Though their strategies and goals are dramatically different, the process of setting objectives is very similar at these institutions. For instance, it may be unrealistic to expect to recruit fifteen $10,000-a-year donors in less than three years. In fact, you could easily spend most of the first year recruiting only the very first of those donors. So it seems prudent to stretch out the process, using all the available time. After all, if you exceed your objectives, the board isn't likely to complain!

TABLE 12.5 Emerging Strategic Plan of the Silver City Symphony
           Orchestra.

Vision	Organizational Goals	Fundraising Goals	Fundraising Objectives
To help contemporary music lovers find new meaning in the classical symphonic repertoire.	Expand the orchestra's repertoire, attract world-class guest artists, launch a recording program within two years, and double the number of public performances within four years.	Launch a $10,000-per-year Conductor's Club that will meet the budget for the recording program and permit paying higher fees to guest artists, double the number of donors to support additional performances, and increase the budget by 10 percent annually.	Year 1. Launch Conductor's Club with first three $10,000 gifts and increase active donors from 500 to 650. Year 2. Recruit five new Conductor's Club members and increase active donors from 650 to 800. Year 3. Recruit seven new Conductor's Club members and increase active donors from 800 to 1,000.

Notice, please, that, concrete and measurable as they are, the
fundraising objectives spelled out for each of the five hypothetical
nonprofits don't explain *how* the job is to be done. They merely
define the dimensions of the job. Such instructions as "increase
active donors from 2,000 to 2,500" sidestep the question of
fundraising methods and techniques. After all, by what means are
you to increase the number of active donors? Special events? Telemarketing? Face-to-face solicitation? What do you actually *do* to
achieve your objectives? Read on. That's the topic taken up in
Chapter Thirteen.

13

Understanding the Ten Most Common Fundraising Tactics

My premise in this book is that how you raise funds for your organization—that means the fundraising tools (or tactics) you select and how you use them—can help or hinder you in the pursuit of your mission. This and the following chapter look at this issue from a strategic perspective. This chapter examines a menu of ten of the most commonly used fundraising methods, and Chapter Fourteen returns to the five hypothetical examples of the preceding chapters and takes a closer look at how the ten techniques might be put to work in each of these cases. Following these chapters you will find five self-assessment worksheets designed to help you determine your organization's readiness to benefit from five of the riskiest and most demanding fundraising techniques: the capital campaign, special events, planned giving, direct mail, and telemarketing.

Ten Tools You Can Use

Broadly speaking, there are three kinds of fundraising:

• *Institutional fundraising* involves asking for money from organizations such as charitable foundations, churches, corporations and other businesses, and public agencies. In general, this type of fundraising is remarkably cost-effective. In other words, a small investment in a good proposal and appropriate follow-up can pay off in a big grant or contribution.

- In *major-donor fundraising*, nonprofits seek gifts from individuals of means. (Call them "rich people" if you want, but most of them don't think they're rich. That's especially true if you're talking about grassroots organizations, where $500 might constitute a major gift. Gifts of that size are frequently made by people with incomes under $30,000.) Like institutional fundraising, major-donor fundraising is typically very efficient from a financial standpoint. It doesn't cost a whole lot to dial the phone or even pick up a lunch tab.

- *Small-donor fundraising*, by contrast, is usually much less efficient than either institutional or major-donor fundraising—at least at first. Most of the methods employed—particularly direct mail, telephone outreach, and special events—are all costly, and none of them works in a vacuum. Their success requires reinforcement from the organization in such forms as advertising and public relations activities, as well as donor newsletters or other means of cultivating donors.

It's obvious, then, isn't it? Because institutional and major-donor fundraising are so much more efficient than small-donor fundraising, shouldn't we all confine ourselves to those lusher pastures?

Well, no.

Actually, there are five reasons why it makes sense for most nonprofits to conduct small-donor fundraising programs, messy though they may be:

- Almost ninety cents of every dollar raised in the United States is estimated to come from individuals, not institutions. Most of this amount—nearly eighty cents—comes from living individuals. The rest is from donors' estates.

- About sixty cents of every dollar comes from individuals or families with incomes of $50,000 and under.

- Major-donor fundraising isn't practical for every nonprofit. Some groups hold no attraction for upper-income people. Others aren't ready to pursue, much less accept, large gifts. Even institutional fundraising opportunities may be severely limited. Modest gifts from middle- and low-income individuals and families may be your only recourse. (In any case, small donors sometimes become large donors—most often by leaving bequests.)

• A nonprofit that demonstrates broad community support is almost always stronger as a result. Both institutional and major individual donors frequently demand evidence of such support before they'll dig really deeply into their resources.

• In grassroots nonprofits, the organization's character or strategy may *require* broad-based financial support. It may be inappropriate for such an organization—for example, a community-based organization lobbying for legislation by the city council—to secure the bulk of its funding from major or institutional donors.

There is an abundance of fundraising techniques. I'll confine this discussion to ten of the most commonly employed methods of meeting nonprofit budgets. Very broadly speaking, they fall into two categories: big gifts and little gifts.

Big Gifts

Methods commonly used to secure *big gifts* include the following:

1. *Foundation grants.* Foundation grants account for roughly ten cents of every dollar raised by nonprofit organizations in the United States in recent years. However, many nonprofits subsist largely—even entirely—on the largesse of public foundations. (As the discussion of the five strategies, especially Stability Strategies, has shown, this is not a healthy situation.) Noncorporate foundation giving has been growing by double digits in recent years. The stock market's continuing rise has ballooned the assets of some foundations to unheard-of levels, and spawned a rush of new family and personal foundations, often linked with people who have become wealthy almost literally overnight.

2. *Corporate support.* Corporations contribute a little more than five cents of every dollar donated to U.S. nonprofits. There are four distinct sources of this corporate money:

• Charitable gifts from in-house corporate foundations

- Support for cause-related marketing programs, usually from a company's marketing, public relations, or community relations budget (But don't get your hopes up; it's hard to find willing companies. You'll net only a small amount unless yours is a national campaign. You're unlikely to acquire the names of new donors in the process, and the corporation's commitment will wane quickly if sales volume doesn't measure up to its targets.)

- Employee contributions secured through workplace giving programs, usually for the United Way or the Combined Federal Campaign

- In-kind gifts of products or services

This discussion refers to only the first two of these three sources. The third source, residing in a gray area, is more properly thought of in connection with individual small-donor fundraising efforts.

3. *Major gifts.* For the majority of charities in North America, major-donor fundraising yields the lion's share of income. In other words, a few individuals underwrite most of the charity's costs.

In a small organization, an "angel" or a small group of deeply committed founders may be largely self-motivated. There may be no need for a staff member or program dedicated exclusively to the care and feeding of major donors. In fact, major donors tend to be board members themselves, for reasons that will surprise no one, and an estimated four out of five gifts of $1 million or more come from trustees.

4. *Capital campaign.* The need to build a building (or an endowment) affords a uniquely attractive fundraising opportunity for a nonprofit organization. Unlike day-to-day operational costs, these needs are relatively easy to raise money for—at least in theory. Some people love to have their names (or those of their loved ones) emblazoned on the portals of proud new buildings, or even just on plaques. The appeal of immortality is irresistible to many folks. To many others, a capital campaign simply affords an opportunity to make a big difference.

A well-established charity may be limited to raising modest sums in most of its fundraising endeavors. But with a strong place in the community and a broad base of individual support, the organization may be able to raise millions through a capital campaign. In theory, it's simple: design a process with a beginning, a middle, and an end; plot it out on the calendar; and start. That's all there is to a campaign after all! But there's a catch: it might not work.

That's why every intelligently run nonprofit conducts a feasibility study before risking the embarrassment or ruin of a failed capital campaign. Almost always this involves retaining outside counsel to bring specialized assessment tools to bear, along with an outsider's fresh perspective.

A capital campaign feasibility study successfully conducted along traditional lines is more than an insurance policy against failure. Done properly, it virtually guarantees the campaign's success. That's because the process unearths commitments for leadership gifts—frequently a third or more of the money to be raised.

5. *Planned gifts (including bequests)*. The scope and complexity of the field within a field that is now increasingly called *gift planning* is vast and the techniques employed are not widely understood. The term covers everything from codicils in wills to life insurance and annuity deals to a wide array of trust arrangements. Trusts and annuities may be designed to suit the donor's convenience, the vagaries of the income and estate tax laws, or the cash flow requirements of charities.

Bequests—the legacies that donors leave by writing your organization into their wills or living trusts—are far and away the most common form of planned gifts. Specialists estimate that at least eight out of ten planned gifts come in this straightforward fashion. (Some say nine out of ten.)

More and more these days, the $15,000 or $30,000 bequests that drift over the transom from time to time are the real reason that some nonprofits continue to invest so heavily in direct mail and telephone fundraising, despite their high fundraising ratios. All that contact and cultivation over the years can pay off in a very big way!

In fact, bequests now account for nearly eight cents of every dollar raised by charity in the United States.

Where do bequests come from? If mention of wills and bequests conjures up visions of the idle rich, consider this story: an organization working to end hunger received a check in a plain envelope one December. The amount? $100,000. It was a bequest from a Carmelite nun who had made modest gifts over the years.

In the same vein, planned-giving specialists report that their organizations frequently encounter donors with records that look a lot like those in Table 13.1.

Small Gifts

Methods frequently used to secure what I've loosely called small gifts include direct mail, telephone fundraising, Web sites, special events, and merchandising. We'll examine each in turn.

6. *Direct mail.* Direct mail is essential to the fundraising programs of most nonprofit organizations. Few groups, however, will admit they use direct mail to raise money.

More typically, a nonprofit operates an annual fund and just "happens" to solicit and receive the preponderance of gifts through the mail, or the effort might be referred to as a membership program based on dues or an annual contribution.

How are dues customarily sought and obtained? By mail, of

TABLE 13.1 The Giving History of a Loyal Donor.

1989	$100
1990	$50
1991	$100
1992	$100
1993	$25
1994	$25
1995	$106,511

course! Even many organizations that survive on the less pre-dictable cash flows of an unstructured individual-giving program rely largely on the mail to communicate with their donors. But they wouldn't be caught dead calling the process direct-mail fundraising.

Like it or not, whatever you call it, it's direct mail, and your organization must come to terms with the complexities of this poorly understood set of fundraising tools.

7. *Telephone fundraising.* Despite the bad reputation generated by legions of telemarketers peddling credit cards, aluminum siding, and questionable causes, the telephone has proven to be a consis-tently useful tool for a host of nonprofit organizations. Like direct mail, telephone fundraising, or *telefundraising*, is a flexible tool that fundraisers use in multiple ways, including the following:

- Membership or annual fund renewal
- Recruitment for high-dollar giving clubs
- Reactivation of lapsed (inactive) members or donors
- Recruitment for monthly sustainer (pledge) programs
- Special appeals
- Donor upgrade solicitations
- Emergency appeals

In-bound telemarketing—using a toll-free number and an answering machine or a professional service bureau—may also be useful for scheduling appointments for service, providing informa-tion, or selling tickets to events.

8. *Web sites.* Increasingly, the world's attention is turning to the Internet. Almost every self-respecting nonprofit organization of any substantial size now maintains its own site on the World Wide Web. Some have several sites, and a few organizations have man-aged to use them effectively as part of the mix of communications media employed in their development programs. More and more, nonprofit Web sites are used to recruit new members or donors and

to provide a host of services to existing members, in addition to public education, community service, and many other important applications. Inevitably, the Web will loom progressively larger in the fundraiser's toolbox as the years go by.

9. *Special events.* For every nonprofit organization that thrives on the basis of a multimillion-dollar annual telethon, long-distance race, or star-studded gala dinner-dance, there are thousands that might well be content to break even at a spaghetti feed or barbecue. And not every event is designed as a fundraising event. In fact, a Visibility Strategy or Growth Strategy might induce an organization to stage an event expressly designed not to yield an immediate profit. Community building, public exposure, name identification, or positioning—in short, putting the organization on the map—may be reason enough to swallow the costs of a high-profile event not fully covered by the price of admission. For the most part, however, special events tend to be viewed simplistically as an easy way for a nonprofit to make money. They're not. Too often overconfidence or lack of sophistication results in disappointing proceeds or even losses. Still, properly managed special events are an indispensible fundraising tool for tens of thousands of nonprofit organizations. And they will continue to be, as long as people band together in common cause in private, voluntary organizations to address the problems of their communities. Successful special events typically raise the lion's share of net money from sponsors or underwriters, and they make extensive use of in-kind gifts as well as volunteers to plan and execute the program and to solicit sponsorship gifts.

10. *Merchandising.* A great many nonprofits earn income from merchandising, which usually capitalizes on the organization's logo and its goodwill. Net income may be meager, but merchandising potentially offers other benefits as well. The display of branded merchandise is free advertising. Members' or donors' sense of belonging may be reinforced by using a backpack, mug, T-shirt, or a windbreaker bearing the organization's logo.

Don't make the mistake of thinking that these ten fundraising methods are equally important. They're not. As in most human affairs, some things are more important than others.

Take major donor fundraising, for example. Major gifts rarely come out of the blue. They're usually the product of a long process of education, involvement, and cultivation. That's why major gift fundraising takes so much time and energy.

If it's so hard to secure major gifts, why do it? Because you probably have no choice.

Major-donor fundraising comes the closest of all the instruments on the fundraiser's workbench to being indispensable. Why? Principally for two reasons:

• Major gifts often set off a waterfall effect, causing lots of less well-off (or less generous) donors to join the cause. Major donors can lend credibility to an organization.

• With the possible exception of planned giving, major-donor development and capital campaigns are typically an organization's most cost-effective fundraising programs. It's common for major gifts to be brought in at a cost of no more than a few pennies on the dollar.

If your organization hasn't at least explored the potential of securing large individual gifts, you're making a big mistake.

Now let's put these ten widely employed fundraising methods to work. Chapter Fourteen examines what these tools can do to advance the fundraising strategies elected by the five hypothetical nonprofit organizations discussed in the preceding chapters.

14

Choosing the Right Tactics for Your Fundraising Strategy

Your vision is clear, your goals are compelling, your strategy is obvious, and your objectives are bold and explicit. You know what fundraising tools are available to support your development campaign. Now what? How do you identify the right tactics for pursuing your strategic goals? To shed some light on this question, let's turn once again to the five hypothetical nonprofit organizations.

Institute for Advanced Cancer Research

When the sun last established on the Institute for Advanced Cancer Research, it had established unusually ambitious goals and was contemplating a five-year fundraising campaign to realize them (see Table 14.1 on page 130).

The heightened visibility that the new research wing will bring and the need for substantially more money than the institute has previously raised in a similar period lend themselves perfectly to a *capital campaign*. The catch, however, is that the institute's current donor base is too small to provide the breadth and depth of community support that the campaign's goals require, and the institute is simply not well-enough known to attract the support it needs.

Growth, then—attention-getting growth that's focused on the capital campaign's need for a much larger number of major donor prospects—is paramount. The ultimate objective is to broaden the

TABLE 14.1 Institute for Advanced Cancer Research: GROWTH + visibility.

Vision	Organizational Goals	Fundraising Goals	Fundraising Objectives
To shine a beacon of hope into the lives of cancer patients everywhere.	Advance the science of cancer research by attracting and retaining the world's best-trained and most insightful oncologists and treating more than 1,000 of the most challenging cancer cases each year for the next five years.	Triple the number of donors, secure at least ten mega-gifts ($1 million plus), and increase the institute's annual budget from $20 million to $55 million.	Year 1: Increase active donors from 2,000 to 2,500; identify and begin cultivating 100 new megadonor prospects. Year 2: Increase active donors to 3,500; identify top 50 prospective megadonors. Year 3: Increase active donors to 4,500; secure first megagift; identify top 30 other prospects. Year 4: Increase active donors to 5,500; secure two more megagifts. Year 5: Increase active donors to 6,500; secure seven more megagifts.

institute's financial base. At the same time, the institute must reach higher and farther than ever before for the multimillion-dollar gifts that are essential to building the new wing.

Many of the other techniques examined in the previous chapter will prove useful in the course of the institute's capital campaign. Let's review each of them briefly:

• *Foundation grants.* The institute must demonstrate substantial community support to succeed. However, foundation grants may provide a significant number of the ten megagifts that are central to the success of the campaign.

• *Corporate giving.* Corporations, especially pharmaceutical companies and two local Fortune 500 companies concerned with good community relations, might also become megadonors.

• *Major gifts.* Generous individual contributions, including some of those ten megagifts, will have to account for a very large share of the total funds raised in the campaign. A focus on major gifts is almost always central to a capital campaign, which is designed around a "gift table" that allocates half or more of the goal to a handful of major donors.

• *Planned giving.* Gift planning can be a useful tool in discussions with many major donors. But only certain planned giving instruments—investment mechanisms through which donors transfer cash to the institute rather than merely promise an ultimate gift—will be directly useful in the capital campaign if all funds must be in hand within five years. (In some circumstances, a firm pledge will suffice.)

• *Direct mail.* Aggressive community outreach via the mails is the primary tool the institute can use to expand its donor base. Direct mail can be used to build community awareness of the project, to keep the institute's profile high as the construction proceeds, and to recruit new donors. Early in the campaign, high-dollar direct mail might be especially useful in enlisting potential major donors. More extensive use of mail—to the community at large—would make especially good sense later in the campaign, once the goal is in sight.

- *Telemarketing*. Telephone contact with new donors—merely to thank them, for example, or to invite them to join a giving club—should strengthen the institute's small-donor program and heighten the chances that some of those small donors might become good prospects for major contributions before the campaign ends.

- *Web site*. Potential on-line applications in the institute's capital campaign include daily updates on the campaign's progress, public recognition for major donors (including foundations and corporations), live-action scenes of the construction once it is under way, and a free educational e-mail newsletter to donors and the community at large.

- *Special events*. For a regional institution such as the Institute for Advanced Cancer Research, special events can play a large role. Events can be used to cultivate and reward donors, to augment the visibility of the institute, and to mark milestones in the campaign. A gala fundraising event held each year might even contribute a significant share toward the campaign goal.

- *Merchandising*. In all likelihood, merchandising will not be useful as an element in the institute's capital campaign.

On the basis of this menu of useful fundraising techniques, the institute's development staff can construct the broad outlines of a plan as well as a time line calculated to achieve the objectives and ultimately the goal set for the campaign. Other nonprofit organizations setting out a growth trajectory would be likely to look on the same list of techniques in a similar fashion. Their options might be those outlined in Table 14.2.

One for All

Table 14.3 (on page 134) portrays the scene at One for All when we last checked in there.

One for All's mission—fighting racism—requires intensive, ongoing efforts to involve members of the community as intimately as possible. This overarching theme colors the group's choice of

TABLE 14.2 Potential Applications of Fundraising Tactics
to Promote Growth.

Tactic	Application(s) in a Typical Growth Strategy
Foundation grants	If available, foundation funding may support capacity building. Foundation giving per se doesn't support growth.
Corporate giving	If available, corporate gifts may support capacity building. Corporate giving per se doesn't support growth, except where members or constituents are corporations.
Major gifts	Major gifts are almost always attractive but usually have little to do with growth.
Capital campaign	A planned capital campaign may require growth in order to build a base of campaign prospects. Often a capital campaign is a useful growth vehicle.
Planned giving	Encouraging bequests and other forms of planned giving may make eminently good sense but is not a likely vehicle to realize growth.
Direct mail	Traditionally direct mail has been—and will be for many years to come—the centerpiece of a growth strategy. Used both to recruit new members or donors and to cultivate, educate, and resolicit them.
Telemarketing	This is a risky approach to growth per se because phone-acquired donors usually require expensive subsequent phoning to renew, but it is extremely useful in specialized applications in coordination with direct mail.
Web site	Increasingly, this is an attractive way to increase growth in membership or a donor base.
Special events	These are sometimes useful for local and regional organizations as a prospecting device (with the risk that donors' motives for giving may be mixed and thus a poor predictor of future behavior).
Merchandising	In direct marketing programs—mail, telephone, and Internet—merchandising is often helpful as a source of premiums (membership incentives). In itself, merchandising doesn't directly support growth.

TABLE 14.3 One for All: INVOLVEMENT + visibility.

Vision	Organizational Goals	Fundraising Goals	Fundraising Objectives
To bring closer the day when racism no longer poisons our lives.	Conduct antiracism workshops for every significant community group within the next three years, distribute "Teach Understanding" kits to every fifth-grade teacher in town, and secure agreement from the County Board of Supervisors to rename a major highway in honor of Dr. Martin Luther King, Jr.	Within the next three years, secure grants of at least $10,000 each from three new foundations or corporations, double the number of Penny Potluck fundraising events each year, recruit a group of politically savvy donors (a community advisory council) who will fund the drive to lobby the board of supervisors, and raise the yearly budget by $25,000 per year.	Year 1: Secure $10,000 corporate gift for Teach Understanding kits from one of three local companies, increase number of Penny Potlucks from 12 to 16, and recruit first three members of new $500–per-year community advisory council. Year 2: Bring in $10,000 grant from one of five new foundations, increase number of Penny Potlucks from 16 to 20, and add three members to the community advisory council. Year 3: Bring in $10,000 grant from another new foundation or corporation, increase number of Penny Potlucks from 20 to 24, and add four members to the community advisory council.

fundraising tactics. As much as possible, One for All will favor those fundraising methods that in themselves help to involve and educate the community. For example, here's how One for All might look on the ten common fundraising techniques we've been considering:

- *Foundation grants*. If any local foundation is deeply interested in combating racism in the community, it would certainly be natural for One for All to turn to them for help. However, if One for All has produced encouraging results to date, it might consider approaching that foundation, along with others, as part of a collaborative through which One for All would have the opportunity to train other local groups in replicating its work. A collaborative approach may also be inherently attractive to local foundations interested in community building.

- *Corporate giving*. Cash-and-carry corporate gifts would, of course, help underwrite One for All's efforts. How much better, though, to approach sympathetic local corporations and propose some form of on-site program involving corporate employees as part of the deal! In other words, a corporation might not just contribute the cash One for All needs to operate. By organizing antiracism efforts in its offices or plants, the company also might directly help advance the group's agenda.

- *Major gifts*. For a small grassroots organization such as One for All, especially one grappling with an issue so ringed with controversy, very large gifts are unlikely. The Institute for Advanced Cancer Research might expect seven-figure gifts from some of its donors. One for All can't. However, some of the more well-to-do activists in the community might reasonably be asked to contribute, say, $500 per year—hence One for All's new Community Advisory Council. For members of this high-dollar giving club, such active efforts as meetings with local elected officials might be very attractive, an inducement to give while also, of course, calculated to further One for All's work.

- *Planned giving*. One for All is the sort of organization that may encounter difficulty seeking bequests and planned gifts. Most donors will question whether the organization is likely to remain in existence for more than a few years.

• *Direct mail.* If the community where One for All is located is large enough, well-enough educated, and sufficiently affluent, direct mail fundraising may be effective. In smaller communities, however, direct mail for a group such as One for All is likely to be limited to a newsletter and occasional appeals mailed to previous donors.

• *Telemarketing.* Donor contact by phone may be useful. For example, a senior staff member might phone to thank a donor upon receiving any gift of, say, $100 or more. Telefundraising in its professional form probably won't be productive—unless some local, headline-grabbing crisis has forced the issue into people's awareness and One for All wants to complete the phoning faster than its volunteers are capable of doing.

• *Web site.* With sufficient staff resources, a Web site can be useful in cementing relations with Internet-savvy donors—a fast-growing lot. E-mail bulletins can be productive, too, either as a supplement to or (eventually) instead of mailing invitations to special events. More importantly, a well-maintained Web site could serve as a means to permit donors to participate in ongoing program and issue discussions at One for All.

• *Special events.* For a community-based organization such as One for All, special events are a natural if not central component of the development program. The group's Penny Potlucks serve a dual function—raising modest amounts of money while directly involving contributors in activities that exemplify the work against racism.

• *Merchandising.* Merchandising is unlikely to be useful as an element in One for All's fundraising program. The requirements for maintaining inventory and managing sales can be taxing and are probably not a good use of the group's limited staff time and money.

In similar fashion, as shown in Table 14.4, other nonprofit organizations committed to an Involvement Strategy might choose among these fundraising techniques.

TABLE 14.4 Potential Applications of Fundraising Tactics to Promote Involvement.

Tactic	Application(s) in a Typical Involvement Strategy
Foundation grants	Except as a possible source of funding for new programs, foundation grants are not often directly applicable to donor or member involvement.
Corporate giving	Except as a possible source of funding for new programs, corporate giving is not often directly applicable to donor or member involvement.
Major gifts	Personal notes and phone calls, face-to-face solicitation, intimate major-donor events, and other involving activities are frequently important in a donor Involvement Strategy.
Capital campaign	Usually, heavy donor (volunteer) involvement is useful—often, indispensable—in a capital campaign. The converse isn't necessarily true, however. A capital campaign may actually distract donors from other forms of involvement.
Planned giving	Except as a possible source of funding for new programs, planned giving is not often directly applicable to donor or member involvement. (Encouraging planned gifts is an inherently involving activity, however.)
Direct mail	For a large or widely scattered membership or donor base, direct mail may be extremely useful if communications (both solicitations and newsletters) actively encourage direct donor action and feedback.
Telemarketing	For a large or widely scattered membership or donor base, telemarketing may be extremely useful if phone calls encourage direct donor action and feedback—perhaps soliciting opinions as well as gifts.
Web site	This will increasingly prove to be a valuable adjunct to any involvement strategy. A Web site offers endless opportunities for participation and two-way communications—that is, direct donor involvement—at extremely low cost.
Special events	Particularly useful may be a donor benefit or special gift acknowledgment. Volunteer-run events may encourage deeper involvement.
Merchandising	Merchandising involves donors or members only if it affords opportunities for them to pursue efforts that support the organization's mission.

Citywide Community Hospital

Table 14.5 depicts the scene we last viewed at the Citywide Community Hospital.

To promote its visibility-centered fundraising strategy, the hospital's development staff might look on the available fundraising techniques as follows:

- *Foundation grants.* Local foundations or those with special interest in health care may be good prospects. Perhaps a foundation might be located to endow a resident fellow's chair, university-style. Few foundations, however, would be interested in underwriting a brand-X community hospital—and probably only to back specific new programs or projects. In any event, the hospital's big challenge is twofold: to build awareness of the newly merged institution throughout the community and to lay the groundwork for efficient fundraising operations in the future. These ends will be better served by other, more public fundraising methods.

- *Corporate giving.* The prospects for corporate gifts are roughly analogous to those for foundation grants. However, perhaps a local pharmaceutical or medical supply manufacturer would take special interest in supporting the Citywide Community Hospital.

- *Major gifts.* Where appropriate, the hospital's development staff will presumably seek out large individual contributions—perhaps from a wealthy physician or ex-patient. Job one, however, is to make the hospital visible.

- *Planned giving.* Perhaps a few farsighted donors will consider leaving bequests or looking into other forms of planned giving. For the most part, however, donors are likely to withhold such generous support until the hospital has established an institutional identity and a favorable track record of service. Thus, activities to promote planned giving probably won't be fruitful.

- *Direct mail.* Direct-mail contact, supplemented by both free and paid media, including the local newspaper, selected radio and TV stations, and billboards, will be indispensable for the Citywide Community Hospital. A community health care survey to raise

TABLE 14.5 Citywide Community Hospital: VISIBILITY + stability.

Vision	Organizational Goals	Fundraising Goals	Fundraising Objectives
To sustain a state-of-the-art health care facility to heal the sick and injured in the local community, regardless of financial circumstances.	Within five years, merge the community hospital with two specialized clinics, contract with a major HMO to provide inpatient services, and upgrade the staff by launching a resident fellows program in cooperation with the nearby medical school.	Blanket the community with dual-purpose appeals (playing a public relations function as well as a fundraising role), highlight the hospital's contributions to the community through frequent public events that bring citizens into the facility, and secure major gifts from leading citizens to to expand women's health programs, especially those related to childbirth, and launch a regional marketing and promotion plan for those services.	Year 1: Mail community health care surveys to all 50,000 households at six-month intervals, organize first annual $100-minimum gala with top film star, and launch lecture and workshop series featuring hospital staff.

Year 2: Mail one community health care survey to each of 50,000 households launch community health care newsletter, hold second annual gala, continue lecture and workshop series, and recruit lead donor for women's health program.

Year 3: Mail one community health care survey plus two issues of community newsletter to each of 50,000 households, hold third annual gala, continue lecture and workshop series, and recruit lead donor for women's health program. |

awareness of the newly merged institution and to solicit feedback (and secondarily, gifts) may be an ideal way to take the hospital's awareness campaign directly into people's homes. A practical, easily readable newsletter on health care issues is another potentially useful tool.

• *Telemarketing*. For the hospital, the telephone is most likely to be useful as a means to *receive* calls from interested members of the community rather than as a way to call out to them. A toll-free number (if necessary) could be prominently displayed on all promotional material, inviting inquiries about the merger, the hospital's expanded services, or even selected health care issues.

• *Web site*. Referrals to a toll-free line could also be promoted on the Web. Perhaps the hospital would find it useful to package readily available information about common diseases and medications and promote its availability throughout the city. If the hospital possesses special knowledge, such as cutting-edge research results or data about the state of health in the city, a Web site might help stimulate additional interest.

• *Special events*. Splashy, widely promoted special events are an excellent way for the hospital to get out the word and to build goodwill in the community. In the early years, however (assuming that events are intended to be held annually), it seems unlikely that they would be highly profitable. Their principal function is to support the visibility effort.

• *Merchandising*. Premiums bearing the logo and name of the newly merged hospital may be useful, especially in conjunction with special events (golf jackets at a golf tournament, for example, or branded wineglasses at a banquet). But unless there's a volunteer-run gift shop that's a profit center for the hospital, the sale of merchandise is not a likely source of financial support.

Table 14.6 lists how other organizations seeking visibility are likely to regard the same ten fundraising techniques.

TABLE 14.6 Potential Applications of Fundraising Tactics to Promote Visibility.

Tactic	Application(s) in a Typical Visibility Strategy
Foundation grants	Except as possible sources of funding for new attention-getting efforts, foundation grants are not often directly applicable to visibility.
Corporate giving	Except as a possible source of funding for new attention-getting efforts, corporate giving is not often directly applicable to visibility.
Major gifts	Except as a possible source of funding for new attention-getting efforts, major gifts are not often directly applicable to visibility.
Capital campaign	Visibility may be the centerpiece of a capital campaign's public phase, and a capital campaign—especially with highly visible bricks-and-mortar products—may be useful to focus attention-getting efforts.
Planned giving	Except as a possible source of funding for new attention-getting efforts, planned giving is not often directly applicable to visibility.
Direct mail	Often expensive, though potentially effective, direct mail is a means to gain visibility. Added capital is required to fund attention-getting mail that doesn't necessarily bring in lots of gifts.
Telemarketing	Because of its high cost per contact, telemarketing is not often useful for gaining visibility.
Web site	This is an excellent tool for Internet-based promotional efforts.
Special events	Events are frequently very useful for spotlighting an organization or a campaign, especially with celebrity support.
Merchandising	Merchandising may help gain visibility through such means as decals, calendars, mugs, and T-shirts.

Potential Plus

This residential facility for developmentally disabled children faced the situation depicted in Table 14.7, the last time we looked.

Here's how Potential Plus might analyze the ten fundraising techniques we're examining:

- *Foundation grants.* All forms of institutional fundraising are likely to be highly efficient for any nonprofit that's a good candidate for institutional support. Potential Plus might approach a local foundation or a regional or national one dedicated to issues that include support for developmentally disabled children. With a capital campaign in the offing, the chances of receiving such a grant are probably greater. In any case, there's little lost if the answer is no. Foundation fundraising doesn't usually cost a lot.

- *Corporate giving.* All forms of institutional fundraising are likely to be highly efficient for any nonprofit that's a good candidate for institutional support. In general, local corporations may be more interested in investing their community relations money or foundation funds in causes that have broader impact and greater visibility in the community. However, the Potential Plus capital campaign—with its inevitable naming opportunities—increases the likelihood that local companies will be interested in helping.

- *Major gifts.* Generous individual support will likely bear the brunt of Potential Plus's financial needs. One or more major donors—perhaps one with a child or a sibling who faced challenges similar to those of Potential Plus's clients—could account for a large share of the budget and be solicited at a very low cost. In any event, the capital campaign requires bold leadership from one or more major figures in the community.

- *Planned giving.* Any major donor to Potential Plus—in fact, almost any donor over the age of fifty—is a reasonable prospect for a bequest or other planned gift. Donors will realize that there is always likely to be a need for such facilities, so a perpetual gift could be a wise investment. For some donors, too—even those who

TABLE 14.7 Potential Plus: EFFICIENCY + growth.

Vision	Organizational Goals	Fundraising Goals	Fundraising Objectives
To help developmentally disabled children live full and productive lives.	Bring scattered and uncoordinated services for "mentally retarded" children under one roof in a new, $10 million facility largely supported by private gifts.	Merge the individual agencies' development programs into a united effort, sparked by a $10 million capital campaign and continuing with a donor-acquisition program designed to enlist support from at least ten thousand new donors, and increase aggregate annual income by 10 percent per year.	Year 1. Consummate merger, conduct capital campaign feasibility study, and launch 60,000-piece donor acquisition test mailing. Year 2. Secure $2–3 million lead gift for capital campaign and mail 300,000 letters to recruit 2,000 new donors. Year 3. Secure $4–6 million in additional leadership gifts and mail 500,000 letters to recruit 4,000 new donors. Year 4. Launch public phase of capital campaign for last $1–3 million and mail 1,000,000 letters to recruit 6,000 new donors. Year 5. Reach $10 million campaign goal and mail 600,000 letters to recruit 4,000 new donors to replace those lost through attrition.

haven't previously contributed large gifts—the capital campaign may offer an attractive opportunity to make a lifetime gift.

• *Direct mail.* By and large, direct mail is not efficient compared with big-gift and institutional fundraising. However, growth is the secondary characteristic of the Potential Plus fundraising strategy, the capital campaign requires beefing up the donor list, and direct mail is unavoidably an important means to recruit new donors. Properly managed, a donor-acquisition program conducted with a steady eye on the long-term value of donors may prove to be extremely profitable over the long run.

• *Telemarketing.* As a supplement to direct mail and to special events, highly selective telemarketing may make sense for Potential Plus. It's a costly way to raise money, however, and is unlikely to be broadly usable.

• *Web site.* At low cost, Potential Plus can use its Web site to reinforce donor relationships (through e-mail bulletins to major donors about the progress of the capital campaign, for example). On-line fundraising is highly efficient, and as use of the Internet for institutional advancement becomes more broadly accepted, on-line techniques may eventually come to account for a large share of the funds raised by Potential Plus.

• *Special events.* Receptions, dinners, and tours of the new facility while it is under construction will be especially useful to Potential Plus as donor cultivation devices. Intimate big-ticket dinners—especially if held in a donor's private home with donated food and service—may help, too, especially at a crucial point in the progress of the capital campaign. In general, however, special events are not particularly efficient.

• *Merchandising.* Selling merchandise will be of little or no value to Potential Plus.

So it goes for Potential Plus. Other nonprofit organizations dedicated to efficiency in fundraising may take a similar view, as shown in Table 14.8.

TABLE 14.8 Potential Applications of Fundraising Tactics to Promote Efficiency.

Tactic	Application(s) in a Typical Efficiency Strategy
Foundation grants	All fundraising from institutions tends to be (or ought to be) highly efficient.
Corporate giving	All fundraising from institutions tends to be (or ought to be) highly efficient.
Major gifts	Major gifts are often a very efficient way to lower the cost of fundraising.
Capital campaign	By offering donors incentives to give larger gifts, a capital campaign may be especially useful in gaining efficiency.
Planned giving	In the long run, where planned giving is applicable it is typically the most efficient form of fundraising.
Direct mail	Direct mail is usually not very efficient, though there are exceptions, such as monthly sustainer programs and high-dollar giving clubs.
Telemarketing	Telemarketing is a high-cost fundraising technique. It promotes efficiency only by supporting a monthly sustainer program or a high-dollar giving club.
Web site	A Web site is potentially very efficient, but it usually requires up-front investment.
Special events	These are rarely efficient unless underwritten.
Merchandising	Most often, merchandising is a low-margin (that is, inefficient) activity.

Silver City Symphony Orchestra

Let's refresh our memory about the state of affairs at the Silver City Symphony Orchestra when we last visited that dynamic organization (see Table 14.9 on page 146).

For this orchestra, the central preoccupation is stability. This strategic choice shapes the uses to which available fundraising techniques might be put. For example:

TABLE 14.9 Silver City Symphony Orchestra: STABILITY + Growth.

Vision	Organizational Goals	Fundraising Goals	Fundraising Objectives
To help contemporary music lovers find new meaning in the classical symphonic repertoire.	Expand the orchestra's repertoire, attract world-class guest artists, launch a recording program within two years, and double the number of public performances within four years.	Launch a $10,000-per-year Conductor's Club that will meet the budget for the recording program and permit paying higher fees to guest artists, double the number of donors to support additional performances, and increase the budget by 10 percent annually.	Year 1. Launch Conductor's Club with first three $10,000 gifts and increase active donors from 500 to 650. Year 2. Recruit five new Conductor's Club members and increase active donors from 650 to 800. Year 3. Recruit seven new Conductor's Club members and increase active donors from 800 to 1,000.

• *Foundation grants.* Local foundations or national foundations with special interest in music might be a large though still limited force in the orchestra's fundraising program. With some notable exceptions, foundation funding is episodic and project oriented. Foundations in general cannot be counted on to supply the lion's share of funding over the long term. However, smaller foundations might be good prospects for the orchestra's new $10,000-per-year Conductor's Club.

• *Corporate giving.* A special local corporation might be willing to fund a music outreach program, either as a philanthropic effort or out of desire for recognition by the community (or both).

But funding from corporations won't directly support the orchestra's Involvement Strategy.

• *Major gifts*. An Involvement Strategy requires special efforts to cultivate and, yes, involve major donors in the orchestra's work. There must be a single, consistent message: The Silver City Symphony Orchestra wants you to be part of our family.

• *Capital campaign*. A capital campaign structure probably won't lend itself well to the orchestra's current expansion plans because such a structure lacks focus. It's difficult to translate an expanded repertoire and a lengthened performance schedule into concrete enough terms to motivate large numbers of donors.

• *Planned giving*. Gift planning is not, in and of itself, likely to be widely useful in executing the orchestra's Involvement Strategy. (However, one or more individual major donors might be excellent prospects for a trust arrangement to guarantee their $10,000-per-year Conductor's Club gifts for a long time to come.)

• *Direct mail*. Specialized applications of direct mail will prove useful. In expanding the donor base over the next three years, high-dollar direct mail can be used to introduce the Conductor's Club to prospective donors or to follow up personal visits. Any such mailings will be most effective in the long run if they call for active participation as well as large gifts. Direct mail can also be used selectively to help increase the number of donors to the orchestra. For example, attention-getting mailings to the patrons or members of other local arts and cultural organizations (such as public television) could attract a lot of new donors, effectively assuming the role as the growth engine in the orchestra's strategy of INVOLVEMENT + Growth. (However, donor acquisition mailings should solicit participation as well as financial support.)

• *Telemarketing*. Telephone contact with existing or new donors might be very fruitful on a selective basis. For example, current top-tier donors might be notified by telephone—as "insiders"—of the new expansion plans. Selected individuals (or a particular segment of the donor file) might be approached to be asked for "leadership gifts" to kick off the new strategy.

• *Web site.* As a donor involvement device, a Web site will prove increasingly useful as the years go by. For instance, such amenities as concert program notes or advance notice of special events sent via e-mail could help cement relationships with the orchestra's most responsive donors.

• *Special events.* For a regional cultural organization—especially a performing arts organization with the capacity to stage private entertainment—special events are a natural. The Conductor's Club, in particular, lends itself very well to an exclusive annual or even twice-yearly reception with the music director and other luminaries. And small ensembles composed of orchestra members can make highly visible appearances at such venues as schools, nursing homes, and fundraising events sponsored by other nonprofit organizations—thus expanding appreciation of the arts by a wider audience.

• *Merchandising.* Selling goods is not likely to be a lucrative source of funds for the orchestra. However, selected branded merchandise—such as the ever-reliable T-shirts and tote bags—might help heighten the orchestra's visibility. In some circumstances, such items might prove to be good premiums (or rewards) for generous donors.

So much for the Silver City Symphony Orchestra. For other nonprofits embarking on an Involvement Strategy, the options might look something like those listed in Table 14.10.

Following this chapter are five step-by-step self-assessment worksheets to assist you and your colleagues in determining whether your organization is ready to make use of an unfamiliar fundraising technique. To my mind, the fundraising methods that most commonly raise questions and entail the biggest risks and rewards are capital campaigns, special events, planned giving, direct mail, and telemarketing. Each is the subject of its own self-assessment.

TABLE 14.10 Potential Applications of Fundraising Tactics to Promote Stability.

Tactic	Application(s) in a Typical Stability Strategy
Foundation grants	These are very useful as part of a diversified, broad-based fundraising program designed to gain or sustain stability.
Corporate giving	Corporate giving is very useful as part of a diversified, broad-based fundraising program designed to gain or sustain stability.
Major gifts	These are almost always an indispensable part of the mix when seeking stability.
Capital campaign	A capital campaign is very useful as part of a diversified, broad-based fundraising program designed to gain or sustain stability.
Planned giving	Planned giving is almost always an essential part of the mix when seeking stability.
Direct mail	Direct mail can help in gaining stability only as a means to diversify by building an individual membership or donor base where that's lacking or to launch other efforts to diversify (such as monthly giving or a high-dollar club).
Telemarketing	Telemarketing is useful in gaining stability only as a means to diversify by building an individual membership or donor base where that's lacking or to launch other efforts to diversify (such as monthly giving or a high-dollar club).
Web site	A Web site is almost always an indispensable part of the mix when seeking stability, which requires maximizing efforts to communicate with donors or members.
Special events	Donor-acknowledgment or donor-participation activities are particularly useful, though not necessarily as means to raise net cash.
Merchandising	Selling merchandise is irrelevant to a Stability Strategy, except where merchandise helps strengthen donor or member relationships.

Self-Assessment 2

Is Your Organization Ready for a Capital Campaign?

Capital campaigns have traditionally been used to build buildings or endowment funds, or both. Increasingly, however, nonprofits include funds for maintenance or special programs in their campaign goals. It's no secret why. The hoopla and the intensity of a capital campaign frequently move donors to dig far more deeply into their pockets than they do for annual fund appeals or other workaday solicitations—giving gifts perhaps ten to fifteen times as large.

There's something very special about a capital campaign. Regrettably, however, capital campaigns also require special conditions and special preparations. Completing the following checklist will give you a preliminary indication of whether it's worthwhile for your organization to explore a possible campaign in depth.

Be sure you don't take a passing grade on this self-test as adequate proof that your organization is indeed ready to launch a capital campaign. If you get a green light from this exercise, it's time to organize a thorough feasibility study. The stakes are high in capital campaigns. Failure can be more than costly. It can destroy an organization.

But here's a good way to start.

Jerry Panas's Assessment of Campaign Timing (ACT) is an instrument that measures twenty independent criteria of an organization's readiness for a capital campaign. Separately, each criterion is of consequence. But together, at the right levels and in the proper combination, they ensure the success of a capital program.

ACT is most effective when completed individually by board members and then discussed in a group session. It is the candid, thorough, and public examination of each item that helps strengthen understanding and initiate appropriate action.

The first column in the test calls for your subjective rating. The highest score is 10, the lowest is 1. Where you feel your organization deserves a top rating, give the item a 10. Where you feel there is room for improvement, make an assessment of how serious the deficiency is and determine the rating. Use the following definitions as a guide to your evaluation:

10	Best possible rating
9	Excellent but not perfect
8	Very good but requires some attention
7	Good but needs improvement
6	Satisfactory but not good enough to do the job
5	Less than satisfactory; needs serious work
4 or less	Unacceptable; immediate correction is called for

Factor	Score	Weight	Total
1 During the past twelve months, you've operated under a written plan to cultivate your top two hundred sources, and you've made a significant contact with each of them at least twice during the year. It's not good enough just to have the list. You need to be in contact with these sources, romancing your cause and your case. Give yourself a 10 if you have an active and effective program of prospect management and cultivation.		× 5 =	
SUBTOTAL THIS PAGE			

Factor	Score	Weight	Total
2 The board and staff have individually committed in an open meeting, with full discussion and open voting, their dedication to give and work sacrificially. It starts with the board and staff. If the organization's family doesn't care, why should anyone else?		× 4 =	
3 The board is able to give individually (and corporately if it is a personally or family-held company) 10 percent of the campaign objective. Not every board is able to give as much as 10 percent. There have been many successful campaigns where this has been the case. But if the board is able to give 10 percent or better, it helps ensure a victory for the campaign. If you believe that board members will be able to give 15 percent of the campaign objective, give yourself a rating of 10. If they will be able to give 10 percent, give yourself a 9. Anything lower than 10 percent should be evaluated accordingly.		× 4 =	
4 You are able to determine or identify the twenty major gifts that will produce 40 percent of your objective. The campaign cannot be successful without major gifts. If within your donor constituency there isn't the potential to give 40 percent of your objective in twenty large gifts, your campaign is very likely moribund. And if you can't identify these sources, you haven't started the campaign process. Give yourself a 10 if you have isolated these twenty sources. (If you're able to generate 40 percent of your objective with fewer than twenty sources, all the better!)		× 3 =	
SUBTOTAL THIS PAGE			

Factor	Score	Weight	Total
5 There is wholehearted agreement between the staff and the board regarding the worthwhileness of the project and they are willing to work together to bring the project to fruition. It's not uncommon for staff to initiate ideas and be the inspiration behind a campaign project. You hope to have a staff that provides leadership and motivation. It is unacceptable, however, to have a capital program that is entirely staff driven. There must be a sharing of vision and dreams. The board must accept the project as its own. Give yourself a 10 if there is total and wholehearted agreement and a sense of excitement and high expectations. If these don't exist, or if some board members aren't enthusiastic advocates of the project, give yourself less than a 10. Either the situation needs to be corrected or the apathetic (or negative) directors need to determine whether they can continue to stay on the board and remain effective.		× 3 =	
6 The project meets a valid need. The completed project will fill a justifiable and urgent need and has been tested in such a way that there is some substantiation. Further, the project helps fulfill your mission and is in keeping with your philosophy of operation. Give yourself a full 10 if it meets all these criteria.		× 3 =	
7 The case for the program has emotional and dramatic appeal. To raise important funds a project must be compelling and have sizzle! Otherwise, no matter how valid the need, you won't raise funds. If you feel the case can be dramatized in such a way that it tugs at both the heart and the purse strings, give yourself a 10. If a sense of urgency and excitement is lacking, lower your score accordingly.		× 3 =	
SUBTOTAL THIS PAGE			

Factor	Score	Weight	Total
8 On your board you have a person of sufficient strength, stature, influence, and affluence that he or she will be a desirable candidate to head your campaign. It isn't necessary to choose your chair from the board roster, but this often makes the selection easier and certainly makes it more natural. If you do have a person of this caliber on your board, it also says something about the power of your group.		× 3 =	
9 The organization has successfully met its object-ive in its annual support campaign in the past two years. A group that cannot raise annual support will not be able to mount a major capital campaign. If you have gone over goal in the campaign, give yourself a 10. If you have just met goal, give yourself a 9. If you've done anything less than that, begin decreasing accordingly. If you do not have an annual campaign for sustaining funds, give yourself a 1.		× 2 =	
10 In the past two years you've operated within a balanced budget. People give to organizations that are fiscally responsible and that demon-strate proper financial stewardship. A balanced budget provides evidence of sound management and board accountability. Give yourself a 10 for a surplus and grade lower for an operating deficit.		× 2 =	
11 You have carefully developed a pro forma bud-get and have projected that when the facility is completed the project will generate sufficient income to make it self-supporting. Funding for the operation has become increasingly more difficult and income has to be won. Major credit goes to the operation whose budget is self-		× 2 =	
SUBTOTAL THIS PAGE			

Factor	Score	Weight	Total
supporting to a significant degree. If the project demonstrates that it will generate significant income over expense, give yourself a 10—and congratulations! If the campaign includes funds for an endowment, increase your rating.			
12 A general rule of thumb is that you will be able to raise ten to fifteen times the funds in a capital campaign that you have been raising annually. Take the more liberal figure, fifteen, for instance. If your project needs more than fifteen times what you've been raising annually, you'll find it difficult to meet your objective. You're going to have to do better on your annual campaign. If the total capital project equals fifteen times your annual giving (or less), give yourself a 10. The higher the numerical ratio between your capital effort and your annual giving, the lower your rating.		× 2 =	
13 You have identified and listed the two hundred sources that are most likely to provide the largest gifts for your program. It's quite likely that 80 to 90 percent of your funds will come from your top two hundred sources. You need to determine now who these sources are. Your top leadership should be developed from these sources. This truly becomes the heart and spirit of your successful campaign.		× 2 =	
14 If you are able to identify someone of sufficient strength, stature, influence, and affluence who you feel will accept the chairmanship of your campaign program, and if that person has already accepted the responsibility, you get roaring applause, and a 10. Even if you haven't posed the question but you feel fairly certain that the man or woman of the caliber described will accept, give yourself a 10, and cross your fingers.		× 2 =	
SUBTOTAL THIS PAGE			

Factor	Score	Weight	Total
15 You will be able to recruit sufficient volunteers to mount a successful campaign effort. While it's clear that your largest gifts will determine the level of your success, you'll still require a broad base of giving to ensure a victory. You will need a well-trained, enthusiastic, and happy worker for every five to eight prospects. Give yourself a full 10 if you will be able to recruit the workers you need.		× 2 =	
16 No campaigns in your service area should be planned for the same period that will cause a serious conflict. For your effort you'll require all the dedication possible of volunteers, donors, and media coverage in order to win. There are some campaigns, even of a major size, that won't interfere with yours. But if there are other organizations with campaigns similar to yours, this could cause a problem. If you don't anticipate a conflict, give yourself a 10.		× 2 =	
17 If your executive director has been on the staff for a minimum of twenty-four months, grade this a 10. Deduct a point for every three months less than twenty-four months.			
18 Your board is up to the full complement of membership allowable in your bylaws. Grade this a 10 if you have no vacancies. For each vacancy, give yourself 1 point less. For instance, if you have two vacancies, give yourself an 8.			
19 Board attendance during the past eighteen months has averaged 80 percent or more. Total all the board meetings you've had during the past eighteen months and compute the			
SUBTOTAL THIS PAGE			

Factor	Score	Weight	Total
attendance. If it's 80 percent or more, give yourself a10. For every 5 percent less than 80 percent, deduct 1 point. For instance, if you had an average of 63 percent attendance, you should receive a 5. (Note: If your attendance averages less than 50 percent for regularly scheduled meetings, you are in serious trouble as far as the vitality and commitment of the board is concerned. You should probably not even be thinking about a campaign!)			
20 The organization has a challenging annual dollar objective in its annual campaign, which forces it to stand on tiptoe to achieve its objectives. It's not enough merely to reach your annual campaign goal. Your objective must push you.			
TOTAL			

Source: Copyright © 1984 by Jerold Panas. Reprinted with permission.

Scoring

Each item in the ACT is given a weight. The higher the weight, the greater the consequence of the criterion for the success of the campaign. Each item has been measured carefully for its significance.

Multiply your rating in the first column by the weight in the second column. Indicate the total in the third column. When you're finished, total the third column. Your total score is _____. Here's how to interpret your score:

Score	Interpretation
299 or less	You're not ready—not nearly so. You need to spend time improving in the critical areas that will determine your ability to reach the goal.

Score	Interpretation
300–399	You're close. You still have some work to do before you can be assured of success. Begin now to make the necessary changes.
400–449	You'll almost certainly have a successful campaign. Take time to correct the few deficiencies you have.
450–500	You're ready. What are you waiting for?

Self-Assessment 3

Do Special Events Make Sense for You?

Special events such as dinners, cocktail receptions, golf games, and telethons yield millions in revenue for well-organized charities. Smart nonprofits also design special events to serve other purposes—to cultivate donors, improve public relations, and boost staff morale, to name a few. If your organization wants to make money from a special event, focus first on factors that will increase your profits. Then plan for ways to meet your other, nonmonetary goals.

Joan Flanagan prepared the following checklist in response to my own, inadequate draft. Use it and you'll discover some of the elements that may make or break your event.

Yes = 1

No = 0

Factor	Score	Weight	Total
1 The organization's leadership is personally committed to meeting a specific dollar goal.		× 5 =	
SUBTOTAL THIS PAGE			

Factor	Score	Weight	Total
2 Six months in advance of the event you have written contracts for underwriters or sponsors to defray all the costs.		× 5 =	
3 Two volunteer cochairs and most committee chairs are veterans of previous years' events.		× 3 =	
4 One hundred percent of the tickets are sold four weeks before the event. All sales at the event are gravy.			
5 Your leaders each buy ten tickets and, six weeks before the event, commit to sell ten to fifty tickets each.			
6 You have a written contract, with a substitution clause for a star of equal or greater magnitude, with a celebrity who is popular in your market, who will not have performed in the area for at least six months, and who is sympathetic with your mission.			
7 Your organization has a tradition of doing a great event on the same date every year, and the date connects to your mission—such as Valentine's Day for the Heart Fund or Lincoln's Birthday for handgun control.			
8 Your organization has a tested list of donors from previous events.			
9 Your organization has high visibility. (Controversy is especially helpful.)			
10 The date, place, and cochairs for next year's event are selected and will be announced at this year's event.			
SUBTOTAL THIS PAGE			

Factor	Score	Weight	Total
11 You have planned for ways to meet other, non-monetary goals of the event (for example, hoopla and publicity, leadership development, membership sales, fellowship and solidarity—and fun!)			
TOTAL			

Scoring

For the questions to which you answered no (0), write 0 in the right-hand column, regardless of that factor's weight.

For the questions to which you answered yes (1), write 1 in the right-hand column, unless there's a weighting factor in the second column from the right. If there is a weighting factor, enter that number instead in the right-hand column.

Here's how to interpret your score:

Score	Interpretation
0–10	Forget it. Don't waste your time. This event might accomplish lots of good things, but it's not likely to make any money for your organization.
11–15	This event might make money, or it might not. You're leaving a lot to chance.
16–20	You've probably got a winner on your hands, but there's still risk in this venture. Not all the bases are completely covered.
21	Really? Really? Well, all I can say is, if this event doesn't make you a bundle, you ought to be ashamed of yourselves!

Self-Assessment 4

Is Planned Giving Within Your Reach?

Gift planning, more commonly known as planned giving, has seized the attention of fundraisers everywhere. For some it's the magic elixir—the ingredient in the fundraising mix that can justify all the time, effort, and money invested by a charity in recruiting, educating, and cultivating donors. After all, it doesn't take many $250,000 bequests to defray several years' expenditures on a quarterly newsletter or even a direct-mail donor acquisition program. And both fundraisers and donors are becoming steadily more comfortable with the exacting requirements of gift planning.

The upshot is that bequests accounted for approximately 7.8 percent, or $13.62 billion, of the $174.52 billion estimated to have been contributed to nonprofit organizations in 1998 (the most recent year for which statistics were available at press time), according to *Giving USA*. Bequest-giving increased by 7.8 percent in that year, following a 10 percent increase in 1997.

Bequests currently account for more than four of every five planned gifts in the United States (some say nine out of ten). But the very biggest individual gifts come through other forms of gift planning: charitable remainder trusts, charitable lead trusts, annuities, pooled income funds, and other creations of lawyers and accountants.

So how does your organization get onto this gravy train (assuming you're not already on board)? In fact, is planned giving an appropriate fundraising option for you? The following self-assessment will help you get a handle on your organization's planned giving potential.

Many nonprofit organizations don't have a prayer of raising significant sums through bequests and other forms of planned gifts. For others, the field of gift planning may be only marginally useful. In fact, a great many nonprofits can raise significant sums only through bequests, not by means of other types of planned giving. This self-assessment will help you determine whether your organization is likely to reap big rewards from a gift planning program.

Tip: Use the spaces labeled *action* to jot down notes about concrete steps you can take to move your organization closer to readiness for planned giving.

To answer each question, place a check mark or X in the appropriate column on the right.

Question	Yes	No	Not sure
1 Is your organization old enough and well-enough established to inspire confidence that it will survive for decades to come? Action:			
2 Is yours a long-term mission that justifies a multigenerational perspective? Action:			
3 Is your organization a likely vehicle by which donors may see their gifts to you as a legacy for future generations? Action:			

Question	Yes	No	Not sure
4 Does your organization have a reputation for integrity, frugality, and effectiveness? Action:			
5 Do you possess a large enough pool of committed individual donors from whom you might seek planned gifts? Action:			
6 Do you have in place a donor communications and cultivation program through which planned giving may be readily promoted (newsletters, donor briefings, and so on)? Action:			
7 Do you have available the necessary legal and accounting resources to ensure that questions from donors or their financial advisers will be promptly and accurately answered? Action:			
8 If you hope to secure planned gifts in forms other than bequests, do you have the staff capabilities necessary to deal face-to-face with individual donors—to cultivate, discuss, and follow through on the inevitably unique aspects of each planned gift? Action:			
9 Does your organization view planned giving as a vehicle for donors? As philanthropic intentions rather than a means to gain individual financial advantage?			

Scoring

It may be pointless to proceed with a gift planning program unless you have answered yes to all nine of these questions. However, some of the weaknesses you might have uncovered are correctable.

For example, if you lack a large-enough pool of individual donors, your organization can invest in acquiring donors—and years later launch a very successful planned giving program. If your donor communications and cultivation program is inadequate, you can bolster these activities by investing the necessary resources in such activities as donor newsletters, open houses, selective donor briefings, and the like.

As a result, a charity that's ill-suited for gift planning today can develop enormous potential that might pay off tomorrow.

Self-Assessment 5

Should Your Organization Launch a Direct-Mail Campaign?

Research repeatedly confirms that the majority of first-time gifts to charity are made by mail. Why? Because direct mail has long been the most cost-effective way for most nonprofit organizations to identify and acquire new donors. And because these donors are principally acquired by mail, it's usually most effective to inform, cultivate, and upgrade them by mail, too.

It's a little like what democracy is sometimes called: the worst possible form of government, except when compared to all the others.

Now, let's be clear about what I mean by *direct mail*. Almost every nonprofit organization communicates with, even solicits, its donors by mail. But some charities maintain continuing efforts to acquire new donors from "outside" lists—members of other organizations, for example, or subscribers to suitable periodicals, or homeowners in selected neighborhoods.

That's what I mean by direct mail: a conscious effort to use the technique as a strategic tool in an organization's development program—first as a way to recruit donors, then as a means to build lasting relationships with them.

That kind of direct mail has its risks. A strategy may be ineptly designed. Mailings may be poorly conceived or badly executed. Unfortunate timing could undermine success.

Even for organizations that make no mistakes at all, the cost of direct-mail fundraising may be out of proportion to its potential yield. There are many possible reasons for that:

- There may not be enough people who agree that your organization fills an important need, or it may be difficult to find or assemble mailing lists on which their names and addresses appear.

- People may agree that the work you're doing is important, but not care strongly enough to send money.

- The ever-fickle public may feel that the need you're filling has passed, or simply that it isn't urgent enough to require immediate support.

- Your constituency or market may be too small to support an ongoing program of donor acquisition.

The self-assessment provided here will help you determine whether your organization is ready to undertake a full-fledged direct-mail fundraising program.

Warning: Organizations that operate on a small scale may have an especially difficult time launching the type of large direct-mail fundraising programs I'm referring to—for example, those with annual budgets of less than $300,000, or those with potential constituencies of fewer than two million people. (Admittedly this rules out statewide or provincial efforts in some parts of North America!)

Although there are important exceptions, for the most part the market for a local public interest group in all but the largest metropolitan areas may simply be too small to apply these techniques. Professionally managed direct-mail fundraising is built on economies of scale.

This does *not* mean, however, that the techniques of direct mail are worthless to small groups. Every nonprofit uses the mail to communicate with and solicit its donors. Many of the methods employed in large-scale direct-mail fundraising programs are indeed transferable to the efforts of small organizations.

The Questions

The questions in the self-assessment examine eight factors (adapted from my book *Raising Money by Mail: Strategies for Growth and Financial Stability*):

> *Question 1: Do you have the necessary capital to invest in an initial test mailing, and to expand and sustain the program if the test is successful?*

It's possible for an organization to mount an initial test mailing for $10,000, or even less, but that's not usually advisable. For a fair test—one that will yield statistically valid results—you'll need to mail at least thirty thousand letters with samples from half a dozen lists. (Fifty thousand or more and ten lists are usually far better.) That's likely to cost $20,000 at a minimum. With professional assistance where it counts the most—on strategy, the creative work, and list selection—it's more realistic to think of investing twice that much.

And the capital for the test mailing is only the beginning. Usually, additional (and larger) infusions of capital are essential or the program dies. Direct mail is capital intensive. Its hunger for cash never stops.

> *Question 2: Can you bear the risk of an unsuccessful test mailing?*

Face it: the money you invest in an initial test mailing is risk capital. You can't count on getting back even a nickel.

The odds are, of course, that you'll recover a significant proportion of your investment. These days, somewhere between one-third and two-thirds of the outlay will probably return immediately in gifts sent in response to your test appeal. A few organizations—but very few—are still able to launch direct-mail test programs at breakeven, or even turn a modest profit. But unless your organization has a strong track record in fundraising and terrific name recognition, you can't count on receiving even one-third to two-thirds of the investment. There are too many start-up costs, and too many things can go wrong. It's far more prudent to write off the money you put on the table to take your first crack at direct mail.

Question 3: Can you effectively distinguish your organization from others serving the same constituency by identifying something dramatic or unique about your organization or its work?

Lots of worthy charities labor valiantly for years to perform valuable services for an appreciative public. But only those that can set themselves apart from the rest in some obvious way have a chance to derive significant amounts of net revenue from direct mail: perhaps through the personality or reputation of the chief executive or a key board member ("Oh, yeah? I've heard of them! They're the people who work with so-and-so."), perhaps through something unique in their programs or through their results, or perhaps because they're the only organization of their type serving a particular region or constituency. There's got to be something that will sustain public interest and respect throughout a long-term campaign.

Question 4: Are your mission and strategy clear so that your programs can be packaged for a wider public?

There's nothing deadlier than a direct-mail campaign built around "a little of this and a little of that." Your mission must sing out from the written materials. And what you ask of prospective supporters must be immediately apparent in every single letter you send. (Are you asking them to join as members? To support a particular campaign? To sign a postcard to the governor? To send $250 rather than $25?)

Question 5: Does your organization have the track record, name recognition, prestige, or credentials necessary to establish your credibility?

Stop for a second. Think how crazy it is for people to send money through the mail to support organizations they may never have heard of before. Many of us do that every day of the year. Why? Because the written materials are credible. They tell a story in evocative words, images, and other symbols that persuades readers that the cause or institution really is and does what it says. Unless readers are familiar with something in the materials you send, they'll throw them away with a snort. You need to convert readers into believers—instantly—by referring to the names of leaders or supporters or to the group's history of accomplishment. And that won't work unless there's something there to begin with.

Question 6: Do you have sufficient staff (or an outside firm) to ensure that donors will get the service they need?

The job of managing a direct mail program only begins when gifts arrive in the mail. If you're not ready before you mail to take the next step—acknowledging and processing those gifts and building the donor history database—you're not ready for direct mail.

Even more important, if your organization isn't equipped to manage relationships with the donors you recruit through the mail, there's no point in bringing them in the door. Almost regardless of how big it is, the first gift means little. The true rewards will come only with time, in the form of subsequent (and sometimes larger) gifts.

Question 7: Are the issues involved in your work specific, compelling, and of concern to a broad public?

Some charities get all the breaks! They do things with unfailing public appeal—saving puppies and kittens, for example, or preserving the rainforest, or helping cancer patients. Even (sometimes) feeding starving children.

But most nonprofits face a harder sell. For some, the challenge may be (or at least seem) insurmountable. The harsh reality is that not all issues or causes will work in direct mail. Whatever you ask donors to support must be urgent, easy to understand, and have obvious, significant impact on people's lives. Otherwise, you'll be better off trying to coax out gifts face-to-face.

Question 8: Is your organization committed for the long haul? In other words, are you considering the long-term value of donors, and are you prepared to do what it takes to cultivate and upgrade those donors?

Direct mail yields up its treasure only in the long run. It's rare nowadays for a charity to make a profit on its first outings in the mail (prospecting or donor acquisition campaigns). Usually the profits come only after one or more subsequent appeals (as well as warm gift acknowledgments and plenty of information about the charity's work).

To answer each question, place a check mark or an X on the checklist in the appropriate column on the right.

Tip: Use the spaces labeled *action* to jot down notes about concrete steps you can take to move your organization closer to readiness for direct mail.

Question	Yes	No	Not sure
1 Do you have the necessary capital to invest in an initial test mailing, and to expand and sustain the program if the test is successful? Action:			
2 Can you bear the risk of an unsuccessful test mailing? Action:			

Question	Yes	No	Not sure
3 Can you effectively distinguish your organization from others serving the same constituency by identifying something dramatic or unique about your organization or its work? Action:			
4 Are your mission and strategy clear so that your programs can be packaged for a wider public? Action:			
5 Does your organization have the track record, name recognition, prestige, or credentials necessary to establish your credibility? Action:			
6 Do you have sufficient staff (or an outside firm) to ensure that donors will get the service they need? Action:			
7 Are the issues involved in your work specific, compelling, and of concern to a broad public? Action:			
8 Is your organization committed for the long haul? In other words, are you considering the long-term value of donors, and are you prepared to do what it takes to cultivate and upgrade those donors? Action:			

Source: Copyright © 1995 by Mal Warwick.

Scoring

All eight factors are essential for success in direct mail fundraising. However, if you're not sure how to answer the last two questions but you answered "Yes" to all the rest, a test of your organization's direct mail potential may be wise anyway. That will be especially true if your fundraising strategy requires either growth or the diversification necessary to achieve stability.

Self-Assessment 6

Is Telephone Fundraising Right for You?

Many fundraising managers dismiss telephone fundraising out of hand because of personal bias or resistance from board members. If you're caught in this trap, you may be leaving a great deal of money on the table, and foregoing other valuable benefits besides.

Charities that include the telephone in their toolbox of fundraising techniques learn more about their donors, foster increased donor loyalty, and enjoy rising revenues—a share of the billions raised every year through this fast-spreading fundraising method.

Of course there are some forms of telephone fundraising you're probably wise to reject. Selling merchandise by phone isn't likely to lay a firm foundation for a long-term philanthropic relationship. Nor is using unqualified callers to read mechanically from a script (even if the callers are volunteers).

It's also wise to tread cautiously into the fields of telephone prospecting. Acquiring new donors by telephone is most successful when you have access to phone-responsive people on lists of inquiries, donors, or prospects who have some relationship with your organization—such as those who call your toll-free number for information to become members. Calling everyone in the phone book is a waste of time for most nonprofits (and a public nuisance, too, as far as I'm concerned).

But I believe it's highly likely that your organization will benefit from a program that employs the building blocks of professional telephone fundraising:

- Highly motivated callers
- Thorough training
- Careful supervision
- Precise selection of the target audience
- Scrupulous attention to fundraising ethics
- Compliance with all legal requirements, including registration with state charities regulators

The Questions

The following self-assessment asks eight questions you can answer to determine whether professional telephone fundraising is right for your organization. A single answer in the affirmative may be enough to justify the time and expense required to undertake a telephone fundraising program.

Question 1: Does your organization have large numbers of lapsed or former donors?

If you answer yes to this question, a telephone reinstatement program may be in order. Nonprofit organizations routinely discover that lapsed and former donors or members can be cost-effectively reactivated by phone long after direct-mail efforts cease to be worthwhile. A far larger percentage of lapsed or former donors are likely to resume their support when contacted by phone than will respond to even the most effective letter. Sometimes even long-lapsed donors—those whose most recent gift was received three or more years ago—can be reactivated by telephone at breakeven.

Question 2: Is your organization launching (or building)
a monthly sustainer program?

Charities throughout North America are turning to monthly giving programs to upgrade donors who aren't responsive to appeals for large, lump-sum gifts. Time and again, calling them on the telephone has proven to be the most effective way to persuade such donors to take the big step of pledging monthly gifts. The target group typically includes both long-time donors of small, frequent gifts and new donors whose first gift was only recently received.

Question 3: Does your organization want to set up (or expand)
a high-dollar gift club?

A great many nonprofits identify prime prospects for major gifts by inviting their more generous direct-mail-acquired donors or members to join giving clubs, usually at the $500 or $1,000 level. Telephone fundraising can be used—often in combination with specially tailored, upscale direct-mail packages—to boost the recruitment effort. Because of its directness and potential for meaningful interaction, the telephone is one of the best ways to induce donors to upgrade dramatically.

Question 4: Is the response to your direct-mail appeals declining?

A telephone fundraising campaign may bring new life to your donor development program and provide you with a wealth of unfiltered, up-to-the-minute feedback from your donors.

Question 5: Is your first-year donor renewal rate disappointing?

Many organizations have concluded that the competitive pressures of today's nonprofit fundraising environment require them to increase their investment in educating, cultivating, even pampering their donors. In addition to such devices as warm, speedy gift acknowledgments and sometimes lavish new-donor welcome packages, some charities are systematically calling new donors simply to say, "Thank you." The cumulative impact of such efforts may have a dramatic effect on your renewal rate.

Question 6: Does your organization appeal to its most active donors less often than six times annually?

Focus groups reveal that direct-mail donors greatly *underestimate* the frequency of charities' contact with them. Research consistently shows that donors may say they want only one or two appeals per year, but they're usually unaware of receiving regular solicitations if mailed less frequently than every couple of months. Committed donors want and expect frequent contact with the organizations they support.

If you're not mailing at least once every two months to the most supportive donors in your file, you're probably passing up a major opportunity and jeopardizing the chances of securing bequests or other planned gifts. A telephone fundraising campaign targeting donors whose gifts are recent, frequent, and decent will help build relationships with them while generating substantial net revenue. And one that takes other factors into account as well may be even more productive. (For instance, it's now possible, with the aid of sophisticated database management software, to track donors who respond to phone appeals versus those who respond only to mail appeals, or to track people who make credit card gifts—just to name a couple of important pieces of donor history.)

Take care: such frequent contact is not advisable with all donors. Only those whose individual donor histories reveal a particular level of interest justify the expense and invite the higher volume of information.

Question 7: Is there an emergency, an expiring challenge grant, or some other looming deadline that requires your organization to raise substantial new sums?

The speed and immediacy of telephone contact mix well with the quick turnaround required to confront emergencies and with deadlines of all sorts. If there's time, the combination of direct mail and telephone contact—with one preceding the other by a few days or a couple of weeks—may be the best response to a fundraising challenge.

Question 8: Are there at least one thousand persons who may be called?

If there are at least one thousand individuals who may be included in one or another specialized telephone fundraising program, your organization will likely find it cost-effective either to hire a telephone fundraising consultant for on-site assistance or outsource the campaign to a professional firm. (If the number of donors in your potential pool is smaller than one thousand, it may still be possible for you to obtain professional assistance in designing an in-house operation and training volunteers, but a fully professional operation is probably beyond your organization's means.)

To answer each question, place a check mark or an X on the checklist in the appropriate column on the right.

Tip: Use the spaces labeled *action* to jot down notes about concrete steps you can take to move your organization closer to readiness for telemarketing.

Question	*Yes*	*No*	*Not sure*
1 Does your organization have large numbers of lapsed or former donors? Action:			
2 Is your organization launching (or building) a monthly sustainer program? Action:			

Question	Yes	No	Not sure
3 Does your organization want to set up (or expand) a high-dollar gift club? Action:			
4 Is the response to your direct-mail appeals declining? Action:			
5 Is your first-year donor renewal rate disappointing? Action:			
6 Does your organization appeal to its most active donors less often than six times annually? Action:			
7 Is there an emergency, an expiring challenge grant, or some other looming deadline that requires your organization to raise substantial new sums? Action:			
8 Are there at least one thousand persons who may be called? Action:			

Your initial investment in telephone fundraising—especially the time and effort required to design and manage the first campaign—may seem steep. But telephone fundraising, like any form of fundraising, requires taking the long view. The advantages will increase as your organization learns how to use telephone contact to best advantage, and economies of scale will become apparent over time.

Telephone fundraising is not a panacea for all that may ail your development program. But a great many nonprofits have found themselves in far better financial health through careful application of professional telephone fundraising techniques. If you're still in doubt that telephone fundraising is right for your organization, take another look at these eight questions. You may be missing a lucrative opportunity!

PART FOUR

Evaluating Your Success and Moving On

15

The Ten Benchmarks of Successful Fundraising

The first three parts of this book discussed the five strategies and how to put them to work in a real-world fundraising program. But what happens next? What happens if we actually follow all these steps and set a new strategy in motion? How will we know whether our strategy is working?

How, for example, will the staff of the Institute for Advanced Cancer Research know whether its adoption of a GROWTH + visibility strategy was a wise decision? How can the folks at One for All determine their progress as they pursue a development program built around INVOLVEMENT + visibility?

Indeed, how do you or I know when we're succeeding and when we're falling flat on our faces, whatever fundraising strategy we elect?

At least two possible answers to this question come quickly to mind:

- It's obvious. We just *know* when things are working, and when they're not.
- We've set down objectives and goals on paper. All we need to do is compare our hopes with reality.

The impish side of me delights in these transparent answers, but I know better. I'm sure you do, too. Intuition and bottom-line accounting are inadequate. To get to the root of fundraising dynamics—to determine what's going right, what's going wrong, and how we can fix whatever's broken—we need much sharper analytical tools.

That's why I've developed my ten benchmarks of successful fundraising. In this chapter I explain nine of them in detail and suggest how you might use them as points of reference to track the progress (or problems) that surface in your fundraising program. Chapter Sixteen explores the tenth and most revealing of the lot.

As we make our way into the uncharted territory of evaluation, we'll leave behind the five hypothetical nonprofit organizations that have served us so well in the preceding pages. Here we'll be dealing with reality—your organization's reality. There's nothing hypothetical about the measurements you'll need to make on a continuing basis to assess the effectiveness of your fundraising efforts. It's time to turn away from make-believe and take a cold, hard look at the nitty-gritty facts of your development program.

The ten benchmarks of successful fundraising will help you track the following aspects of your development program:

1. Revenue growth

2. Donor renewal

3. Donor attrition

4. Returns per donor

5. Donor upgrades

6. The donor "graduation" count

7. The number of donors

8. Fundraising costs

9. Market share and market penetration

10. Return on investment

Together these ten measurement tools constitute a kind of thermometer you can use to take the temperature of your fundraising program. With a clear understanding of your fundraising strategy—

and with care, persistence, and a little perspective on how to read the temperature scale—you can put an appropriate subset of these ten benchmarks to work to assess the overall health of your fundraising program.

The ten benchmarks grew out of five years of effort to nail down a broadly useful set of yardsticks that fundraisers might use, whatever their strategy. During those years I polled colleagues, clients, and participants in many of my fundraising workshops around North America, and of course I spent a lot of time crunching numbers. Others might drop a couple or three of the ten in favor of somewhat different measurements. But I'm confident that these ten will enable you to capture the gist of your fundraising reality.

Now, before we plunge into exploring the ten benchmarks individually, I want to confront a question that frequently arises when I introduce this topic:

Can one size possibly fit all?

If you're affiliated with a not-for-profit hospital or with a college or university, you probably think of your organization as a hospital, college, or university, not as a nonprofit.

Even if your organization is a community health agency, a ballet company, or a research institute, chances are you identify with other, similar nonprofits. You may have trouble discerning what you have in common with the more than one million tax-exempt organizations in the United States and Canada as a group or class.

In most ways, you're wise to narrow your vision to the field immediately surrounding you. After all, a hospital has little in common with a ballet company. Even your fundraising efforts will present a stark contrast.

For example, at the hospital, private voluntary contributions may account for no more than 2 or 3 percent of the revenues. The ballet company might require two or three dollars in gifts for every dollar received at the door. So the role and impact of fundraising in those two organizations are dramatically different. Any assessment of the two development programs must take these differences into account. Otherwise, the assessment will be worthless.

By the same token, an organization funded by a half-dozen generous major donors cannot be compared with one that's dependent on hundreds of much more modest gifts. The comparison is meaningless.

Yet there are common elements in fundraising programs of nearly all types.

There are lessons to be learned about the enduring realities of fundraising that will benefit the leaders and managers of almost every sort of nonprofit organization. For starters, at any type of not-for-profit, it's often well worth taking a look at revenue.

Benchmark 1: Is Your Revenue Climbing or Falling?

The revenue growth rate may be the first and most obvious place to look for signs of the health of your organization's fundraising program. This may be particularly true if your strategy is Stability, because revenue will have to grow at least at the rate of inflation.

There are no surprises here. If you're raising more money this year than last, something's going right.

If you're raising less money now than you did before, there'd better be a good explanation!

Reviewing the rate of revenue growth is the simplest and most straightforward early signal of the state of your fundraising program. The overall revenue numbers need to be tracked—and remembered—from year to year.

For instance, let's say your organization's strategic plan—built on a Growth Strategy—calls for you to double revenue in five years by dramatically expanding the donor base. Last year's growth rate was only 5 percent, so you're behind schedule. (Either the plan will have to be revised or the staff or board may need to be shaken up.)

However, if your strategy is instead driven above all by a quest for stability, your goal may be to achieve just enough revenue growth to keep pace with inflation. In that case, increasing revenue by 5 percent is growing a little too fast. You're sacrificing efficiency (needlessly raising your cost ratio). Instead, you might be wise to

invest in diversification the same funds you've plowed into generating more revenue.

The important thing is to think this way. Look for the Big Picture!

But there are other important lessons to be learned in examining your fundraising results. The most important of them involve
the people who help you get where you're going: your donors.

Benchmark 2: Are Your Donors Coming Back for More?

Taking the temperature of your fundraising program requires you to
assess the state of your donors' health. And one measurement above
all others will help you get a fix on that all-important question: your
donor renewal rates.

Donors are fickle.

If you haven't been involved in fundraising long enough to
learn that lesson, stick around. You'll pick it up fast.

The harsh truth about fundraising is this: most first-time donors
never give a second gift. Even the most artful development director
is unlikely to secure additional support from more than a slender
majority of first-time givers.

Ah! But that terrific old woman who walked in off the street
three years ago *did* give a second gift—followed by a string of increasingly generous contributions. So did a few others. And a larger
number have continued giving with regularity without enlarging
the size of their gifts. Clearly, all these people became donors in a
meaningful sense of that word.

The crux of the matter is this: Did the subsequent support from
that generous old woman and other repeat donors add up to
enough? Has all your time, sweat, and money paid off, or was it
expended in vain? To make this judgment, you first need to answer
a fundamental question: *During the past twelve months, how many of
your donors from the previous twelve months have given you gifts?*

The answer, expressed as a percentage, is the renewal rate. For
many organizations, this benchmark is the single most important
indicator of the health of the fundraising program.

For example, let's say your organization received gifts from a total of 5,000 donors two years ago. This past year, 3,500 of those donors gave again, for an overall renewal rate of 70 percent.

That sounds pretty good. But it may be a little misleading—or at least not revealing enough. Calculating a single renewal rate requires that you throw all donors into the same statistical pot, treating them as equals.

Yet you and I know that these donors are very different from one another. If nothing else, these renewing donors are each at different stages of the fundraising cycle. Some had previously given only a single gift. Others had been loyal supporters for many years.

You don't have to ponder this matter very long to realize that you should determine separate renewal rates for first-time givers and multiyear givers. Chances are that the two rates are dissimilar, and viewing them separately can point the way to entirely different strengths and weaknesses in your fundraising program.

So, let's break down that 70 percent renewal rate into more meaningful components. Assume that 1,000 of the 5,000 people who gave gifts to your organization two years ago were first-time donors, but only 200 of your 3,500 donors during the past twelve months were among those one-time givers. In other words, your first-year renewal rate is 20 percent (1000/200). The multiyear rate, by contrast, is 82.5 percent (3,500 – 200 = 3,300 renewing multiyear donors). The previous year, 4,000 (5,000 – 1,000) had given gifts for more than one year (4,000/3,300 = 82.5 percent). (All of this is summarized in Table 15.1.)

TABLE 15.1 Calculating Renewal Rates.

Segment	# Donors 2 Years Ago	# Donors Last Year	Renewal Rate
First-year donors	1,000	200	20.0 percent
Second-year donors	4,000	3,300	82.5 percent
All donors	5,000	3,500	70.0 percent

Now the picture of your organization is very different. The multiyear renewal rate is encouragingly high. You must be doing something right to keep all those donors coming back for more year after year! But the first-year renewal rate is—dare we say it?—pathetic. You're getting a lot of one-time gifts—a thousand of them two years ago—but precious few of these one-time donors are developing any signs of loyalty. Why? You're probably not doing all you could do to involve and inform them. The 20 percent first-year renewal rate suggests that you'd better figure something out fast! Otherwise, much of your investment in recruiting new donors will continue going down the drain. (See Sidebar 15.1 [on page 190] for an example of "typical" donor renewal rates.)

Tracking your renewal rates over time, year after year, will illuminate the trends in your development program. You'll be able to discover the answers to such questions as these:

- Is your multiyear renewal rate trending downward? Should you therefore invest more time and effort to promote long-term donor loyalty? Or reexamine your case statement to be certain it still seems fresh and relevant?

- Is your first-year renewal rate moving upward from year to year? Does that mean that the steps you've taken to involve new donors are paying off? Or do you need to do much more?

- Is the imbalance between your first-year and multiyear renewal rates so great that your donor base is aging fast? Should you exert special efforts to recruit younger donors?

These are fundamental questions. But renewal rate calculations can lead you to an even more significant question: Will your organization survive?

Benchmark 3: How Long Can You Last Without New Donors?

The flip side of the renewal rate is the attrition rate. Expressed most simply, it's the inverse of the renewal rate—the percentage you get

SIDEBAR 15.1 TYPICAL DONOR RENEWAL RATES

There's rarely anything really typical when it comes to fundraising. With as many as one million organizations raising funds—and more than 100 million givers—there's more variation from one nonprofit to another than hairs on a dog (a long-haired dog).

But you don't want to hear that from me. You want to get some idea of what your organization's donors are likely to do when you ask them to renew their support. So, based on experience with hundreds of nonprofits and millions of donors, here are what I believe to be reasonably typical renewal rates in a well-managed small-donor fundraising program.

# Years Donor Renewed Annual Support in Previous Years	Renewal Rate During Current Year
0 (recruited last year)	40–60 percent
1	60–70 percent
2	68–78 percent
3	75–85 percent
4	80–87 percent
5	83–90 percent

Now, please don't despair if your organization's renewal rates happen to fall below these ranges. Of course there may be some good reason—or rather, a bad reason—that explains it, such as asking only once each year that your donors renew their support. In such cases, you'll want to take corrective action—fast.

I've seen genuinely healthy nonprofit organizations with lower renewal rates. Most of them experience lower first-time renewal rates. They find it difficult to convert newly recruited donors into consistent givers, because it takes a special kind of person to support the organization. But once that hurdle is passed, those very special donors may become ferociously loyal—for exactly the same reason they joined in the first place.

Demographic factors also play a role in this arithmetic. Some groups of donors have more stable lifestyles than others. Most of the donors to a chamber music ensemble may be homeowners who change address infrequently, while the supporters of an aggressive environmental action group may be much younger on average and typically renters rather than owners.

Mortality rates can also affect the degree of donor attrition. (In other words, donors to some organizations are a lot older than donors to other groups—even older enough to die a lot faster.)

by subtracting the renewal rate from 100 percent. In other words, it's the proportion of donors who don't renew.

Viewed as a percentage, however, the attrition rate doesn't help much. It's far more useful to calculate it in absolute numbers. For instance, to continue the hypothetical example cited earlier, your organization lost 1,500 of 5,000 donors from the year before last to last year. Those 1,500 people who chose not to give again constitute your donor attrition.

Now let's make a further assumption. Your program plans— grounded in a search for stability—require that you maintain a donor base of at least 5,000 people every single year. So you must recruit 1,500 new donors this year to make up for the nonrenewers. You must! If you fail to recruit another 1,500 givers, you won't have 5,000 donors next year—and you won't meet your budget.

Unfortunately, most donors don't upgrade. The amount of their first gift is the amount they keep giving. In fact, some donors give smaller gifts. Thus, even if you want only to maintain the same level of income for your organization, you'll have to keep increasing the donor base. Merely keeping the donor base the same size entails risk!

The implications of this conclusion can be sobering, but they must be faced—now, not next year. Next year will be too late.

The harsh reality is that to recruit 1,500 new donors every year, you'll almost certainly have to spend a bundle. Now you can see how very important it is to boost that first-year renewal rate! If you can cut first-year attrition from 800 out of 1,000 to, say, 400—raising the first-year renewal rate from 20 percent to 40 percent—that's 400 fewer new donors you'll need to recruit next year. That in turn can reduce your investment in donor acquisition. After all, it should be a lot cheaper to recruit 1,100 donors than 1,500!

Extend the logic of donor attrition just a bit further and the result can be downright scary. If you need 5,000 donors to keep your head above water and you lost 1,500 of them last year without recruiting new people to replace them, you've only got 3,500 donors this year. Even if you assume that without donor acquisition your renewal rate will go up (because it's not dragged down by a low first-year rate), you'll still lose another 612 donors this year (3,500 times the attrition rate of 17.5 percent, which is 100 percent minus the multiyear renewal rate of 82.5 percent).

The upshot is, next year you'll have only 2,888 donors—barely more than half the number you've calculated you will need to meet minimal income targets.

The following year—after just three years—assuming the same rate of attrition, your donor file will shrink to 2,382. That's less than half the 5,000 donors you'll need to sustain your operations!

And that process will continue until there's hardly anything left of your donor base. But you may have to close your doors long before then.

Think about it.

Don't imagine for one minute that I'm crying wolf. I've seen nonprofit organizations literally disappear from the face of the Earth because they decided they couldn't afford to prospect for new donors.

Never forget: fundraising is a complex, long-term process. Here's one of the fundamental truths of development: Not all fundraising activities raise funds.

In fact, the process includes many pursuits that themselves are not profitable. For most organizations, new-donor acquisition is the most significant of these money-losing but absolutely essential activities.

To sustain the health of your fundraising program, you'll almost certainly have to maintain at least as many active donors next year as you've got this year.

If you want your revenues to climb, you'll need more donors. That means spending money on acquisition.

But it doesn't take much brain power to realize that the sheer number of donors means little. Obviously, because some donors are more equal than others, you have to take into account how much money each donor gives. (See Sidebar 15.2.)

SIDEBAR 15.2 WHAT HAPPENS IF YOU DON'T REPLACE DONORS LOST TO ATTRITION?

When	# Donors	1.5 Gifts per Donor, Avg. $100	Fundraising Revenue
Last year	5,000	× 1.5 × $100	$750,000
This year	3,500	× 1.5 × $100	$525,000
Next year	2,888		$433,200
Two years from now	2,382		$357,300

What happens, indeed? Sooner or later, the organization goes broke!

Benchmark 4: How Much Do Your Donors Give?

There are two numbers that together will give you an insightful peek at the responsiveness of your donors:

- How many gifts they give in a year, on average
- How large those gifts are, on average

Individually, these two measurements are of relatively limited use. Their diagnostic value increases when the two numbers are seen as twin dimensions of donor responsiveness. That's especially true if your fundraising strategy is founded on involvement. By contrast, these numbers may be of little or no use in tracking a Growth or Visibility Strategy.

Now let's look at each of the two components in turn.

The Average Gift

Take the number of gifts you received this year (7,500, to stick to the example) and divide that into the total revenue from them this year ($750,000). The average contribution was therefore $100. Now, what does that tell you?

A lot. And very little.

First, we have to assume that your $750,000 in revenue doesn't include a $250,000 bequest from a former trustee. Obviously, a huge gift like that will skew the average. Eliminating it will drop the average from $100 to $67. So let's assume that those 7,500 gifts don't include a single extraordinarily large contribution. For the sake of argument, say they're all $1,000 or less.

Now what does that $100 average gift tell you?

Just this: you're deriving a whole lot more revenue from each donor than an organization with an average gift of $10, and a whole lot less than one with gifts averaging $1,000. This may be very meaningful if organizations similar to yours are bringing in $1,000 gifts on average (or $10 gifts, for that matter). But, looking at just these figures, it's impossible to know whether you're in better shape than they are, or worse.

For one thing, we don't know what it cost you to generate those $100 gifts. Just as information about fundraising costs is meaningless in the absence of knowledge about fundraising revenue, the revenue figure is worth little except in comparison with costs.

Equally important, even though we've factored out any unusually large gifts, we don't know which donors (or which components of the fundraising program) drive the average up or down.

For example, you could generate about $750,000 in revenue from 7,250 gifts averaging $69 each plus 250 contributions of $1,000.

Or you could realize roughly the same revenue from 700 gifts of $1,000 and 6,800 checks for $7.35.

These two pictures are very, very different, no?

In scenario A, a third of your revenue comes from $1,000 donors, two-thirds from donors of much less than $1,000.

By contrast, in scenario B, nearly all of your revenue ($700,000 of $750,000) comes from $1,000 donors. Only the little bit left comes from donors making very small gifts.

Overall, average gift calculations are of limited value because the figures vary so sharply from one program component to another.

(Direct-mail gifts might average $20, say, while bequests are typically $20,000.) So there are really only two significant things you can learn from the raw average-gift data:

• By comparing the average first-time gift to the average multiyear gift, you'll get a hint of the effectiveness of your development program. For instance, if multiyear gifts average much higher than new gifts, you may be doing a spectacular job of involving and informing your donors.

• By studying year-to-year trends in the average gift—especially when broken down between first-time and multiyear averages—you can determine the effectiveness of steps you've taken to beef up your fundraising efforts. Or you might learn at a glance that you need to take corrective action quickly.

Thus, as Table 15.2 shows, there are really four average gifts (A1, A2, B1, B2). *Note:* The year-to-year change may be measured either in absolute numbers or in percentage terms. However, I recommend you choose one or the other. It's not necessarily useful to look at more numbers!

Frequency of Giving

The other side of the coin of generosity is frequency: how often your donors give gifts.

These two measurements—annual average and frequency of contributions—complement each other. It's no accident that when multiplied together the two numbers yield the total fundraising revenue.

TABLE 15.2 Calculating Average Gift Levels.

	(1) Average First-Year Gift	*(2) Average Multiyear Gift*
(A) Last year	A1	A2
(B) Previous year	B1	B2
(C) Year-to-year change	A1 minus B1	A2 minus B2

In the hypothetical example we've been using, the organization received a total of 7,500 gifts this year from 5,000 donors. That's a frequency of 1.5 gifts per donor.

But here, too, the overall average number is of limited value. It's far more revealing to track and compare the frequency numbers over time, just as we did with the figures for the average gift. Once again we'll be looking at four separate numbers, plus the year-to-year change in each (see Table 15.3).

If subtraction and division bore you—or if your donor file seems too small for such high-powered mathematics—you might approach the question from an even simpler perspective. Instead of dwelling on the average giving frequency of your donors, count the number of donors who have given three, four, five, or more gifts during the most recent period (a year, two years, three). These are significant numbers, because such multidonors tend to be much more responsive than one-time or even two-time donors.

Table 15.4 provides a real-world example of frequency and average gift. The table was part of an analysis that my firm, Response Management Technologies, conducted for a client a few years ago. The data are still valid, despite the passage of time, because we routinely see the same pattern. Note the year-to-year variations in frequency and average gift, but the powerful long-term trend of increasing responsiveness the longer a donor remains active.

Whichever way you analyze the numbers, you're not yet done looking at giving trends over time. To grasp the picture more firmly, you need to add a third dimension to the measurements of frequency

TABLE 15.3 Calculating Gifts per Donor.

	(1) Average # Gifts from First-Year Donors	(2) Average # Gifts from Multiyear Donors
(A) Last year	A1	A2
(B) Previous year	B1	B2
(C) Year-to-year change	A1 minus B1	A2 minus B2

TABLE 15.4 Year-to-Year Variations in Frequency and Average Gift.

Year of First Gift	# Who Joined	# Who Gave in 1994	Percent of Those Giving in 1994	Total # of Gifts in 1994	Gifts per Donor	Total 1994 Revenue	Average Gift
1970	2	1	50 percent	4	4.00	$53,500.00	$13,375.00
1972	1	1	100 percent	3	3.00	$17,750.00	$5,916.67
1977	1	1	100 percent	5	5.00	$12,500.00	$2,500.00
1978	17	12	71 percent	32	2.67	$546,719.87	$17,085.00
1979	7	6	86 percent	23	3.83	$177,700.00	$7,726.09
1980	6	3	50 percent	5	1.67	$10,200.00	$2,040.00
1981	5	4	80 percent	5	1.25	$156,572.86	$31,314.57
1982	18	12	67 percent	40	3.33	$105,049.08	$2,626.23
1983	22	7	32 percent	11	1.57	$56,750.91	$5,159.17
1984	18	5	28 percent	12	2.40	$37,200.00	$3,100.00
1985	12	7	58 percent	12	1.71	$78,442.12	$6,536.84
1986	8	3	38 percent	3	1.00	$3,500.00	$1,166.67
1987	20	7	35 percent	16	2.29	$62,584.00	$3,911.50
1988	88	47	53 percent	79	1.68	$106,550.00	$1,348.73
1989	64	22	34 percent	32	1.45	$8,295.00	$259.22
1990	281	121	43 percent	214	1.77	$371,795.00	$1,737.36
1991	1120	230	21 percent	348	1.51	$353,417.84	$1,015.57
1992	581	169	29 percent	258	1.53	$233,781.08	$906.13
1993	4070	1871	46 percent	2777	1.48	$815,893.00	$293.80
1994	7548	7548	100 percent	8723	1.16	$858,682.32	$98.44
Total	13889	10077	73 percent	12602	1.25	$4,066,883.08	$322.72

and average gift. The changing behavior of individual donors is in some ways even more important than the average contribution. Especially significant is whether they're increasing or decreasing their support.

Benchmark 5: Upgrades and Downgrades

Funny thing: the fundraising process, from A to Z, is posited on the assumption that over time donors will "upgrade" their support. Yet neophytes to the field of fundraising are often shocked to learn that donors rarely start at a minimum contribution level and increase their gifts in a steadily rising pattern from year to year. Sharp variations in gift amount are the rule, not the exception. For instance, a $100 first-time donor may send $25 the second time and $50 the third. Only with the fourth gift, sometimes years later, does that donor upgrade to the $200 level. Fundraising is tough!

Still, we often invest more than we care to admit in recruiting, welcoming, informing, and cultivating donors—all in hopes that their generosity will grow through the years. Yet very few organizations take the trouble to measure the effectiveness of these upgrade efforts.

Don't make that mistake. Assessing the patterns of upgrading (and downgrading) among your donors may lead to considerable insight about the dynamics of your fundraising program. That analysis, perhaps most significant in an Efficiency Strategy, could point to glaring problems—or spectacular new opportunities.

Hyperbole? No!

Consider the scene at our hypothetical nonprofit, with its 5,000 donors and $750,000 in revenue this year. Now let's develop two different scenarios:

• This year you'll receive one-third of the $750,000 from $1,000 donors: the 250 active members of a giving club who receive special privileges for their generosity. But last year, instead of 250 donors at that level, there were 350. In other words, 100 major donors are downgrading their support. Thus your organization may have a very big problem indeed. To compensate for the loss of $100,000 in revenue, you'll have to bring in an additional two thousand smaller gifts. Is that likely? No. Clearly, it's urgent to take a look at the operations of that giving club!

• What if, instead, there were major changes in the giving patterns of smaller contributors? Let's say that this year you're going to generate two-thirds of your $750,000 in revenue from ten thousand gifts averaging $50 each. Assume that the previous year you received about the same number of gifts but their average size was considerably smaller: $40 (being sure to factor out unusually large contributions). It behooves you to examine very, very closely what methods your organization has used to secure those gifts—and to compare what you did the previous year with what you did this past year. An increase in the average contribution from $40 to $50 is dramatic. You've obviously stumbled onto something big. (See Table 15.5.)

It won't take long to figure out that the average gift by itself is an inadequate measure of upgrading or downgrading. After all, we're talking about individual donor behavior. To gain perspective on the true pattern of year-to-year change in giving habits, you'll need to count the number of donors who upgraded their support sometime during the past year and compare that with the number

TABLE 15.5 Comparison of Two Year's Revenue.

Assuming total revenue is constant . . .			
	High-Dollar Revenue	*Small-Donor Revenue*	*Total Revenue*
1 This year	250 × $1,000 = $250,000	10,000 × $50 = $500,000	$750,000
Last year	350 × $1,000 = $350,000	8,000 × $50 = $400,000	$750,000
2 This year	250 × $1,000 = $250,000	10,000 × $50 = $500,000	$750,000
Last year	350 × $1,000 = $350,000	10,000 × $40 = $400,000	$750,000

who upgraded the previous year. Similarly, you'll want to know the number who downgraded in both years. And to round things off, you'll find it useful to calculate the year-to-year change in both these measurements.

All told, that adds six numbers to our growing list of primary benchmarks (see Table 15.6).

But your organization may find it useful to add yet another three numbers—yardsticks that measure what I call the graduation class.

Benchmark 6: The Graduation Class

In most fundraising programs, there is a boundary between the realm of small contributions and the exalted kingdom of major gifts. In some charities, that boundary may be at the $50 level. In others, the dividing line could be $100,000. Wherever the line is drawn, the principle is the same. When a donor passes from one territory into another, bells ring and something happens. Perhaps that level of upgrade will trigger a personal phone call from the president or a member of the board of trustees. Perhaps the donor is automatically admitted to some honorary status, entitling her to special recognition.

Nonprofits take exceptional steps like these because major donors are their lifeblood. They are treasured, pampered, and jealously guarded.

If there's such a clear dividing line in your organization—or if you establish one to help set fundraising priorities—you would do

TABLE 15.6 Calculating Donor Upgrades and Downgrades.

	(1) # of Donors Who Upgraded	(2) # of Donors Who Downgraded
(A) Last year	A1	A2
(B) Previous year	B1	B2
(C) Year-to-year change	A1 minus B1	A2 minus B2

well to count the number of donors who cross the line each year. Then compare that number with the previous year's and look at the difference.

Assume, for example, that the graduation threshold in your organization is $500. You might construct a chart like the one in Table 15.7 to track your donor graduation pattern. What can you learn from this table? Plenty—even without knowledge of the particulars of the organization's fundraising program.

Far more donors are graduating to the $500 level this year than last year. (The number grew from thirty-seven to forty-five, an increase of nearly 22 percent.)

Most of the increase—seven of the eight additional upgrades—occurred in two months: December (which may be predictable, because it falls in the prime giving season) and May (which is a surprise, thus suggesting some unusual and highly successful upgrade effort in that month).

Keep your eye on the graduation rate and you'll understand much more quickly how effective your fundraising program is.

TABLE 15.7 Tracking Donor Graduation (First-Time Major Gifts).

Month	Last Year	This Year	Year-to-Year Change
January	4	5	+1
February	2	1	−1
March	2	2	0
April	3	3	0
May	2	6	+4
June	0	0	0
July	1	1	0
August	2	1	−1
September	4	4	0
October	4	5	+1
November	5	6	+1
December	8	11	+3
Total	37	45	+8

Benchmark 7: Is Your Donor Base Growing?

Clearly, if growth is the central focus of your development efforts, tracking the sheer number of donors or members is paramount. But your fundraising strategy may not require a growing list of active donors. For some nonprofits, efforts to promote involvement, efficiency, or stability may be little affected by the number of donors. However, most nonprofits—facing the need to raise more money each year than the last—strive for at least modest growth in the donor base. (They know there are limits to the potential for upgrading donors.)

Measuring this aspect of growth is fundamentally simple. All you have to do is count the number of people who gave gifts this year and subtract from it the number who gave last year. The difference is the growth—or negative growth (shrinkage), if this year's number is smaller than last year's.

This straightforward measurement is very useful. It will tell you whether your donor base is getting bigger or smaller. But in most circumstances, merely knowing that much isn't enough.

To fathom the dynamics of your fundraising program, it's far more useful to segment your donor list into classes or categories of donors and to track the growth or shrinkage by segment as well as overall.

You might wish to define segments on the basis of donors' highest previous contribution, or on the total number of gifts they've given (perhaps during the past twelve months). Or you may prefer to define donor file segments multidimensionally.

Following is a simple way to track donors by segment.

For example, you could divide the list into four groups of donors. Call them "best," "not quite so good," "okay," and "not very responsive." Label them A, B, C, and D, perhaps (if none of the donors will ever see the labels). Each of those segments or categories might be determined on the basis of, say, three aspects of your donors' behavior: how recently they last gave, how frequently they've given, and how much money they've given in any single gift. The best could be those who've given at least one gift during the past twelve months and given at least three gifts altogether, at least one of which was for $100 or more. Other segments would be similarly defined. Then, using the same definitions, segment the list, year after year (or quarter by quarter), and track the changing numbers or proportions of donors by segment.

If you notice that the number of your best donors is growing, that's good. If the number is shrinking, dig a little deeper. Something's probably wrong.

This way, you might construct a tracking chart along the lines of the one provided in Table 15.8.

What's happening in this hypothetical example?

There's no overall growth in the number of donors for three quarters, then a big spurt in the year's final quarter (from 12,600 to 14,900).

Meanwhile, however, good things were happening in the absence of overall growth. There was a steady pattern of upgrading, with D-level donors moving up to the C level or even the B level at a substantial pace.

However, there was no growth whatsoever in the numbers of A-level (best) donors throughout the year.

TABLE 15.8 A Simple Segmentation Model.

Donor Segment	1st Quarter	2nd Quarter	3rd Quarter	4th Quarter
A	100	100	100	100
B	500	600	700	800
C	2,000	2,400	2,700	3,000
D	10,000	9,500	9,100	11,000
Total	12,600	12,600	12,600	14,900

Benchmark 8: The Fundraising Ratio

This one's simple—or at least that's how it looks at first. (And it may really be simple if your strategy is based on efficiency.)

On the face of things, calculating the fundraising ratio is simply a matter of adding up all your fundraising revenue, calculating all your fundraising costs, and then comparing the two sums.

Let's say you are that lucky. That may be all it takes to compute the ratio, because your organization's fundraising program is so straightforward. Your fundraising ratio (or cost ratio) stacks up as shown in Table 15.9.

There's a strong chance, though, that some factor will compli-cate your life. For example:

• To meet the reporting requirements of the state charities registration office or a particular watchdog agency (not to mention the Internal Revenue Service), your accountant may use some form of joint cost allocation. This is a frequently discussed, some-times controversial procedure through which some fundraising costs are allocated to other aspects of the organization's activi-ties—most commonly, public education. In our simple, hypothet-ical example, half the fundraising cost might be allocated to education. Does that mean, then, that your cost ratio is only half as high—$0.10 to raise $1.00? That depends on your point of view. But I say the answer is yes.

• Laws, regulations, and dogmatic auditors notwithstanding, there's usually some room to wiggle in reporting the overhead costs attributable to fundraising. For instance, do you really track and report all the staff time spent preparing for fundraising events?

TABLE 15.9 Calculating the Fundraising Cost Ratio.

Total Revenue	$500,000
Total fundraising costs	$100,000
Fundraising cost ratio	20 percent, or $0.20 to raise $1.00

(Really?) And do you include fees paid to a fundraising consultant for strategic planning and board training? Or is that expense legitimately allocated to other budget categories, such as organizational development or human resources? In the example I'm using, let's say you doggedly compute that extra investments of staff time in fundraising actually amount to $100,000. So, because your fundraising costs are really double what they seemed, is your fundraising ratio now twice as high—$0.40 to raise $1.00? If you answered yes to the previous question, as I did, then intellectual honesty demands the same answer to this question.

One way or another, you'll resolve these uncertainties. Taken individually, none of them really matters much in an internal assessment of a fundraising program.

I say that with one loud caveat: *Make sure you apply the same criteria to line cost allocations from year to year!* Only if you're consistent will you derive any benefit from tracking the fundraising cost ratio.

Benchmark 9: How Big a Piece of the Pie Have You Got?

Businesses routinely measure their performance against market share. So do big nonprofits.

For example, a well-run hospital development program keeps a sharp eye on any competition from other organizations that actively raise money in the area, especially those involved in health care. The development director particularly needs to know how her program stacks up against those of other hospitals, as well as those of regional or national health-related nonprofits active in the hospital's service area.

The most telling measurement of the hospital's competitiveness is its *market share*. That benchmark is most simply stated as the percentage of all households in the service area that contributed to the hospital during the past twelve months. For other major nonprofit organizations, such as museums, zoos, public broadcasters, or leading charities such as the Salvation Army and the American Heart

Association, market share measurements calculated in the same manner may make compelling reading for executives and trustees.

For a college or university, market share is more meaningfully defined as the percentages of alumni, parents, faculty, and staff members who are active donors. (Usually the measurement looks only at giving to the annual fund, or membership in the alumni association, or both.) Institutions of higher learning routinely track these numbers—as well they should.

What better measurement is there of how effective the development staff has been in persuading the school's key constituencies to contribute to its future?

Caution: measurements of market share are of little use to a small nonprofit in a large community. This benchmark has greatest value for the leaders of a charity with a strong competitive position in its service area.

See Sidebar 15.3 (on pages 208 and 209) for an illustration of one way of determining and using market share.

You can use market share calculations to take stock of the competition and of your potential for growth. Let's say, for example, that you direct the membership and fundraising programs at an art museum. The museum has a strong presence throughout your metropolitan area, which is home to a total of some 3 million persons in 1.2 million households.

Assume further that you've estimated, through extensive direct-mail experience with all the other local arts institutions' membership and donors lists, that the total number of households in the region that are active donors to the arts is about sixty thousand.

In this scenario, you'll do better to ponder the potential for financial growth from upgrading your donors rather than from trying to boost their numbers.

Through painstaking research, you might estimate that your market share stacks up as shown in Table 15.10.

What might these calculations reveal to you? These things, among others:

TABLE 15.10 Calculating Market Share.

Institution	# Donor Households	Market Share (Percent of 1.2 Million)	Market Share (Percent of 60,000)
The opera	40,000	3.3 percent	66.7 percent
The Metropolitan Museum of Art (New York City)	20,000	1.7 percent	33.3 percent
The symphony	20,000	1.7 percent	33.3 percent
Your museum	18,000	1.5 percent	30.0 percent
The ballet	9,000	0.8 percent	15.0 percent
Another local art museum	6,000	0.5 percent	10.0 percent
Other local arts organizations	18,000	1.5 percent	30.0 percent

- Your fundraising presence in the region is indeed strong. Only three other arts organizations have bigger lists of supporters locally.
- So far, you've recruited three out of every ten active local arts donors. That's a great accomplishment, but it's less than half what the opera has managed to do. That means you can probably learn something from the opera's fundraising methods.
- If only three out of ten local arts donors have joined the museum, there should be room for you to grow—a lot of room, actually. It's a little unusual for a strong local art museum to have fewer members than a symphony orchestra and an opera company. After all, a popular museum can draw a crowd every day! Performing arts groups are hard-pressed to go on stage so frequently. Only the biggest performance halls can match the capacity of a museum of respectable size. And admission fees at museums tend to be a lot lower than the price of tickets to a symphony concert.

In this fashion, you can learn a great deal from market-share calculations. But it may also be useful to compute market penetration.

Let's take a look at your museum's market penetration—the proportion of households you reach with your message (see Table 15.11 on page 210).

Now, what does this tell you? Again, lots!

If you're mailing to only 10.0 percent, or one out of every ten households in the region, and you've already built a membership list that includes almost one out of three active local arts donors, you've clearly got a lot of room to grow. With greater market penetration—that is, with a more substantial investment in donor acquisition efforts—you have every reason to hope that your membership will increase by leaps and bounds.

SIDEBAR 15.3 PANNING FOR GOLD IN MERGE-PURGE REPORTS

Studying the "merge-purge" reports you receive after each direct-mail donor acquisition effort may cast light on your market share. A merge-purge report reveals the degree of overlap between your list and the other lists you use, and among the other lists. The following table illustrates a hypothetical example of duplication rates among four lists in a merge-purge.

	Quantity	Your List	Outside List A	Outside List B	Outside List C
Your list	20,000	100 percent	60 percent	20 percent	5 percent
Outside list A	40,000	60 percent	100 percent	30 percent	10 percent
Outside list B	10,000	20 percent	30 percent	100 percent	2 percent
Outside list C	5,000	5 percent	10 percent	2 percent	100 percent

Now, assume for the sake of argument that the size of the market is defined by the aggregate size of the donor lists of the four competing organizations (yours, A, B, and C). Assume also that all four lists are complete—that is, practically no names were omitted from the merge-

After all, you reach only one out of ten households in the area. The opera reaches more than three out of ten!

Using the Ten Benchmarks to Evaluate Your Strategy

That's nine of my ten benchmarks of successful fundraising. The tenth, return on investment, is a little more complicated than the others. An explanation of it follows in the next chapter. But first, I'd like to sum up the relative importance of each of the ten benchmarks as a yardstick for progress in programs employing each of the five strategies. Table 15.12 (on page 211) reveals a number of important lessons:

---

purge—and that no other organization of significant size is competing with the four of you. What insight can you gain about your organization's competitive position?

Lots:

• The market is dominated by Organization A. You share three-fifths of your donors with A. That means it's important for you to keep track of A's doings—close track! You can't ignore what A does. Most of your donors won't.

• Your organization operates in a mature market. Explosive growth in numbers is probably not an option for you. Right now about two-thirds of your 20,000 donors overlap with one or more of the other lists. Conceivably you could add the remaining 16,000 donors to A, the remaining 8,000 donors to B, and the remaining 4,500 donors to C. But that's not a simple matter of addition. There's duplication between A and B, between B and C, and between A and C. Chances are that there are no more than 20,000 people who have contributed to one of the other three organizations but have not contributed to yours.

It's unlikely you can recruit all 20,000. Many people can comfortably contribute to two or more similar organizations, but not everyone. Some people in the market will prove to be died-in-the-wool fans of A, or B, or C and oblivious to your organization's many obvious attractions.

In this scenario, you'll do better to ponder the potential for financial growth from upgrading your donors rather than trying to boost their numbers.

• Each of the five strategies may be evaluated most usefully by *one benchmark* (marked "most important" in the table). For example, the growth in the number of donors is, virtually by definition, the key to tracking a Growth Strategy, while fundraising cost is paramount for an Efficiency Strategy. The other benchmarks are only slightly less obvious: frequency and average gift levels for Involvement Strategies, market share for Visibility Strategies, and Return on Investment for Stability Strategies.

• Three of the ten benchmarks are consistently important, almost regardless of the fundraising strategy: the donor renewal rate, donor attrition, and return on investment.

• Return on investment is, in the final analysis, the most crucial benchmark under any strategy. As you'll see in the next chapter, however, you can interpret that number differently, depending on the strategy you're employing.

The other benchmarks may or may not be of use in assessing a particular fundraising program. In general, you can get a pretty good feel for the success or failure of any particular strategy by tracking no more than four or five of the ten benchmarks.

TABLE 15.11 Calculating Market Penetration.

Institution	Estimated # of Households Mailed or Phoned in Last 12 Months	Market Penetration (Percent of 1.2 Million)
The opera	400,000	33.3 percent
The Metropolitan Museum of Art (New York City)	200,000	16.7 percent
The symphony	400,000	33.3 percent
Your museum	120,000	10.0 percent
The ballet	180,000	15.0 percent
Another local art museum	48,000	4.0 percent
Other local arts organizations	96,000	8.0 percent

From another perspective, however, you may find all ten benchmarks useful. Used consistently as tools to evaluate all the fundraising techniques used in pursuit of any of the five strategies, the ten benchmarks will dramatize the consequences of making both strategic and tactical decisions. For example, the rates of response by direct-mail donors sent a renewal notice and eventgoers invited to a benefit are likely to vary dramatically, even though both means of asking used mail. The direct-mail group is likely to be far more responsive. Viewing comparisons such as this may help you understand how solicitation methods perform differently.

TABLE 15.12 Relative Usefulness of the Ten Benchmarks in Evaluating the Five Strategies.

Benchmark	Growth	Involvement	Visibility	Efficiency	Stability
Revenue growth	Maybe useful	Maybe useful	Unimportant	Maybe useful	Important
Donor renewal	Important	Important	Important	Important	Important
Donor attrition	Important	Important	Important	Important	Important
Returns per donor	Unimportant	*Most important*	Unimportant	Maybe useful	Maybe useful
Donor upgrades	Unimportant	Maybe useful	Unimportant	Important	Maybe useful
Graduation count	Unimportant	Maybe useful	Unimportant	Important	Important
Number of donors	*Most important*	Unimportant	Important	Maybe useful	Maybe useful
Fundraising cost	Unimportant	Maybe useful	Unimportant	*Most important*	Important
Market share	Maybe useful	Unimportant	*Most important*	Maybe useful	Maybe useful
Return on Investment	Important	Important	Important	Important	*Most important*

16

Using Return on Investment to Focus on Results

In this chapter I come to grips with the peskiest of my ten benchmarks of successful fundraising: return on investment. Calculating and tracking this one can be a drag, because it requires knowing both the long-term value of your donors and your acquisition cost. (Please be patient: I'll explain all three concepts.) Yet understanding return on investment is ultimately the key to working successfully with the five strategies for successful fundraising. Only through knowledge of return on investment can you weigh the trade-offs among strategies.

Long-Term Value and How to Compute It

We talk about donors as though they were interchangeable units, or sometimes as inhabitants of a no-person's land called a "segment of the donor file." But you and I know that donors aren't interchangeable. Each individual donor has a personal history; a distinct personality; singular values, beliefs, and experiences; and financial circumstances that apply only to her. We're fools not to take those unique individual facts, feelings, and circumstances into account.

Not now, though.

For the time being, as leaders of a nonprofit organization, we have to stop thinking of donors as those nice people who built the new wing or covered last year's shortfall in the budget. Forget their names, their quirks, their individual uniqueness. Think of them instead as (Dare I say it?) statistics.

Long-term value is the name of this game.

This is where we start getting a fix on the relationship between fundraising costs and fundraising returns.

For starters, we've got two choices:

- Count nickels and dimes—the relatively meager returns from individual donors in response to individual fundraising efforts

- Look for the Big Picture—the aggregate value of all those individual gifts accumulated over time in response to all our fundraising efforts

But you're quite smart enough to know that all the nickels and dimes add up to the aggregate value. In other words, those two choices are no choice at all.

The best way to transcend these choices is by using the term most widely employed to depict the Big Picture: *long-term value*.

Incidentally, long-term value is known to some fundraisers as life-time value. But I prefer to talk about the long term. There are two reasons for this:

- The average donor doesn't stick with a charity throughout his lifetime. A few years at a stretch is more typical.

- Some of the methods used to calculate long-term value look only at a specified number of years—frequently five years, three years, even a single year.

The important thing is to lock your attention onto the results of the fundraising process. For the moment, put aside your natural interest in the returns from individual fundraising projects. Measuring long-term value is a way to assess your effectiveness in building relationships with your donors.

If definitions make you feel more secure, try this one out:

Long-term value is the sum of the net revenue from all your fundraising programs over a given (but long) period, divided by the total number of individual donors included in the calculation.

If you're more comfortable with equations, this may help:

$$LTV = R/Q$$

LTV is the long-term value, R is the total net revenue from the donors, and Q is the number of those donors.

For example, if an average donor to your organization remains active for five years, you can compute your long-term value by adding up all the net income over those five years from the donors whose worth you want to calculate, then dividing that five-year revenue total by the total number of donors in question. The result is a simple number in dollars and cents. It might be $10, $100, $1,000, or much more. You won't know until you take the trouble to do all the addition and division.

Computing long-term value can thus be tedious. But it's worth the time and effort.

Long-term value is the only true measurement of the results of your ongoing efforts to recruit, inform, and upgrade donors.

A word of caution: if your donor development program (or your whole organization) is less than three years old, or if reliable records don't go back that far, it may be pointless to try computing the long-term value of your donors. Five years' data will make the job more manageable. Ten years' would be better.

In a well-developed fundraising program, long-term value may have to take into account the revenue from a large number of programs and communications channels. The list at any given organization might include the following:

- Membership dues
- Annual gifts
- Major gifts
- Bequests
- Monthly sustainer gifts
- Special appeals
- Planned gifts
- Merchandising
- Newsletter subscriptions
- High-dollar club
- Internet gifts
- Direct mail
- Telephone outreach
- Newspaper ads
- Radio public service announcements
- TV public service announcements
- TV talk-show correspondence
- Convention and conferences
- Magazine blow-in cards
- Point-of-purchase displays

To complicate matters, many of these efforts overlap. For example, you may acquire monthly sustainers largely but not exclusively through the mail. Others may be recruited by telephone, at special events, or at house meetings. It's essential to keep the distinctions straight. In evaluating the performance of the monthly sustainer program, it's crucial not to lump all the sustainers together as direct-mail acquired. Their behavior—expressed in such ways as renewal rates and donor loyalty—could differ significantly. Sustainers recruited face-to-face or by telephone could prove far more valuable—or far less. Don't put apples and pineapples into the same basket and call them all fruit! Count them together, if you must. But know what you're counting.

It's essential to understand clearly, or to decide arbitrarily, which donors to include in the formula. People who've given this year only? Over the last two years? Everyone on the mailing list? Direct-mail-acquired donors versus eventgoers versus newsletter subscribers?

To determine the long-term value of your donors requires precise and highly detailed records. At a minimum, you'll need to know to the penny how much money you've raised from the activities you want to include in the calculation, precisely when you raised it, and from whom.

Remember: money raised from people who aren't included in the calculation will distort the picture if those funds are included!

Warning: this is where we've got to grit our teeth and deal with numbers. Lots and lots of numbers. If numbers make you cringe, you won't like what comes next in this chapter. I'm sorry about that. There's no way around it. Calculating long-term value, for example, is not a matter of guesswork. It's a quantitative exercise. If this stuff gives you real trouble, find someone who can set it all up for you on a big spreadsheet.

Calculations of long-term value become more useful the more comprehensive they are, and the longer the period measured. Here's why:

• Assume that you're at the helm of a small museum called History on Parade. You have a marvelously diversified fundraising, marketing, and merchandising program. You generate significant revenue through sales of T-shirts, trinkets, and magazine subscriptions. You also operate a wide range of development programs, notably including a monthly sustainer club and a legacy society that persuades members to remember History on Parade in their wills. All these activities yield, say, $6 million per year, divided almost equally between fundraising programs (conducted by the development department) and merchandising activities (assigned to the marketing department). Call it $3 million produced each year by each of the two departments (see Table 16.1).

• Assume further that your members, donors, and customers come to you through a wide variety of sources. That is, some members (not all) become donors, customers, or both. Some donors have never formally joined the organization, so they're not counted in the membership rolls. And many customers have only purchased T-shirts or trinkets or subscribed to the magazine. They've never become members, much less donors.

Now, how on earth do we calculate the long-term value of all these supporters? Which ones do we count? What revenue do we include? If we toss them all into the same pot, an overview of the picture would look like Table 16.2. (Assume for simplicity's sake that the revenue numbers represent net revenue, or profits, over a five-year period.)

If we lump together all 62,000 supporters and divide that number into the $30 million revenue total, we'll arrive at a long-term value

TABLE 16.1 Distinguishing Between Fundraising and Merchandising Revenue for History on Parade.

Department	Yearly Revenue	5-Year Revenue
Fundraising	$3,000,000	$15,000,000
Merchandising	$3,000,000	15,000,000
Total	$6,000,000	$30,000,000

TABLE 16.2 Segmenting History on Parade's Fundraising and Merchandising Revenue by Source.

	Fundraising	Merchandising	Total 5-Year Revenue
10,000 Members	$4,800,000	$2,000,000	$6,800,000
2,000 Donors	$10,000,000	$200,000	$10,200,000
50,000 Customers	$200,000	$12,800,000	$13,000,000
All 62,000 Supporters	$15,000,000	$15,000,000	$30,000,000

of approximately $484. ($30,000,000/62,000 = $484.) That's about $97 per person per year on average for the five years in question.

But is this a meaningful average? Is it really appropriate to include both a six-year-old child who bought a T-shirt and a loyal major donor in your calculations?

Obviously we've got to be a little more selective to derive meaning from this exercise!

If we look at fundraising revenue alone, we'll miss half the picture. Each of the two departments brings in a total of about $15 million over the five-year period.

If we factor out all of History on Parade's customers—counting only the revenue from members and donors—we'll achieve almost the same negative effect. And who decides which people fell into which category anyway? There's a lot of overlap!

Warning: don't understate long-term value just because it's difficult to measure the proceeds from merchandising, special events, subscription sales, or other collateral money-making activities. And don't overlook the potential value of bequests and other planned gifts simply because you haven't yet begun to tap those rich sources of support. Long-term value is future value. It's vital to take all the possibilities into account.

Now let's try some quick calculations:

• Take all revenue sources into account and figure the long-term value of your ten thousand members:

Long-term value: $6,800,000/10,000 = $680

Average annual value: $680/5 = $136

But are you sure you're counting the income you receive from those several hundred people who originally joined as members but are now classified as donors? Some signed up more than five years ago and would thus be reclassified as donors, but others didn't.

• Now look at your two thousand donors:

Long-term value: $10,200,000/2,000 = $5,100

Average annual value: $5,100/5 = $1,020

But what about the $5 million lead gift you received from a single family in last year's capital campaign? Including that gift—which you'll recall is what you have done—doubles the apparent long-term value of all the rest of your donors! Does that make sense?

The long-term value of History on Parade's fifty thousand customers is $13,000,000/50,000 = $260.

Their average annual value is $260/5 = $53.

It's problematic to lump these customers together with your members and donors. They don't give money. But who's to say that much of the revenue from your members and donors—even possibly that $5 million lead gift—didn't come in part because of the attractiveness of your merchandising program? And that program wouldn't even be self-supporting, let alone hugely profitable, if you didn't welcome large numbers of customers who never become members or donors!

There are no simple, straightforward answers to these questions. Calculating long-term value may require exercising judgment at many stages. And your calculation of your donors' long-term value may mean something wholly different from the measurement made by a colleague in an organization very similar to yours. It's difficult to compare these numbers from one nonprofit to another. But certain guidelines apply broadly:

• Factor out gifts of exceptional size. Certainly, don't include any single gift that by itself will significantly raise the average.

• Work with the longest period that's practical for your organization. If all you've got is three years of reliable records, that's not great, but it's better than nothing. (Next year's measurements will be better still, won't they?)

• Be certain to include all forms of income—bequests, for example. Yes, they're exceptional gifts. But bequests may be the principal justification for the investment you make in donor acquisition and cultivation. In most circumstances, it's probably best to evaluate long-term value both with and without income from bequests and other planned gifts.

• Leave out nondonors (that is, those who don't send voluntary gifts). If it's useful to count the financial benefits you receive from nondonors such as merchandise sales to customers, count them, but separately.

In the orthodox approach, developed for the insurance industry decades ago, long-term value is known as the net present value. This concept takes into account the cost of money (inflation and interest) over time. In other words, using a formula your accountant would be happy to show you if necessary, you deduct from the long-term value the expected amount of inflation over the donor's "lifetime" and the interest you would earn if you were to invest your money in, say, a money market fund instead of using it to acquire new donors.

To the extent that your calculation of long-term value is accurate, you'll be in a position to evaluate the return on your investment in acquiring new donors. We'll take a look at that not-so-simple computation after the following section, which relates the tale— mercifully less complicated—of acquisition cost.

Acquisition Cost

Are you paying too much to acquire new donors? Are you paying enough?

Acquisition cost is the net amount a charity spends to recruit a new donor. (Remember, that's a donor-as-statistic, not a real person.) Calculating your acquisition cost is an exercise in elementary school arithmetic.

In the course of a year, Save the Wombat mails 200,000 letters to prospective donors. One thousand of them respond by sending gifts. (That's one-half of one percent—much closer to reality for most nonprofits than the proverbial one percent return that's widely taken as a conventional rule of thumb.)

Now, those 200,000 letters cost a total of, say, $75,000. And the one thousand gifts generated by the letters produce a total of $40,000 in immediate cash gifts. So the net cost of a year's worth of direct-mail donor acquisition efforts for Save the Wombat is $35,000 ($75,000 minus $40,000.)

In other words, it costs $35,000 to bring in one thousand new donors, or $35 per donor. That $35, then, is Save the Wombat's acquisition cost—at least for direct mail conducted in that year and using the particular mailing lists involved.

Simple enough, right? Now the plot thickens.

How do you determine whether it makes sense for Save the Wombat to spend $35 to acquire a new donor? What's the formula to use?

Bad news. No formulas need apply.

To evaluate Save the Wombat's $35 acquisition cost means comparing that figure with the long-term value for similar donors. The only generalization I feel comfortable applying here is the following:

Your group's long-term value ought to be greater than your acquisition cost.

In fact, I can think of exceptional circumstances where even that rule might not be useful! For example, let's say Save the Wombat is three years old. Its development program is only gradually introducing new donor options, including a bequest program, which has just been launched. The demonstrable long-term value of Save the Wombat donors over the three-year period to date may be only $25 or $30. But a wise development director may conclude that it's still worth paying $35 to acquire a new donor. It won't take many $25,000 bequests to make that short-term investment pay off! He'll just have to wait a while (probably quite a long while) to realize the return.

But let's assume you're not dealing with exceptional circumstances. It's clear enough that your long-term value needs to be greater than your acquisition cost. How much greater? That's a judgment call. Naturally it depends on your strategy.

For instance, if Save the Wombat is hell-bent on growing a donor base as quickly as possible and receives the necessary capital from other sources, its $35 acquisition cost may simply be the price it has to pay for growth—even if the long-term value is only $35.50!

If, instead, Save the Wombat is a mature organization dependent on generous membership support and focused on a Stability Strategy, a $35 acquisition cost may make sense to its leadership only if the long-term value is $100, $150, or more. And if they're concerned about mounting criticism of the group's high fundraising ratio and determined to increase the efficiency of the fundraising program, the board might even insist that every dollar yield four or even six dollars in revenue, requiring a long-term value of as much as $210 per donor.

In any event, this process of weighing the trade-offs will help you avoid extreme and illogical courses of action, such as the one described in Sidebar 16.1 (on pages 224 and 225).

I regard this ratio of long-term value to acquisition cost as the simplest and most useful measure of return on investment in fundraising.

This concept deserves more attention.

Return on Investment

People with MBAs have lots of complicated ways to determine return on investment—a measure of whether a particular investment is a financially sound proposition.

Your organization's financial affairs may be of such great scope and complexity that you need to use one of these methods. For the overwhelming majority of nonprofits, however, something simpler will do just fine.

After all, we've already knocked ourselves out calculating long-term value and acquisition cost. Isn't that enough trouble for one lifetime?

Because we already know our acquisition cost and long-term value, it makes good sense to compare the two and call the result return on investment. (Purists will shudder, but I'm used to that.)

For example, let's take another look at History on Parade. You've learned that the five-year value of your ten thousand members is $680. If you root around in the records of the museum's membership recruitment efforts you'll find that the acquisition cost in recent years has leveled off at about $34 per member. In a typical year you acquire two thousand new members to replace those lost to attrition, keeping the membership file steady at ten thousand. If you stick to this course, acquiring new members at about the same rate, over five years History on Parade will likely generate $20 in revenue from every dollar invested in acquisition.

But wait a minute. Let's play with the assumptions.

• If analysis shows that History on Parade's membership is shrinking—a serious threat over the long haul—you might elect to invest enough money to acquire, say, three thousand new members this year. If we are so foolish as to assume that you can recruit an additional one thousand members at the same $34 rate, your net investment in acquisition will increase by 50 percent, from $68,000 to $102,000 (2000 × $34 = $68,000; 3,000 × $34 = $102,000). In reality, it's usually costly to step up membership acquisition because the more widely you range in search of members, the harder you have to look. (As economists say, the marginal cost increases with volume.) So, to be safe, let's assume that recruiting three thousand members will cost twice as much as recruiting two thousand. Those three thousand members will come in at a cost of $136,000, or approximately $45 each ($136,000/$3,000 = $45.33). If we can further assume that those three thousand members will generate the same long-term value of $680—also a risky assumption—then the 20 to 1 return-on-investment ratio will decline to about 15 to 1. In other words, a Growth Strategy will make History on Parade's membership program about 25 percent less efficient (15/20 = 75 percent).

• Try another scenario: analysis shows that History on Parade's long-term-donor value is rising because of several donor upgrade initiatives recently undertaken by the development department. A modest additional investment in major donor fundraising, planned giving, and a high-dollar giving club seems likely to continue this trend. Instead of having a long-term value of $680, members of History on Parade should be worth on average $1,020 after two to three

SIDEBAR 16.1 WHY NOT SIGN UP THE WHOLE HUMAN RACE?

Having 200 donors is better than having 100 donors, right? Twenty thousand is better than 10,000? And 200,000 is better than 100,000?

Well, maybe not. Because you won't profit from every new donor.

Regrettably, fundraising takes place in the real world, not in the make-believe universe of mathematical models and computer projections. No matter how much social scientists would have it be otherwise, the human species doesn't quite measure up to the expectations of dreamers. There are practical limits to just about everything involving people, and that definitely includes your donor acquisition program. Here's why:

The reach of your donor acquisition program is only as broad as the mission, the reputation, and the track record of your organization.

In your neighborhood, the Shark River Toxic Waste Coalition may be a household word. There may be members on every block. Even so, you can't persuade everyone in the neighborhood to join, because some people choose to be ornery, a few others disagree about the toxicity level in the Shark River, and others won't join anything, no matter what. You all live close to the Shark River, and to the plastics factory down on the bank. The coalition can hardly expect to recruit members so successfully in a sheltered neighborhood on high ground all the way across town.

In other words, you can't realize a profit on every new donor. Acquiring new members or donors outside your neighborhood will first become expensive, then impossible. You can extend your reach only so far.

But that's only part of the story.

Some of the techniques you select to acquire new donors will be more cost-effective than others. For instance, the Shark River Toxic Waste Coalition may do just fine recruiting new members by mail. When all the numbers are in and the books are closed, you might find that the acquisition cost is just $10 per member. With a long-term value of $35, there's no question that direct mail is profitable for you.

Not so recruiting via TV. Aunt Hilda's bright idea to put membership recruitment spots on late-night cable TV ("because it's so cheap") could soak up thousands of dollars in dribs and drabs of $25 and $30 each—and yield only a handful of new members. (Lots of good word-of-mouth on the street, though: "Gee, I saw you on TV last night!") In recruiting by TV, the coalition might be paying $50 or $150 per new member. That doesn't stack up so well against a $35 long-term value.

Then there are seasonal variations. The acquisition cost might be $5 per member in the spring, when the Shark River is at floodtide, noses twitch, and eyes turn red. In the depth of winter, shrouded by ice and snow, the Shark River is out of sight, out of mind, and out of smell. Response to membership-acquisition letters plummets. The result is an acquisition cost of $30 per member—barely less than the demonstrable long-term value.

These are some of the external factors that limit donor acquisition. Often there are internal factors, too.

For example, the coalition may be able to scrape together $3,000 to mail a membership invitation to every household in the neighborhood. But that money has to cover other expenses as well: printing leaflets and a newsletter, phone service, insurance, and airfare for the chairperson to fly to the state capitol to testify at a legislative hearing. So, even though spending all $3,000 on that membership invitation might be profitable, it's not possible. The cash flow won't support it.

years of intensive upgrade efforts. Meanwhile, the acquisition cost has stayed constant at $34. Thus, this new emphasis on efficiency and stability will raise the return-on-investment ratio from 20 to 1 to 30 to 1.

The ratio of long-term value to acquisition cost is a fair, ballpark way to express how much value each investment dollar brings to your organization. It's easy to compute and easy to understand, once you wrap your mind around the concept.

Much more important, that ratio will give you a pretty fair indication of how well your fundraising strategy is working (or for that matter, whether the strategy you think you're pursuing is the one you're really involved in).

Here are a few considerations that come to mind.

How Growth Affects Return on Investment

A Growth Strategy—when intelligently applied by an organization with legitimate potential for growth—will usually lower the ratio of long-term value to acquisition cost. In other words, return on investment will decline. In some cases, aggressively pursuing donor-base growth will consume all the profits from current fundraising activities. As a result, in start-up organizations and occasionally in other cases, the ratio may be less than 1 to 1 for a time. That is, the organization will make a net investment in donor acquisition, sacrificing current revenue for future potential. The payoff will come later.

For instance, consider the experience of Puppy's Heaven, a shelter for abused and abandoned dogs. The shelter's staff has been recruiting new donors at $10 and deriving $50 in long-term value from each. The shelter is overcrowded, though, and the trustees have resolved to expand the facility. A major donor will advance half the amount needed, but the other half will have to come from individual donors over the next five years. The development director is doing all she can to generate revenue from the existing donors to Puppy's Heaven. So, inevitably she must accelerate the donor acquisition program and build a bigger base quickly.

Fortunately, the board and the executive director understand the realities of fundraising. They authorize the development director to spend up to $50 per person to acquire new donors. This will permit her to recruit at least twice—and possibly three or more times—as many new donors as last year. (Recall that the marginal cost of acquiring new donors is likely to rise with the volume of acquisition efforts.)

In other words, by expanding the donor base, she'll ratchet down her expectations of return on investment from 5 to 1 to as low as 1 to 1. But the extra funds invested by Puppy's Heaven, and the stepped-up donor acquisition efforts, will eventually result in a substantial increase in net revenue and a return to a more comfortable return-on-investment ratio. Why? Because the larger number of donors will permit greater economies of scale and perhaps more sophisticated, higher yielding fundraising programs as well.

The Financial Consequences of Involvement

If the principal purpose of an organization's fundraising program is to involve donors—or nondonors, for that matter—in some high-priority activity such as grassroots lobbying, it's likely that the ratio of long-term value to acquisition cost will be low, possibly even less than 1 to 1. Return on investment for an organization guided by an Involvement Strategy is limited, because so many resources are being devoted to involving donors.

If involvement is just one (but not the principal) goal of the program, a higher ratio is possible. However, promoting involvement costs money in any event. The resulting program can't have a cost per dollar raised as low as a program focused squarely on fundraising efficiency. That's a matter of definition.

Take a look, for example, at WorldShakers, a nonprofit political action group formed to engage young people in effective citizen action—often grassroots lobbying. Until recently, WorldShakers has been guided by a conservative board, which has insisted that the cost of acquisition not rise above $10 per member on average.

This benchmark is based on the knowledge that the group's long-term value is approximately $50. The board feels that it's inappropriate to spend more than $10 out of every $50 to acquire new members. As a result, WorldShakers is small—in fact, it is far too small to shake the world (or any appreciable corner of it).

A new board chair and the activist majority behind her decide that the organization has been failing in its job. Clearly, they assert, WorldShakers must expand its membership base, and that will obviously require an investment of additional funds in new-member acquisition. However, that investment will do double duty. The organization's member-acquisition packages include a petition to the governor about an important new piece of legislation, and WorldShakers' top priority this year is to deliver lots of petitions on that issue.

Accordingly, the board has concluded that it makes sense to spend an average of $50, $75, even $100 per person on donor acquisition. The resulting return-on-investment ratio may be as low as $50 to $100, or 0.5 to 1. To state the case baldly: this year, and for as long as involvement continues to be the centerpiece of its membership development program, WorldShakers may recoup only 50 cents of every dollar invested in new-member acquisition. But assuming that the capital is available to fund the campaign, that's okay. WorldShakers will be doing its primary job of involving the public.

At the same time, with its membership growing, the organization will be increasingly able to raise its donors' long-term value. With greater numbers on board, WorldShakers can educate, resolicit, and cultivate its members more cost-effectively. Also, eventually the group can launch more lucrative fundraising programs such as a high-dollar club or a monthly giving program that wouldn't be feasible with the current narrow membership base.

Caution: certain types of donor involvement, such as brief questionnaires in telephone fundraising calls or so-called involvement devices in direct-mail packages, may directly promote higher rates of donor response. In such cases, involvement is a way to raise more money, not a costly requirement imposed by the organization's leadership to pursue its mission. There are circumstances, then, in which you can achieve both involvement and growth (because more new donors may be attracted in these ways). Nonetheless, this is not likely to be the most efficient way to raise money, because the higher response rate promoted by involvement devices usually comes at the price of a lower average gift.

Visibility's Impact on Return on Investment

Visibility is typically even more costly than involvement, because fundraising efforts undertaken with a view toward raising an organization's public profile are less likely to yield immediate gifts. In fact, some direct-mail, telemarketing, or television fundraising programs designed primarily to foster an organization's (or an issue's) visibility are merely image advertising programs masquerading as money-making efforts. The ratio of long-term value to acquisition cost will thus be very low.

Does this course of action seem unlikely? Think again.

Assume that a virulent new disease attributed to environmental factors suddenly breaks out in one major city in the United States. The Centers for Disease Control (CDC) determine that this frequently lethal disease, known as Kentucky Flu, is likely to emerge from similar environmental conditions in other cities, and quickly. Kentucky Flu threatens to reach epidemic proportions nationwide within a few years. Clearly, the CDC, the U.S. Public Health Service, and other governmental entities at all levels are now on alert and doing everything possible to educate the public about the factors that commonly give rise to this disease. But government action isn't enough. The public is slow to take the Kentucky Flu threat seriously, and the country may have to suffer the consequences for decades to come.

Enter a private, nonprofit organization called To Your Health. With seed money furnished by health care providers, both public and private, supplemented by an emergency appropriation of federal funds, To Your Health sets out to tackle the challenge of educating the public about Kentucky Flu. However, the conditions set by the organization's funders require that To Your Health become financially self-sufficient within five years. The plan is modeled on the successful, privately supported nonprofits devoted to AIDS research, education, and services.

To Your Health's mandate is clear: first, get the word out. That means a fundraising strategy centered on visibility. It's important to begin building a base of individual donors who will sustain the organization in years ahead; but it is even more important to launch an intensive public-education campaign designed to teach people how to prevent Kentucky Flu.

Back-of-the-envelope calculations suggest that eventually To Your Health donors may be worth $50 or more on average. Clearly, however, the organization's donor-acquisition program must not be limited by an arbitrary ceiling of $50 per donor. To Your Health will have to invest in visibility.

As a consequence, the newly hired development staff requests and secures a commitment from the board to spend several million dollars on mass media advertising, including direct mail targeted at neighborhoods that are judged to be at greatest risk of harboring Kentucky Flu. The number of donors acquired in the course of this campaign will initially be meager. For donors with an estimated long-term value of $50, To Your Health might pay $100, $200, or more. Thus, the group's return on investment ratio may be $50 to $200, or as low as 0.25 to 1.

However, in the process, To Your Health will create millions of advertising impressions on TV and radio, and mail millions of direct-mail packages. The development staff is serving the organization's purpose by doing these things, even though its fundraising program is horribly inefficient, at least temporarily. At a later stage, once public recognition of the danger is widespread, To Your Health's fundraising strategy can shift course and begin to harvest the financial benefits of its Visibility Strategy.

Efficiency and Return on Investment

This one's easy. The more efficient your fundraising program is, the higher will be your return on investment.

At Metropolitan Prep, a venerable, well-endowed private secondary school with substantial alumni support, a reassessment of the fundraising program has convinced the board that a long-standing strategy of INVOLVEMENT + stability has outlived its usefulness. Metropolitan must economize in its fundraising program, reducing the amounts spent to romance the alumni (who yearn for less attention, not more) and pay heed to the efficiency of the school's development department. The overriding consideration must now be to generate gifts at the lowest cost per dollar raised.

Metropolitan's fundraising program is already relatively efficient. With its donor-acquisition cost in the vicinity of $50, the school calculates that the long-term value of those donors is at least $300. The return-on-investment ratio, then, is an enviable 6 to 1. But it's not necessary for Metropolitan to continue spending even as little as sixteen cents to raise a dollar. The preliminary target for the newly designed EFFICIENCY + involvement strategy is a ratio of 20 to 1—three times the current level.

The means toward this end seem clear to the school's development department. Begin by asking alumni which forms of involvement are meaningful to them and which are not. Ask a number of the major donors what motivates them to give and what might discourage them. Look for evidence that suggests what action or offer might induce donors to give substantially bigger gifts. Then craft a more modest fundraising program based on those findings. Chances are that the new strategy will result in greater emphasis on Metropolitan's endowment and on planned giving. Perhaps a major challenge-grant campaign will figure into the picture, too.

There's usually a way to get from point A to point B. The only indispensable requirement is that you know where you're going.

What Stability Means for Return on Investment

The most stable fundraising program of all is one that relies exclusively on an endowment. Such a program is, of course, equally efficient. Stability and efficiency often go hand in hand. But not always.

A nonprofit organization is likely to be a candidate for a Stability Strategy if its finances are too heavily dependent on some relatively unreliable source. That source may be institutional funding—from government, the United Way, public foundations, or corporations—or it may be a small-donor fundraising program reliant on direct mail, telemarketing, or both. In any case, the organization's future is uncertain, because no such source of funds can be relied on indefinitely. Diversification is essential in such circumstances.

Consider the plight of Nature Forever, a nonprofit membership organization devoted to restoring the environment. For years, Nature Forever has operated a successful and unusually efficient membership program. The popularity of its mission and the skill of its staff in getting out its message to the public have enabled the group to build a membership base of more than fifty thousand. New members are acquired at an average cost of $10. Their long-term value exceeds $100, due in large part to the organization's well-developed monthly giving program, a successful $1000-a-year high-dollar giving club, and resourceful use of telephone fundraising techniques. So Nature Forever's return-on-investment ratio is $100 to $10, or 10 to 1. This is truly excellent, given Nature Forever's INVOLVEMENT + efficiency strategy. So far so good.

But trouble is brewing here. The new-member acquisition cost appears to be rising, a sign that public response to the group's message may be waning. Membership development programs now contribute more than 80 percent of Nature Forever's operating budget, so any decline in response could have nasty long-term consequences. The group's president concludes that this calls for an effort to broaden the financial base to diversify Nature Forever's funding so that it is less dependent on direct response.

The ultimate result of this course of thinking is a new fundraising strategy of STABILITY + efficiency.

In the new approach, Nature Forever will spend some of its revenues on financing new fundraising programs—principally major gifts and planned gifts (to build an endowment). The key to the group's future, as it turns out, is still the membership—but with selected members treated as potential sources of large or planned gifts, not merely dues and special contributions.

For a time—probably several years—Nature Forever will invest heavily in the new development initiatives, including a feasibility study for the endowment, heavy marketing of bequests in particular and planned gifts in general, and several newly hired major gift officers. Results from these activities may be spotty for awhile. Such investments often take time to pay off. As a result, Nature Forever's return-on-investment ratio will very likely decline in the short run. Eventually, however, once these new efforts bear fruit, the long-term value of the members will rise substantially. Even if the new-member acquisition cost also continues to rise, Nature Forever's return on investment ratio will likely climb. At some point, it may even exceed the current 10 to 1 ratio. More importantly, by diversifying its funding sources, Nature Forever will help ensure its long-term survivability, despite the vagaries of direct mail.

Table 16.3 approximates the experience of three nonprofit organizations with which I have worked.

TABLE 16.3 Return on Investment for Three Real-World Nonprofits.

Organization	Strategy	Acquisition Cost	Long-Term Value	Ratio of Long-Term Value to Acquisition Cost
A	Growth	$35	$45	9:7 = 1.29
B	Efficiency	$3	$40	40:3 = 13.3
C	Involvement	$15	$22	22:15 = 1.47

Organization A, committed to a fast-growth strategy, was happy to settle for a low ratio of long-term value to acquisition cost—just 9 to 7, or only 29 percent above breakeven.

Similarly, Organization C, whose strategy required involving large numbers of people in grassroots lobbying efforts, was content to use its fundraising program (primarily direct mail) largely as a vehicle to recruit and activate grassroots supporters. For C, the ratio of just 22 to 15 (or 47 percent above breakeven) was adequate because its larger organizational purpose was well served.

Organization B's efficiency-driven fundraising strategy stood in sharp contrast to those of A and C. Pursuing its mission required the lowest possible cost per dollar raised. Thus Organization B sought—and achieved—a ratio of 40 to 3 (or more than 13 to 1) between long-term value and acquisition cost.

Thus each fundraising strategy will dictate an appropriate range of ratios of long-term value to acquisition cost. Determining where within that range you should set the goal for your own organization's ratio is purely a matter of judgment. Table 16.4 illustrates typical return-on-investment ratios for the five strategies. *These ratios are not intended as rules*. Rather, they suggest the range of expectations I've encountered among the diverse group of nonprofit organizations with which I have worked over the years—large, small, national, local, and involved in every conceivable cause or pursuit. If your organization's ratio falls outside the range indicated in the

TABLE 16.4 Typical Return on Investment Ratios for the Five Strategies.

Strategy	Ratio of Long-Term Value to Acquisition Cost
Efficiency	4:1 or higher
Stability	2:1 to 4:1
Growth	1:1 to 3:1
Involvement	0.5:1 to 3:1
Visibility	2:1 or lower

table for the fundraising strategy you've elected to pursue, that's not necessarily bad. It's merely food for thought.

What's critical is that the leadership of every nonprofit organization must *think* about these issues. Setting the return-on-investment ratio is one of the most important policy decisions any board of trustees can make.

Unfortunately, the decision is rarely made consciously. Most boards, executive directors, and development directors make such decisions by default. They're influenced by pressures from donors, charities regulators, legislators, and their own, often untrustworthy instincts and preconceptions. They enact policies they think they ought to pursue—or still more often, no policy at all.

That's no way to run a railroad—or a nonprofit organization.

Measuring long-term value and acquisition cost are vital first steps toward taking the destiny of your organization into your own hands (assuming, of course, that your fundraising track record is long enough and that sufficient data are available).

However, concepts like *destiny* and fundraising *policies* may leave your trustees cold. Perhaps all they want to know is, "Why are you spending so much money on fundraising?" (See Sidebar 16.2 [on page 236] for a discussion of one aspect of this question.)

OK. If that's what you're up against, here's something you can try. Take care, though. You'll have to join me on another trip into the forest of statistics. We're going to look at the contributions made to your organization by a "typical" group of one thousand donors.

What One Thousand Donors Can Do for Your Organization

Forget fundraising costs, if you can. Think for a moment about fundraising revenue instead.

Consider all the varied sources of revenue from individual donors or members. If your organization is like most nonprofits I've known, you've probably got half a dozen or more different fundraising "tracks" (even if you don't call them that).

SIDEBAR 16.2 WHAT ABOUT RETENTION COST?

Explaining away high fundraising costs by comparing acquisition cost to long-term value frequently causes a problem.

By focusing so squarely on acquisition, we might think we obscure some—possibly a lot—of the real fundraising costs that are incurred later.

What about the costs of renewing, educating, cultivating, and upgrading donors?

These costs are taken into account in most long-term value models. Sometimes they're even given a category of their own—something like "retention cost."

In other words, gross revenue per donor – (acquisition cost + retention cost) = long-term value. The approach works, as long as you take care not to understate the true financial implications. For example:

- Are all the data processing costs factored in? (Really?)

- Does the retention cost include the costs of producing and mailing newsletters (which may be under some other department's budget)? In a system using joint cost allocation, it may be inappropriate to attribute all of these costs to fundraising. But some surely apply.

- What about the costs associated with events, such as college reunions? They're probably budgeted elsewhere. They're a factor nonetheless.

- Are you including at least some of the cost of marketing and public relations activities designed to support the fundraising program but also tucked away somewhere else in the agency's budget?

Many of these expenses are subject to joint cost allocation, because the activities often fulfill program goals—many, but not all.

As a practical matter, it's probably safe under most circumstances to exclude from retention cost any expenses for which the board and the chief executive don't hold you responsible. For example, yours is a membership department, and a separate unit—say, the communication department—produces and pays for the newsletter. Lucky you! That's an offer not to be refused. But don't be lulled into thinking that the newsletter is really free. Its cost should still be included as a rentention cost—even if you're the only one in the organization who knows it.

The key to an honest assessment of your fundraising program is to face the truth squarely, even if it makes you uncomfortable. Don't be gulled into thinking "everything's just fine" because you've closed your eyes to reality.

Let's assume, for the sake of argument, that those distinct tracks, or sources of individual gifts, include all of the seven categories listed in Table 16.5, which illustrates the revenue generated by one thousand typical donors to or members of a reasonably well-managed nonprofit organization.

Annual gift appeals. Your own overall renewal rate may be higher or lower than the 65 percent figure in this hypothetical example. Your average annual gift may be different, too. But these numbers are representative of many nonprofit organizations all over North America. Typically, a nonprofit organization supported by a large number of people will receive one gift per year (and only one) from some 65 to 70 percent of its donors. Only a third, in round numbers, will give more than one gift per year.

Newsletters and thank-yous. Some nonprofits successfully raise significant amounts of money through appeals featured in (or accompanying) their newsletters or donor acknowledgments. However, in organizations that operate active direct-mail fundraising programs, it's more typical that such appeals raise only enough to cover some of the mailing costs. Most often the fundraising manager has to decide whether the returns from such appeals are worth the possible sacrifice of donor goodwill. In the long run, the orga-

TABLE 16.5 Revenue Generated by One Thousand "Typical" Donors.

Source	# of Donors	Average Amount	Total Giving
Annual gift appeals	650	$25	$16,250
Newsletters and thank-yous	50	$20	$1,000
Special appeals	200	$30	$6,000
Monthly giving	30	$180	$5,400
High-dollar club	10	$1,000	$10,000
Major gifts	2	$10,000	$20,000
Subtotal	1,092	$56	$61,650
Planned gifts	?	?	?
Total	?	?	?

nization might benefit more from sending information-only news-letters and limiting requests for money to appeals and renewals.

Special appeals. Fundraising solicitations built on special needs, imminent deadlines, and particular projects may elicit generous support over and above the annual gift or membership dues from 30 or 35 percent of active donors in a given year.

Monthly giving. Monthly pledge or sustainer programs are play-ing an increasingly large role in membership or small-donor–based organizations. Why? A donor who's accustomed to giving two $20 gifts per year may frequently be persuaded to contribute $10 or $15 per month. That's three or four times as much money per year! This fundraising model assumes that 5 percent of the active donors enlist in the monthly giving program. In some organizations, 10 percent, 15 percent, or more may join, while others are able to enlist only 2 or 3 percent.

High-dollar club. In an organization with the donor dynamics displayed in this model, it's reasonable to expect that 1 percent of the active donors will sign up for a $1,000–a-year giving club or gift society. A much larger percentage would be normal in an environ-ment where typical annual gifts are $100 or more.

Major gifts. Here's a useful rule of thumb to keep in mind when planning a major giving campaign: about one in five of the donors who give you $1,000 per year are fully capable of giving you ten times as much (and if they're adequately cultivated as major donors, they're likely to develop the willingness to do so).

Subtotal. Note that the total number of gifts received in a year from one thousand donors is more than one thousand, even though fewer than two-thirds of the donors have contributed that year. Although only 30 to 35 percent of donors give two gifts per year, many of them may contribute numerous gifts.

Planned gifts. Planned gifts are usually simple bequests made through a donor's will. In fact, a typical bequest amounts to some-where between $15,000 and $30,000—and it's most likely to come from a $10 or $20 donor. (Often an inactive $10 or $20 donor, at that! Why? Because disposable income normally shrinks with age—but not a donor's desire to support her favorite charities.) It's generally a safe bet that a bequest promotion program that's been in place for a number of years will generate substantial revenue each year. But it's perilous to make revenue projections based on previous years' experience. And keep in mind that most planned gifts are revocable. In other words, the donor can change his mind!

Total. Because of the uncertainties inherent in planned giving, it's not practical to project how much a typical one thousand donors will give altogether. Over time, however, it's virtually certain to be far more than what's generated through other fundraising activities.

Also, please note that the median (or mode) gift is often much more useful than the average. One group might report its average gift as $44 when they receive fifty gifts of $25 and one of $1,000, then use the $44 figure as the basis for the amounts they request in their direct-mail appeals. The results aren't likely to be good. A request for an amount closer to the median ($25) may be much more productive.

It doesn't take hours of study of numbers like these to conclude that an investment in recruiting, educating, and cultivating donors may pay off in a great many ways. Such investments—sometimes difficult to quantify—are the subject of the following chapter.

17

Building Relationships

The Key to the Future

Throughout this book (and at every other opportunity) I emphasize that the key to fundraising is building relationships with your donors. This is true regardless of which of the five strategies you elect to pursue:

• *Growth.* Doubling the size of your donor base will do you little good if too many of your new "donors" never choose to give again.

• *Involvement.* Members or donors who feel mistreated are unlikely to continue responding faithfully to your appeals for volunteer support or participation in grassroots fundraising efforts.

• *Visibility.* What's the value of making your organization much better known if people distrust the face you show to the public? In the nonprofit sector, any news at all is not necessarily good news!

• *Efficiency.* It's obvious, isn't it? There is a straight-line correlation between donor loyalty and responsiveness—and treating donors as they wish to be treated. Donors who feel slighted, left out, ignored, or unappreciated are unlikely to become loyal and consistently responsive.

• *Stability.* If the success of your development program depends on the continuing productivity of diverse fundraising activities, how stable will your finances be if donors constantly pass through a revolving door, leaving almost as quickly as they arrived?

This chapter focuses on several essential elements in the relationship-building process: donor thank-yous, donor education, and donor cultivation. Sound a little dull? Well, there's good news! This chapter is not about numbers. In fact, you'll find nary a number here.

Instead, I'd like you to join me in examining the *nonfinancial factors* that are all too often overlooked by fundraisers. These factors— usually intangible and often hard to discern— ensure that any analysis of a fundraising program must look at a whole lot more than the bottom line. (See Sidebar 17.1 [on page 242].)

Let's examine first the often-neglected subject of donor acknowledgments.

Donor Thank-Yous: Politeness Goes a Long Way

Almost all for-profit companies face a number of significant but unavoidable costs—for example, letterhead and business cards, telephone service, and liability insurance. These items may seem minor, even inconsequential—but woe to the company that ignores them! They're all part of the cost of doing business. (So, too, for nonprofits, of course.)

In the nonprofit world—what management guru Peter Drucker aptly calls the "social sector"—donor acknowledgments are another of the fundamental, unavoidable costs of doing business.

Yes, you may be able to accomplish several desirable ends simultaneously if you cut back or eliminate thank-you letters to donors. For example, you'll lower your fundraising costs, making your program more efficient. And you'll probably make life easier for the people in the development department—all to the good.

However, the option not to thank donors is unavailable in two instances: receipts are required for any benefit event with a ticket price of $75 or more, and for every gift of $250 or more.

If you ignore the demands of civility and stop thanking donors for their gifts, you'll also be undermining the foundation of your fundraising program: the goodwill of your donors.

SIDEBAR 17.1 WHAT IS THE BOTTOM LINE?

The private sector is waking up. Most large, traditional companies tenaciously cling to the notion that the welfare of the business world—and society's common good—is best measured by the latest quarterly profit-and-loss statement. But more and more businesspeople throughout North America—representing thousands, maybe tens of thousands of companies—are dedicating themselves to the concept of social responsibility. They believe that business involves a whole lot more than making a buck.

Ben Cohen, cofounder of Ben & Jerry's (the ice cream company), frequently speaks about the "double bottom line." For his company, and for a growing number of others—including big firms with recognizable names like Levi's and Reebok—social responsibility means that the company's performance is measured not just by net profits but also by its success in making the world a better place. At socially responsible companies, large sums (often including lots of paid staff time) are invested in efforts that benefit the environment and the local community, support voluntarism and philanthropy, and enhance employees' quality of life. Few, if any, of these companies are angelic. Undoubtedly they all have their faults. But their actions are guided by more than just the single bottom line.

This double-bottom-line analysis focuses on the company's long-term survival and profitability. It's based on the commonsense notion that what goes around, comes around.

Now, wouldn't it be ironic if, just when the private sector is starting to wise up, the social sector (nonprofit organizations) were to go off half-cocked and "businesslike," enslaved to our own numbers-driven equivalent of the bottom line?

Like any business, your nonprofit organization is a corporate citizen. If you haven't already considered your corporate impact—on your employees, on the local communities where you operate, on society at large, and on the natural environment we all share—it's high time to do so.

Doesn't your organization, as a not-for-profit enterprise supported by the public through your tax-exempt status, bear an even heavier responsibility than any business to trod lightly on the Earth and contribute to the betterment of humankind?

Think about it.

For more information, contact Business for Social Responsibility, 609 Mission Street, Second Floor, San Francisco, CA 94105–3506, phone (415) 537–0888, fax (415) 537–0889, Internet <www.bsr.org>.

In fact, to involve and cultivate donors, you should probably be spending more time and money on your donor acknowledgment program, not less. Few nonprofits routinely have thank-yous in the mail (or on the phone) within seventy-two hours of the receipt of gifts—and I regard three days as a requirement, not a goal.

Don't be fooled into thinking that donors don't notice. In truth, they probably notice—and remember—the absence or tardiness of a thank-you note more readily than they notice almost anything else. Long after she's forgotten what you said you were going to do with that $25 she sent you, the donor remembers that you never sent her a thank-you note!

Don't believe me? Sit in on a few focus groups with donors. That will have you ready to beef up your donor acknowledgment system in no time flat! (See Sidebar 17.2 [on page 244].)

Thank-you letters and phone calls aren't just required by the near-universal expectation of politeness in North American cultures (even more intense in Canada than in the United States). They're a wonderful opportunity to inform, educate, and involve donors.

The Secret Value of Donor Cultivation

Most aspects of fundraising are quantifiable. Much of the time we live and die by the numbers. But not always.

To evaluate the cost-effectiveness of thank-you letters, for example, you can easily structure a test. It takes a lot of time and patience to do this, but it's possible. All you need to do is identify one group of under-$250 donors to whom you send thank-you letters and another under-$250 group to whom you do not send gift acknowledgments. (Both groups must be statistically identical, of course, and other formalities need to be observed to ensure the validity of the test.)

Chances are you'll find that over time the donors you thank are more generous and more loyal than those you don't thank. You can even measure the difference in renewal rates, frequency of giving, and average gifts between the two groups. In other words, you can measure precisely the cost-effectiveness of a donor acknowledgment program. So you can actually prove it's shortsighted to cut back on thank-yous.

But you'll find it a lot harder, and maybe even impossible, to quantify the value of donor education and donor cultivation programs.

Undeniably, the cost of building relationships with your donors will be high. Producing detailed annual reports, staging quarterly donor briefings, and funding membership benefits is expensive. And how on earth do you prove the connection between last year's lovely annual report and the surge in year-end gifts or that huge planned gift you just received?

Quantifiable or not, donor education and donor cultivation programs are essential for most nonprofit organizations. Fundraisers

---

SIDEBAR 17.2 THE DONOR IS ALWAYS RIGHT

You don't have to go to the extent of staging an expensive series of focus groups to learn that donors like to be appreciated. Simply asking them for their opinions will achieve the same end. And if you switch into question mode—calling your donors to solicit their advice, not their money—you'll probably learn a lot more than you asked for.

I routinely advise my clients to call their donors. Of course, you need to be in frequent contact with your top ten (or twenty, or five) major donors. But it also pays to pick one or two dozen names at random from among your rank-and-file donors and call them, too. Ask their opinions. Probe for impressions of your organization's program—and for attitudes about your fundraising methods. Most donors are flattered to be asked. And the experience will add another rich dimension to your evaluation of your fundraising program.

Like it or not, your nonprofit organization is a business. Your customers include the donors who help sustain your operations—and they'd better be happy customers! They've got to feel at all times that you're delivering a valuable service. If they don't think there's a need for your business, you're going to lose their support, sooner rather than later.

know that such efforts are frequently effective. Why? Because they seem to lead to more and bigger gifts over the long haul, and because donors tell us these efforts are effective.

If visibility is your paramount goal, the subtleties of your relationships with your donors may not matter a whole lot to you. But under almost any other strategic standard—in fact, in any program where you hope to receive more than one gift from your donors—you need to budget for donor cultivation and donor education.

Even if these efforts take a big bite out of your revenue, cutting sharply into the bottom line, they come with the territory. Donor cultivation and donor education are part of what it means to be a nonprofit organization.

Investing in your future requires more than money. There are other external or intangible factors you'll want to take into account when assessing the effectiveness of your fundraising program. Among them are the following:

- *Your organization's name recognition.* Is your name a household word, or are you just another Brand X charity?
- *Your organization's track record, and the confidence that constituents have in you.* Does everybody know that you deliver on your promises, or is there the stench of scandal wreathing your reputation?
- *The fundraising climate in the nation, and in your community.* Are happy days here again, or is the economy in a tailspin and the big Ford Motor plant outside town about to shut down? Are these real (or misperceived as real) problems?
- *The extent of direct competition for donors' dollars.* Does your organization fill a unique niche or dominate the field or issue you're involved in? Or is it just one more look-alike group addressing a familiar problem in an all-too-familiar way?
- *The quality and reputation of your organization's leadership.* Will donors flock to your leader's banner if they learn the true story of the miracles she works? Or will they head for the hills, suspecting a scam?
- *Your own personal determination to succeed.* Willpower works.

Collectively, these factors will influence the success or failure of your fundraising program more than any methods or devices you might employ in your resource development plan. Just one of these factors may individually outweigh anything you can say or do.

None of us raises funds in a vacuum.

To assess the effectiveness of your fundraising program, then, you have to weigh your organization's plans and performance not just in relation to each other but also against the real-world factors that set the context and the tone of all your efforts.

Don't lose sight of the Big Picture.

We're all in this business because we want to make the world a better place. We're in for the long haul. And we all know that how we conduct ourselves is just as important as what we accomplish.

Never forget: the single most widely cited reason that donors don't give gifts is that "nobody asked."

Almost always, fundraising efforts fail because staff, board members, or other volunteers (or even consultants) just didn't do what they said they would do:

- "We didn't get the mailing out on schedule."
- "He never made the phone call."
- "The meeting just fell through."
- "Nobody followed up."
- Most often, "She didn't ask."

Philanthropy is voluntary. People want to support good causes and build important institutions. In fact, sometimes donors give despite our best efforts to deny them the opportunity. But there's a limit.

In fact, most gifts come in the final stage of a long, arduous process. Someone—and that means you—has to identify prospective donors, then inform and involve them, and eventually persuade them to invest in your vision.

Most of the time, that takes a lot of work. Hard work.

Remember: fundraising, like genius, is 1 percent inspiration and 99 percent perspiration.

Just do it!

Resource A

Thinking Strategically About Fundraising Costs

This section deals with the sticky subject of fundraising costs. It's included in this book because (1) people get hung up on this topic, (2) fundraising costs are complex, and (3) misinformation abounds. I want to set things straight. You'll learn here how to estimate the costs of many of the most widely used fundraising techniques, how to put these costs in perspective, and how to factor in the hidden and often ignored but sometimes costly aspects of fundraising.

People have strong opinions about fundraising costs. As a topic of discussion at a party, the cost of fundraising is just as likely to set tempers flaring as politics or religion. Wise hands in the nonprofit world have long since learned not to raise the subject in polite company. They know that

- Donors think fundraising shouldn't cost more than a few cents on the dollar—if indeed they're willing to concede that there are any legitimate fundraising costs at all.

- Fundraisers think they could raise lots more money if only they had greater resources to work with. In other words, the cost of fundraising would be a lot more than a few cents on the dollar, even if only temporarily—thirty cents, maybe, in some nonprofits; perhaps fifty cents or more in others.

- Critics of the nonprofit sector (including some state charities regulators, legislators, and self-appointed watchdog groups) think there should be across-the-board limits on fundraising costs—a maximum of forty cents on the dollar, if you listen to some; others say ten or twenty.

What's the correct view of this perplexing subject?

Is there, in fact, any one correct position on fundraising costs?

After all, fundraising should be essentially cost-free, shouldn't it? When you strip away the mumbo jumbo about fundraising practices and procedures and view the philanthropic act in isolation, it all boils down to one person voluntarily giving money to another person (often enough, another volunteer). Why should there be any costs involved in that?

But there are.

Fundraising starts making sense, in my view, only when we recognize this fundamental truth:

Successful fundraising has less to do with money and gifts than with creating and sustaining lasting relationships among people. If you can measure the quality of those relationships, you'll be able to gauge the quality of your fundraising program.

Now I'd like a chance to prove that proposition.

Fundraising and Friend-Raising: Building Relationships with Your Donors

Two questions:

1. *How long will it take your organization to fulfill its mission?* One month? Six months? A year?

You say your goals can never truly be reached? That there will never be an end to your mission, whether it is to educate the mind, ennoble the spirit, or elevate the quality of our lives? That you envision your organization as an enduring presence, fostering good works for decades to come?

I thought so!

2. *Who's going to pay for all that work over the years?*

For the next three months—or three years—the answer may be simple. Maybe your most pessimistic financial projections show a clear path ahead for even longer than three years. For example, through a combination of fees for service and multiyear corporate and government grants plus endowment income, you're confident that your work can continue for five or ten years ahead.

Then what happens? After that money runs out—after those donors (whether institutions or individuals) crawl off into the woodwork of other priorities or go belly-up or die—where will your funding come from?

The answer, of course, lies in some combination of the following sources:

- Repeat gifts from some of the donors who've supported you in the past
- Bequests and other planned gifts from some of today's donors
- Gifts from new donors
- Other new sources, such as fees for service or merchandising

As you consider these four options, you realize you don't really know where your funds will come from in the future. But you'll have to do several things to keep that cash coming in, year after year:

- Your organization must deliver high-quality, cost-effective services that satisfy well-demonstrated needs. Donors want to support worthwhile causes.
- It is vital that you inform your constituents of the importance and impact of your work. Donors have to know what you've done.

- You need to foster loyalty among your donors. You'll need their continuing support to underwrite the costs of your work for many years ahead.

- Because you understand perfectly that all of today's donors won't go on sending money indefinitely, you'll have to recruit new donors. (Not even the most loyal donor is immortal!)

All of this leads to one simple conclusion:
You can't treat donors as mere sources of money!

Foundations, corporations, major individual donors, patrons, clients—whoever they are, whatever formal relationship they have with your organization, your donors are never just donors. They can't be defined strictly in terms of their willingness to provide you with financial support. They give—and get—something else besides.

Donors give gifts for a great many reasons, but always because they get something in return. That something is most likely to be intangible (such as self-satisfaction, spiritual fulfillment, pride, or dozens of other feelings). Occasionally donors are motivated, at least in part, by more mundane and concrete factors (including public recognition, political influence, access to information, or occasionally tax benefits). But there's always something. Usually, it's a combination of factors.

A successful fundraiser begins with the knowledge that all gifts come from people. Fundraising is the process of building relationships with those people—whether a foundation program officer, a member of Congress, a retired banker ripe for a substantial bequest, or the rank-and-file patrons of a ballet company.

Major donor fundraisers are fond of citing the aphorism, "If you want money, ask for advice. If you want advice, ask for money."

Some donors insist on giving advice, even if you don't ask them for it. (In fact, especially if you don't ask!) Others prefer that you spend your time (and their money) doing something more productive than asking for their advice.

It's important to know the difference.

Understanding what makes your donors tick, treating them as the generous friends they are, and attending to all the important details of your relationships with them, just as you would with coworkers or the members of your family—these are the keys to successful fundraising.

You want all your donors to feel that you've used their money so well they'll extend their support for years to come—and help you secure additional grants from other foundations, agencies, or corporations.

And you want all your individual donors to feel so good about what you've achieved with their money that they'll renew their support, year after year—and eventually name you as beneficiaries of their estates.

Some people speak of *friend-raising*, not fundraising. That's what it's all about.

Fundraising is, pure and simple, a matter of making friends.

Because fundraising also (unavoidably) involves money, it's all too easy to fall prey to the notion that its success or failure can be measured in strictly numerical terms.

Not so. Some aspects of fundraising can't be quantified. And sometimes it pays off in a big way to look past the numbers and consider the central role of intangible and emotional factors. If you don't, you can be sure your donors will!

Now, however, it's time to take a look at those numbers. (I can't stall forever!)

The Fundraising Ratio

If you were one of those millions of kids who had trouble with fractions and ratios, please swallow your pain (and your pride). The so-called fundraising ratio—the most widely accepted measure of fundraising performance—isn't really a ratio at all, if you want to get technical about it.

A ratio is usually stated in the form of 2:1 (two to one). By contrast, the fundraising "ratio" is merely the number of cents on the dollar that goes into fundraising costs, but sometimes it's also stated as a percentage.

For example, if your fundraising expenses total twenty cents of every dollar you raise, your fundraising ratio can be presented as 20 percent. If you spend forty cents to raise a dollar, it's 40 percent.

Now it gets a little more complicated.

Why Fundraising Costs Vary

The fundraising ratio varies widely from one organization to another—and not just because nonprofits choose different strategies. The ratio is affected by such other factors as the following:

• *The popularity of the cause or issue.* If a nonprofit organization addresses a new or notably unpopular issue, it may have trouble raising money from the general public. In any case, it's unlikely to match the fundraising performance of the American Red Cross or the Salvation Army (America's two favorite charities).

• *The organization's age.* Over time, an organization can establish a track record, build name recognition, and assemble a large list of loyal donors. These things are rarely possible in a nonprofit's first couple of years.

• *The fundraising methods used.* The cost of a sumptuous lunch at even the most overpriced Manhattan eatery will be more than offset by a $10 million endowment gift from a generous luncheon companion. But that $15 dinner you served to people paying $25 each didn't stack up quite so well. Neither did those ten thousand fund appeals you mailed at a cost of fifty cents apiece, yielding a grand total of $3,000 in gifts.

• *How much money the organization raises.* Within limits, an institution that raises a great deal of money is likely to do it at a lower cost per dollar than a smaller nonprofit. Small organizations can't easily achieve economies of scale. For example, one staff grantwriter may be able to write ten grant proposals almost as easily as three. And it's usually more efficient to solicit gifts from ten thousand members than from one thousand.

• *The skills and experience of the development department.* A well-organized, professionally managed fundraising staff can reasonably be expected to raise money more efficiently than a start-up operation or an institution with unseasoned fundraising staff.

• *Competition.* If you have to spend thousands on advertising a celebrity golf tournament to get public attention on a weekend when three other charities have scheduled major events, you're suffering from what the business world calls *competition.* Though some people in the nonprofit world are squeamish about that word, we are indeed in competition with one another.

• *The character of the constituency.* A community action agency serving poor people will have a rougher time raising money than the art museum in the same city. Most well-to-do folks may identify with the museum. Few will feel they have a stake in a community action agency unless they're involved as board members or volunteers.

• *The charisma of the leader.* If your boss is Marian Wright Edelman or Lee Iacocca, your organization has a big advantage in presenting itself to the public. Outstanding leaders sometimes attract support regardless of the specific character of their work. Many people welcome opportunities to identify with charismatic figures.

• *The zeal of the fundraiser.* How many universities have gone over the top against all odds in extraordinarily ambitious capital campaigns because of the president's passionate commitment to reaching the goal? How many churches and hospital wings have been built because of the grit and persistence of a single-minded campaign chair? The difference a dedicated leader can make is incalculable!

These are among the many reasons that the fundraising ratio may vary from one organization to another. That's why I have little patience for the rigid, one-size-fits-all approach that some legislators, regulators, and charitable watchdogs want to bring to this question.

For example, the State of California (like other states before it) enacted legislation in 1994 that would penalize charities if they spent more than fifty cents to raise a dollar. That law was contested in court and was abandoned as unconstitutional by the state's attorney general long before the case went to trial.

The statute violated charities' free speech. But as far as I'm concerned, it's far worse that the law was *unreasonable*. For some organizations at some stages in their development, it costs more than fifty cents to raise a dollar—like it or not. There's just no getting around that.

As far as I'm concerned, the only truly fair generalization you can make about fundraising costs is, *they vary*. But that's no reason not to try developing sensible guidelines.

In 1994, the National Society of Fund Raising Executives (NSFRE) convened a task force to study the cost of fundraising. Its preliminary report was issued September 30, 1994. The task force wrote then:

> The best way to ask the question, "What does it cost to raise a dollar?" might well be "What do we get back from investing in fund raising?" Information about results achieved, the cost to achieve them, understanding where improvements can be made, etc., may be more important than comparison to an arbitrary "bottom line" percentage. Not-for-profit organizations are no more alike in how they provide their client services than are their fund-raising programs; organizations should not expect results to be alike either. It is the responsibility of the board of directors to decide the level of return on investment that is best acceptable to that organization to achieve the established financial goals. They can then establish their own standards of performance to guide them in managing the budget allocated for fund-raising results.

Later, the NSFRE Research Council continued to design a national study of this complex topic. In 1998, the Center on Philanthropy at Indiana University and the National Center for Charitable Statistics at The Urban Institute accepted the assignment to lead this multiyear study, with NSFRE as the originating sponsor. Though there has been progress in defining this study, selecting the project directors, and securing a good amount of the funding required, no further findings are available as we go to press.

Please: don't get hung up on weighing the costs of your fundraising program. There's something far more important than that for you to worry about: assessing the results.

Costs mean nothing unless measured in comparison with returns.

After all, if I asked you to invest $10, you would be a fool not to inquire what you'd be investing in.

And if I told you that a $10 investment would yield you a profit of $5 while a $20 investment would generate $50, wouldn't you be tempted to dig a little deeper into your wallet?

Start-Up Costs: The Role of Time in Fundraising

One of the biggest reasons that the fundraising ratio varies from one organization to another is time. Time is the essence of several of the nine factors listed earlier in this section. An organization's age, the experience of its development staff, even its size, name recognition, and popularity are all influenced, at least in part, by the passage of time.

But time plays an especially important role in the way that most commonly accounts for differences in fundraising ratios from one nonprofit to another: whether the organization is new or old.

Yes, there is a single overriding reason—a good one—why the National Easter Seal Society can raise money more efficiently than the little charity your cousin Sally is running out of her kitchen. That factor is *startup costs*.

Starting from scratch—with no track record, no name recognition, and no donors—a nonprofit organization faces a big fundraising challenge. In fact, if your cousin Sally's experience matches that of countless other nonprofits, she's spending most, perhaps even all, of her time and resources in a search for money.

For a time, Sally's fundraising ratio may well be more than 100 percent. It may take Sally quite a while and maybe even a significant investment of other resources (including lost income) before she secures her first gift.

But startup costs won't stop once Sally lands that first hefty foundation grant. Now (maybe even to meet the terms of the grant) she has to diversify her fundraising program. That effort might include building a base of generous individual donors whose support can be counted on for years to come.

Perhaps Sally has to reach out through the mail to deliver the news about her research and advocacy projects. Direct mail is the most efficient way to reach that relatively small but widely dispersed group of people who are likely to be interested in the disease she has set out to conquer. But Sally's got a problem: direct mail is expensive. It requires capital. And it might take quite some time for Sally to hone her message and figure out which few thousand out of millions of prospects are actually worth mailing to. While Sally's riding up the learning curve, she's probably dropping a whole lot of cash by the wayside!

Meanwhile, the National Easter Seal Society faces similar costs (the costs of "testing"—trying out new messages, new lists, and new formats). But these costs are tiny by comparison with the returns from the society's mature and well-managed direct-mail fundraising program. There's no way that Sally can match Easter Seal's cost-effectiveness. Not yet, anyway. Not until her infant nonprofit has grown up a lot.

Starting anything new costs money. There's no way around that. (And reality being what it is—rude—you can probably count on finding that your start-up costs are also a whole lot more than you expected!)

Would you expect anything different in starting a new business? If so, you won't go far in the world of commerce!

The Costs and Benefits of Fundraising Tactics

Now let's take a look at the costs we might encounter when using the ten fundraising methods or techniques listed in Chapter Fourteen.

Foundation Grants

In many nonprofits, foundation proposals are typically written, in whole or part, by program staffers. It's difficult to quantify those costs. Few charities even try.

Some organizations employ proposal writers, which means (at the turn of the century) paying salaries in the range of $30,000 to $70,000 per year. (Don't forget the benefits and associated overhead costs!)

Freelance proposal writers are also sometimes available. Some of them charge fees for work performed, usually $15 to $50 per hour. Others work on contingency, accepting a percentage of the proceeds—win or lose, a questionable practice, and one with horrific public relations potential. (If the grant fails to come in, the writer isn't paid for what may be a lot of work. If it does, the payment may raise the donor's eyebrows—not to mention yours.)

Apart from the personnel costs, however, there's generally little expense involved in foundation fundraising. Postage stamps, photocopying, and binding costs ordinarily don't add up to a whole lot.

Far more significant is the investment of time and persistence. The executive director or the chair of the board of trustees is likely to play telephone tag for weeks, trying to reach the foundation's program officer.

Corporate Support

Skillful corporate fundraisers are harder to find than good foundation grant writers. Without direct experience of corporate wiles and vagaries, an individual—for example, a poverty-stricken writer

hoping to score a buck by writing a few corporate grant proposals—
isn't likely to strike the right note. Specialists in this field are thus
more highly paid than foundation proposal writers. They may
require $25 to $100 per hour or, contrary to prevailing fundraising
ethics, they may take a bite out of the proceeds.

Fortune 500 companies tend to be formal in their procedures.
They frequently require written proposals, intimidating sit-down
meetings, and very careful forethought about what's in it for them.
But there are only five hundred companies in the Fortune 500—
and there are millions of smaller businesses.

That's why, for most nonprofits, successful corporate fundraising only superficially resembles the write-and-deliver techniques of
the foundation world. In fact, many corporate gifts are simply a way
in which some well-to-do individuals (executives, shareholders,
directors) support their favorite charities.

Sometimes the proposal is a mere formality. Occasionally it's
not even necessary. So, except in very large fundraising programs—
in which a nonprofit might employ a corporate fundraiser at a salary
of $50,000 or more—I regard most corporate fundraising as a spe-
cial case of major donor development. For the most part, it's a matter of knowing the right people—and schmoozing with them
(assuming, of course, that your case is compelling and the donor
knows it).

However, there is one increasingly common form of corporate
support for good causes that isn't charity at all. It's called *cause-
related marketing,* and it involves—unabashedly—a quid pro quo.
Usually this means that a corporation gains the right to identify
itself publicly as a sponsor of the cause. To make the relationship
known as widely as possible, the corporation spends lots of
money—from its marketing budget, not from the company foundation—for advertising, promotion, public relations, or other outreach efforts. For many nonprofits, cause-related marketing has
obvious advantages. For most, it has self-evident disadvantages, too.
In any event, the costs for a nonprofit to secure funds through a
corporate sponsorship are difficult to calculate.

Major Gifts

Most nonprofits have to plan carefully, develop solicitation plans, and work assiduously to secure major gifts. This means that the development director—or the executive director—spends a whole lot of time catering to major donors. Or you may employ one or more major-donor fundraisers (at up to $80,000 per year, sometimes much more)—just to ensure that there's no interruption in the flow of big gifts from individuals.

Major gifts rarely come out of the blue. They're the result of a long process of education, involvement, and cultivation. That's why major-gift fundraising takes so much time and energy.

For many organizations that conduct specialized major-donor fundraising efforts, donor prospect research accounts for a substantial share of the costs. Prospect research may involve a wide range of activities: ferreting out information on donors or prospects from *Who's Who*, corporate reports, newspaper morgues, or the social register; or running sophisticated computer analyses of your donor file, seeking to unmask those wealthy donors who hide behind their $25 checks. (Remember: the ability to give doesn't necessarily translate into willingness to do so.)

If you hire an outside firm or individual consultant to compile detailed dossiers on your top prospects, expect to pay $25 to $50 per hour, or about $300 to $600 per donor researched.

Computer-match services that enhance your entire donor file (often called electronic screening) come much cheaper, when measured on a per-name basis. But they usually charge several thousand dollars at a minimum, just to crank up the computer, no matter how few names are involved. A complete demographic analysis of a donor file of, say, ten thousand names could cost you $30,000 at one service bureau. Another might do a similar job for one-third as much.

You'll find lots of electronic screening options. They vary enormously in character, cost, and quality. But no matter how much the possibility appeals to the information pack rat in you, no matter how well you choose a screening service, remember this above all: you have to know what you're looking for—and what you're going to do with the information!

The Capital Campaign

The cost of a professional capital-campaign feasibility study varies widely with the scope of the campaign and the experience (and reputation) of the counsel. At a minimum you should expect to spend $5,000 to $10,000 for an exceedingly modest first venture into capital campaigndom. If you're thinking about raising millions, be prepared to spend $25,000—even $100,000—for a competent, thoroughgoing feasibility study.

And that's only the beginning. A capital campaign with a goal of as little as $1 million will require at least one fundraising staffer ($30,000 to $50,000) dedicated exclusively to the campaign.

A larger effort may involve opening an autonomous office and staffing it with hot-and-cold-running campaign staff, many of them on loan from your fundraising counsel. Don't be surprised if a three-year campaign to raise a $10 million endowment runs you $200,000 to $300,000 per year. (Costs typically constitute between 5 and 15 percent of the goal.)

Special Events

The only surefire way to make money from special events is not to spend any money to stage them. That's why, for most nonprofits, in-kind contributions are usually the key to successful fundraising events. That way, whatever you take in at the door is all profit.

Or perhaps even better, persuade someone—perhaps a local business—to underwrite all the costs of the event before you commit to producing it.

Of course, it's not always possible to minimize costs. The success of some events demands lavish spending.

You may have concluded from this experience—as I did early in my fundraising career—that special events are often more useful as donor cultivation or public relations opportunities than as revenue generators.

If you venture onto the hazardous shoals of large-scale special events, you'll probably have to contract with an outside agency, or at least an individual. Some event organizers require a monthly retainer that may range from $1,000 to $25,000 or more over several months preceding the event. Others might work on an hourly basis, charging $15 to $50 per hour at the low end and much more at the high end.

There are also event organizers who work on a full or partial contingency basis, taking a cut of the gate (up to 35 percent), possibly in combination with a set minimum fee. (Keep in mind that this practice violates the code of ethics of the NSFRE.)

In any case, be very careful. Get references. And even then, watch out! Fine print can be hazardous to your organization's financial health.

Keep this in mind, too: some consultants can be successful with certain types of special events and certain audiences but not be able to transfer their experience to your event or your organization—or to your constituency.

Direct Mail

How much should direct mail cost? That depends on what you're looking at.

If you mail appeals to a broad public in quantities of ten thousand or more, it's likely you'll spend from fifty cents to one dollar per letter seeking new members or donors. Most of the time, that amount will suffice to cover the costs of list rental or exchange, printing, postage, data processing, and the "lettershop" operation where your appeals are stuffed, sealed, and delivered to the postal service, plus any creative costs.

If you're mailing to your own donors, or to a small segment or subset of your donor file, you'll spend from thirty-five cents to ten dollars or more. As a new century gets under way, most such "reso-licitations" cost between $.75 and $1.75 per piece (including the postage). They generally cost more than letters mailed to recruit new donors because the quantities are typically too low to benefit much from economies of scale in production and processing. Reso-licitations may also be more cost-effective if you spend more on your best donors—for first-class postage and higher quality materi-als, for example.

But these are just the production costs. In an in-house direct-mail program, it's all too easy to forget the creative and manage-ment costs. Writing and designing appeals can soak up a lot of staff time. And the detail-intensive process of direct mail production management can drive the most efficient and compulsive person to tears. Frequently, overhead costs in an in-house program exceed the cost of producing and mailing the appeals!

Then there are the so-called back-end costs most people (even some professionals) forget about—until later, when the bills come due: the cost of processing the gifts, for example, and the thank-you letters that follow, plus the costs of data entry and computer time to build and update the mailing list.

National mailers—even, increasingly, regional and local non-profits—are facing the costs of government regulation. (This ap-plies to other forms of fundraising as well—but state regulators especially love direct mail, because it's easier to identify and reach direct mailers and to quantify what we do.) Registering with the state or local authorities and filing all the necessary paperwork may require many hours of someone's time. Often there are registration fees as well.

All of this helps explain why many nonprofits—including small organizations operating on lean budgets—seek professional help to get the most out of their direct-mail programs.

If you farm out the creative work alone to freelance copywriters and designers, you'll probably pay from $300 to as much as $6,000 (or even, occasionally, more) for the copy, and another $200 to $3,000 for the design, typography, and layout.

If you work with an outside firm that specializes in direct-mail fundraising, you're likely to pay a monthly fee for management and consulting services of between $1,000 and $10,000 (with much higher amounts in very large-scale programs). Two thousand to $3,000 per month is typical. Sometimes creative services are included. Often they're not.

A qualified consultant who can look over your shoulder from time to time and advise you on strategy and creative direction may cost you $500 to $5,000 per month. But don't expect that person to hang out in your office every day, or to lick the stamps. You'll probably pay that much for advice. Your own staff will have to follow through.

Telephone Fundraising

If you think direct mail is expensive, brace yourself before your first exposure to telephone fundraising costs. A contact by mail may cost you $1 to $3, even taking all your overhead costs into account. By contrast, a telephone contact with the same person can easily run $5, $10, or more.

Why does it cost so much just to pick up the phone and punch in a few numbers? Here's why.

Successful telephone fundraising requires a professional approach. And no matter how you cut it, professional help costs money. (Big surprise!) If you maintain an in-house phone bank, you can't estimate costs based only on telephone calling rates and callers' wages (both of which may indeed be zero in a small, local telefundraising program). There's a lot of overhead involved: telephones, space, caller recruitment, training, supervision, mailing gift confirmations and reminders, gift processing, and analysis. A good telephone fundraising program is never free.

If you retain an outside agency to conduct a telephone fundraising program for you—on their premises, not yours—they're likely to determine their fees in one of two ways. They'll either specify an hourly calling rate (typically between $20 and $70 per caller-hour) or ask for a set amount per contact made (usually $2.00 to $8.00 each). Follow-up and fulfillment costs may be extra. (Telephone fundraising service bureaus frequently charge $1.00 to $2.00 per follow-up letter mailed.) And don't forget your own overhead costs that enter into the picture—for example, the development staffer who spends half-time for two months maintaining contact with the outside agency.

Between these two contrasting approaches lies a broad gray area in which outside help plays a role but is less than dominant. For example, a freelancer may join your staff temporarily with responsibility for caller recruitment, training, supervision, reporting, and analysis. This outside contractor may work either from your own office or in facilities borrowed from some other organization. That might set you back several thousand dollars a month for a salary for a period of, say, two or three months. Or the consultant might ask for a percentage of the proceeds (20 to 40 percent) and split fees with the callers she recruits.

When assessing the costs of a telephone fundraising program, remember that follow-up mail is almost always essential to its success. So once again you're caught in the economic challenges of direct mail (even though you may have turned to telefundraising to avoid them).

Planned Gifts (Including Bequests)

Who understands all the complexities of gift planning? You got it: well-informed financial advisers, attorneys, accountants, and insurance agents, as well as a small but fast-growing cadre of gift-planning specialists. If you guessed that all these people come with price tags—sometimes big ones—you're right on the money.

If your organization hires a planned-giving officer, expect to pay between $35,000 and $80,000 per year. (Some earn much more.) If you follow the lead of many other organizations, however, you may choose instead to retain a specialized freelance consultant or agency. Fees charged by these folks vary so much that generalizations mean little.

Generalizing about the other costs of gift planning is also difficult. But there are common cost factors in most programs:

• Donors rarely volunteer themselves for planned gifts, unless they know that your organization is open to such arrangements. Most nonprofits have to spend—sometimes heavily and over a long period—to promote the concept. Planned giving programs generally involve year-round promotion through newsletters and targeted mailings. Such materials are available off the shelf from a great many vendors. Generic planned-giving newsletters and brochures—customized with your organization's name and logo—may cost fifty cents to two dollars apiece, depending on the quantity.

• The donor should always consult independent counsel—his own accountant, lawyer, or financial adviser—before entering into any planned-gift agreement. Inevitably, that will take some of the financial burden and legal liability from your shoulders. Don't practice law without a license! Disclaim any financial advice you might give donors or prospective donors. Often enough, an attorney or accountant on the board can lend you a hand in these matters. But your organization may still need to have a credentialed planned-giving expert on call who can help donors sort through the options.

• Your organization must consult a qualified attorney before publishing any material that promotes (or merely describes) gift-planning options for your donors. Perhaps there's such a person on your board, or even on your staff. But your friendly neighborhood legal aid attorney may be the wrong person to turn to in these matters. Tax law is a demanding field and requires specialized study.

Bequests, however, generally entail few complications and require less help. All that's needed to write an "ultimate gift" into a will is the organization's full legal name and 501(c)(3) designation. Usually all it takes to arrange that is one phone call to a lawyer with minimal legal research skills. And making donors aware of that language may be as simple as filling unused space in your newsletter, including information in thank-yous, or adding an option to the response device in selected donor appeals. In other words, there may be little or no real cost involved.

However, many bequests are anything but straightforward. They may be designed and developed over a number of years of cultivation and sophisticated tax and estate planning. Of course this doesn't necessarily require you to hire a specialized staff person. The donor's advisor will do the heavy lifting.

The generous rewards to be gained from bequests may warrant a more intensive effort, however—specialized brochures, or even a dedicated newsletter, for example, or establishing a legacy society, with all the attendant hoopla and expense of launching any giving club. Costs will vary. But at a minimum you'll need special letterhead and a club newsletter, and probably at least one event per year as well. This can run from a few hundred dollars to hundreds of thousands.

Web Sites

Theoretically, a Web site can be launched and sustained without spending much money at all. A sixteen-year-old volunteer or an avid staff member working after hours may be able to put together a perfectly respectable site, spending less than $100 to register its domain name. The cost of maintaining such a site can be similarly modest—perhaps $25 to $50 per month for a server to host the site. (Sometimes those fees are even waived.)

Unfortunately, however, sixteen-year-old volunteers and Internet-surfing staff persons rarely know much, if anything, about how to use the many interactive tools available on the Web to build relationships with donors. There's a growing body of specialized knowledge in this field, as there is in any field, and those grandiose plans to update the site twice a week and keep improving it often fall prey to distractions, such as the teenager's computer games or the staff person's crushing workload.

For such reasons, most nonprofits eventually conclude that they need professional help with their Web sites. Assistance may entail a cursory "audit" by someone with experience in on-line fundraising, or an ongoing maintenance contract that outsources most or all of the upkeep on the site to an outside firm. The costs of these services vary so widely that generalizations mean little. You could pay a few hundred dollars for an expert to take a quick look at your site and recommend changes, or many thousands of dollars a month to maintain your site and keep it fresh.

Merchandising

The financial structure of a merchandising program may involve one of many possible outsourcing arrangements, or it may be as simple as ordering a few items in bulk from a specialty catalog and promoting them in your newsletter. A word of caution, however: merchandising is business, and businesses fail more often than they flourish.

Advertising and Public Relations

Advertising and public relations can be costly. If you employ a full-time communications director, you may pay a salary of $35,000 to $150,000. If you work with an outside agency, expect costs of at least two or three thousand dollars a month. Hire an individual on an hourly basis, and you're in for $25 to $150 an hour.

If you're limited to free media, there may be no out-of-pocket costs involved. Sometimes a nonprofit can maintain a very high profile in this way—relying on press coverage, free ad space in newspapers or magazines, and public service announcements on radio or TV. However, a full-throated communications program probably involves some media costs—brochures or flyers, for example, or extra newsletters to your constituents; perhaps point-of-purchase displays in local stores; and maybe advertising space or time. All these have their costs. (Hint: they're usually not cheap!)

Now, just when you're about fed up with the subject of fundraising costs, having looked high and low to tally the costs of every aspect of your many-sided fundraising program, there's even more to take into account.

There are all those hidden costs.

Assessing the Hidden Costs in Your Fundraising Program

Listen.

You won't hear one development director in ten include staff or overhead costs when adding up the expenses of a fundraising project.

Yet these costs may actually constitute the lion's share of the true budget. And the most easily identified items in the overhead—such as salary, rent, utilities, and photocopying—are only the beginning.

Consider your tight-fisted executive director.

Ever vigilant, the CEO wants to keep the tightest possible control over the organization's mailing list, so she insists that the development department add three part-time data-entry people to keep the list up to date and crank mailing labels out of the computer.

"It's not just a matter of control," she says. "It saves us a lot of money. All we need are a couple of extra terminals, and three people at six or seven dollars an hour. Maybe we can even get some of the work done by volunteers! That's far cheaper than a service bureau that wants to charge us at least $1,000 per month in addition to processing fees."

But is that true? I say no. Penny-pinching, in this case, is probably dead wrong.

Forget the space they'll occupy and the equipment the data-entry people will use, volunteers or not. And forget for the moment the problems of recruiting, training, and supervising volunteers. (As you're probably aware, just getting volunteers to show up for work regularly may be a chore.) Even when you pay people, you've got most of the same problems. They will cost you, in many different ways:

• Somebody—maybe you, maybe your personnel department— will have to devote many hours to the myriad tasks occasioned by all the additional bodies in your department. Those tasks fall into the categories of recruiting, training, supervision, and management and are all too easily overlooked by nonprofit boards and administrators, especially at small organizations.

• You may need to secure bonding and extra insurance, and to make provisions for the tighter auditing requirements, thereby adding other, unsuspected costs.

• The equipment used for data entry will require maintenance, and so will the software, because of the inevitable bug fixes and upgrades.

• With a maximum of two people working at any given time to keep your list up to date, it's likely you'll fall behind schedule during peak periods. Fundraising events or direct-mail appeals may be delayed, with uncertain but often expensive consequences. Thank-yous will go unsent.

• And what about the unquantifiable cost that comes from adding so many people to a small office? If you've got only two or three people in the development department now, hiring three data-entry people means doubling the size of the staff. Not only that: it also means transforming the character of the workforce. In effect you'll be changing the nature of the business you're in. No longer will you be running a development office. Now it will be a development and data-entry office. That's not necessarily bad, of course. It may even be highly desirable. But it's *different*. And that difference entails consequences—higher costs among them.

What's the problem here? Somehow, that parsimonious CEO forgot that companies in the business of providing such services as data entry and list maintenance often realize economies of scale and other efficiencies. They may work far more productively than a small, nonspecialized office.

Cost-cutting can be deceptive. Sometimes, you'll actually save money over the long haul by spending a little more in the short run. You may even be well advised to consider outsourcing other functions as well, not just data entry and list maintenance. However, cost is just one of many factors in such decisions.

Consider both sides of the cost-benefit equation:

First, make sure you're counting all the real costs. Remember, this exercise isn't for the benefit of the IRS or the National Charities Information Bureau. Your calculations may never see the light of day, because they're strictly for your own good. A heavy dose of reality can carry you a long way toward a workable fundraising strategy.

Second, look for lost opportunity costs and other hidden potential losses from cost-cutting or underspending. For example, it may be cheaper not to hire a major gift specialist. But if you hire the right person, he might build bridges to those donors who can guarantee a brilliant future for your organization.

In a direct mail fundraising campaign, it costs at least a little extra to test unfamiliar mailing lists or two different versions of an appeal. Yet the money might be well spent if the test opens up new opportunities to recruit members or boost the average gift in your direct-mail program.

Marketing, advertising, and public relations campaigns may look like a burden on your budget and easily expendable. But the high public profile such activities gain for your organization could be contributing far more than you realize to your fundraising success.

Processing gifts, thanking donors, and updating your mailing list in a timely fashion will all boost your organization's income. That's because donors respond more generously if their gifts are quickly acknowledged and if the appeals mailed to them include accurate information on their whereabouts and their giving history.

For some organizations, however, the biggest of the hidden or unanticipated costs are those associated with the demanding requirements of fundraising ethics. That important topic merits a discussion all its own, which we'll take up in Resource B.

Resource B

How Much Does Ethics Cost?

Ethical conduct can be a very expensive proposition. Skeptical? Check out these hypothetical situations:

• He had been doing such a terrific job as a major gift fundraiser! With a million here, half a million there, he was bringing in really major bucks—and from entirely new donors to boot! Nobody had the slightest inclination to question his methods—until that story hit the newspaper. Turns out he had been checking out the obituary page on a daily basis, looking for men over eighty who had recently died (the older the better). Then he rushed off to romance the widow, and—well, one thing led to another. That's how, within a few short years, the orphanage has received half a dozen bequests of a million dollars or more. Unfortunately, the *Tribune* has seen to it that his last gift to the orphanage will indeed be his last. Cost: millions (including a contingency fund for the inevitable lawsuits from disappointed would-be heirs).

• Whizbang Motors has one heck of an idea! The good people at the helm of this public-spirited automobile manufacturing company will give your organization one million dollars, free and clear! That's right, no strings attached. You betcha. In exchange for the million bucks, they want absolutely nothing—except the right to use your logo in ads that announce Whizbang's generous gift. Now, what could be fairer than that?

There are several conscience-stricken trustees—and a cautious executive director—who point out that Whizbang Motors has recently been unmasked in a series of television exposés as one of the country's premier corporate criminals. Not surprisingly, their squeamishness about accepting the money carries the day. Cost: $1 million.

• She believes passionately in the value of your agency's work. She says that's why she wants to leave her job as development director of Helpmates, a rival nearby agency, and fill the vice president of development slot you've had open for nearly six months now. Of course she's asking for a whole lot more money than you're offering—$30,000 more per year, to be exact—but that shouldn't pose any problem, should it? After all, she has made absolutely clear that three of Helpmate's top five donors are personally beholden to her and will transfer their allegiance to you without hesitation once she's on staff. However, your personnel director thinks this arrangement is less than kosher, and she's put her own job on the line over the issue. You (reluctantly?) agree not to hire her. Cost: $250,000 to $300,000 per year.

• You can hardly believe it but, after all these years, that ugly old direct-mail donor acquisition package you've been mailing—well, forever—is still going strong. No matter what alternative approaches you test, the old "control" package still brings in new donors cost-effectively. Usually it pulls twice the response of any alternative package! Lately, however, the chairman of the board's finance committee has been climbing all over you about the control package. "It's not accurate," he says. "We're not doing the same stuff we were doing when we started mailing that letter years ago! No matter how much better the control might work, we've got an obligation to tell the truth in our appeals to the public!" Now the finance committee has brought the issue to a vote of the full board—and won. You've got no choice: mail something different. Cost: $300,000 per year? $500,000? More?

• It seemed like a great idea at the time. When you contracted with that woman to raise major gifts for the zoo, you had no money for new salaries in the development department. Not a cent. Zip. Nada. She was willing to work on a contingency basis, accepting 20 percent of the funds she raised, only after the checks cleared the bank. The problem is, she's done too good a job. (One thing she didn't tell you when she started: her uncle chairs the board of the foundation that has become your very biggest donor.) This year she'll clear $300,000. Her conscience is free. "A deal's a deal," she says. But that's not the way your trustees see the arrangement. Nor do many of the major donors, some of whom are becoming restive. Clearly she's got to go. Cost: unknown, but probably sizable.

• A dynamic new telemarketing agency has proposed a deal that sounds too good to be true. They'll launch a telephone fund-raising program for the hospital. (These folks really know how to raise a buck! Client testimonials are positively glowing.) The agency will hire, train, and supervise all the callers, print and mail all the follow-up materials, and handle all the computer work and gift processing. In other words, they'll do all the work—and they'll finance everything. Every single cent's worth. Not only that, they'll *guarantee* that the hospital doesn't lose a nickel. The upshot: about three months after you start work with the agency they'll bring you a check for the program's net proceeds—probably a big check. And there'll be several more checks to follow. Such a deal!

The agency insists on only one thing in return: they'll own the list of donors. But that's no big deal, is it? After all, in conducting their campaign for the hospital, they'll be using donor lists they developed for other local nonprofits. That's just the way they do business. And it works really well!

However, this proposal is greeted with derision by your executive director. She wonders what will happen to you next year, and the year after that, when you want to tap those same donors for renewed support. You'll have to go back to the same telemarketing agency, of course. They'll own the list! On those grounds alone you're forced to turn down the offer. Cost: at least $25,000—the minimum amount the hospital would need to get a telephone fundraising campaign off the ground.

(When a fundraising consultant or service bureau offers to guarantee results or to work free of charge, it's not necessarily too good to be true. Please note that legitimate, ethically run businesses sometimes guarantee their results. Check the fine print in the agreement to learn what you'll be getting into!)

These half-dozen overdrawn examples illustrate some of the more obvious ethical complications in fundraising. Other examples abound—most of them far more subtle and difficult.

Complications and subtleties notwithstanding, nonprofit organizations face three unavoidable realities:

• *Ethical conduct in fundraising is not optional.* Donors and the public at large have every right to expect complete honesty and integrity from us. Their gifts—and the tax advantages they've granted us—are reason enough.

• *Fundraising ethics make good business sense.* For practitioners in private sector agencies as well as nonprofit staffers with fundraising responsibilities, ethical conduct brings real rewards, because a reputation for integrity is a major asset: donors respond favorably over the long haul.

• *If we don't conduct ourselves ethically, government or the donor public will force us to do so,* sooner or later—sooner in certain states where laws or regulations currently in force may proscribe many of the practices that raise eyebrows—or put us out of business. In other states, where no law may yet be in force or exemptions from coverage are more broadly defined, government regulation may come only later. But it's coming.

Resource C

How to Learn More About Strategic Approaches to Fundraising

The field of fundraising is large and growing fast, and the literature on strategic planning for nonprofit organizations is copious. Any attempt to compile a comprehensive list of resources for further investigation of the themes and issues discussed in this book is doomed to failure. The biggest and best libraries that attempt to cover these fields are full of holes, so self-study requires dedication, patience, and resourcefulness.

Web Sites

The best place to start any such course is on-line. The World Wide Web is a boundless source of great (as well as not-so-great) information about fundraising and nonprofit management. Here, in the opinion of my Web-worthy colleague Nick Allen, are a few of the best sites to visit at the dawn of the twenty-first century. (Most of these sites contain links to additional on-line resources on fundraising.)

General News and Information

www.pj.org   The on-line-only magazine *Philanthropy Journal* contains excellent news and analysis on all aspects of fundraising. Their free weekly e-mail newsletter lets you know about their new stories. Updated frequently.

www.philanthropy.com   The on-line version of the *Chronicle of Philan-thropy*, this site carries stories from the print version as well as resource pages with links to many other sites. Updated frequently.

www.fdncenter.org   The Foundation Center's site.

w3.uwyo.edu/~prospect   The Internet Prospector, about donor prospect-ing on-line.

www.nonprofits.org   This site provides information on special events, annual campaigns, major gifts, planned giving, grant seeking, and fund-raising ethics. Compiled from the *soc.org.nonprofit* newsgroup, an on-line discussion about the nonprofit world.

www.malwarwick.com   The site contains hundreds of articles on direct mail fundraising, fundraising on the Internet, and related topics.

www.fundraisingOnline.com   This site provides up-to-date news and tips on using the Internet to acquire new donors and cultivate existing ones.

www.fundraising.com.uk   This British site, edited by Howard Lake, is an outstanding resource on using the Internet for fundraising.

E-Mail Discussion Lists

Note: The following information is from *www.philanthropy.com*, Web site of the *Chronicle of Philanthropy*. Used by permission.

Annual Giving   An on-line forum for discussing annual giving, main-tained by T. Greg Prince, associate director for annual giving at the Uni-versity of North Carolina at Chapel Hill. To subscribe, send an e-mail message to *listserv@unc.edu* that states in the body of the message "sub-scribe annfund [your name]." Leave the subject blank, and do not include e-mail addresses in the body of the message.

CharityTalk   An on-line forum for discussion of nonprofit management, fundraising, and philanthropy, maintained by Stephen Nill, a lawyer and fundraising consultant. To subscribe, send an e-mail message to *Listserv@CharityChannel.com* that states in the body of the message "subscribe CharityTalk [your name]." Leave the subject blank and do not include e-mail addresses in the body of the message.

Consult-l   An on-line discussion group for fundraising consultants. Topics include relations with clients, collection of fees, ethics, marketing, and strategies for working on campaigns. To subscribe, send an e-mail message to *listserv@jtsa.edu* that states in the body of the message "sub consult-l [your name]." Leave the subject blank, and do not include e-mail addresses in the body of the message.

FundClass   On-line Fundraising School, sponsored by Professional Support Software but moderated by volunteers, this list is a forum for discussion of fundraising. Each month the list focuses on a different topic. Previous topics have included direct mail, annual campaigns, and special events. To subscribe, send an e-mail message *to fundclass-request@ fundraiser-software.com* that states in the body of the message "subscribe." Leave the subject blank and do not include e-mail addresses in the body of the message. More information about the list and its archived discussions is available at *<http://www.fundraiser-software.com/ fundclass. html>*.

Fundlist   An on-line forum for discussion of fundraising, maintained by Steve Hirby, director of development at Lawrence University, and administered by the Johns Hopkins University. To subscribe, send an e-mail message to *listproc@listproc.hcf.jhu.edu* that states in the body of the message "subscribe fundlist [your name]." Leave the subject blank, and do not include e-mail addresses in the body of the message.

Fundsvcs   An on-line forum for discussing technical details of fundraising as well as the use of technology in fundraising. Topics include hardware and software issues, accounting rules, and Internal Revenue Service regulations. The list is maintained by John H. Taylor, director of Duke University's Office of Alumni and Development Records. To subscribe, send an e-mail message to *majordomo@acpub.duke.edu* that states in the body of the message "subscribe fundsvcs." Leave the subject blank and do not include e-mail addresses in the body of the message.

Hilaros   An on-line forum for discussing fundraising for Christian organizations and the Christian perspective on fundraising, maintained by
Cliff Glovier, director of donor development at Geneva College. To subscribe, send an e-mail message to *majordomo@mark.geneva.edu* that states
in the body of the message "subscribe hilaros." Leave the subject blank
and do not include e-mail addresses in the body of the message.

Print Libraries

If your blood runs cold at the thought of jockeying around the Internet
and you prefer information in black ink on paper, your first best source is
probably The Foundation Center. This national organization, based in
New York, maintains libraries on fundraising in numerous cities around
the United States. For more information, contact The Foundation
Center, 79 Fifth Avenue, New York, NY 10003, phone (212) 620-4230,
fax (212) 807-3677, e-mail <info@fdncenter.org>, Web site <www.
fdncenter.org>.

I'm told that in Canada the best library on philanthropy and fundraising
is maintained by the Canadian Centre for Philanthropy. For more information, contact them at 1329 Bay Street, 2nd Floor, Toronto ON, M5R
2C4, phone (416) 515-0764 or (800) 263-1178, fax (416) 515-0773,
e-mail <ccp@ccp.ca>, Web site <www.web.net/imagine>.

Periodicals

There are lots of English-language publications that cover (or try to
cover) the field of fundraising. A few are too technical to be of general interest (in which case a Web search or a visit to a library might
turn up a title or two, if you're technically inclined). For the practitioner eager to stay current with trends in the field, there is a handful of newspapers, magazines, and newsletters of continuing value.

Chronicle of Philanthropy.   The best source of news and general information on fundraising in print. Well-capitalized (by *The Chronicle of Higher
Education*) and professionally written, edited, and produced, the *Chroni-*

cle is a must for anyone seriously interested in keeping tabs on the field. It's a tabloid-sized newspaper—often fat with job opportunities and grant announcements—and is published every two weeks during most of the year. For more information, contact *The Chronicle of Philanthropy*, 1255 Twenty-Third Street NW, Washington, DC 20037, phone (202) 466-1200 or (800) 728-2819, Web site <www.philanthropy.com>.

Contributions   Also a tabloid-format newspaper, published monthly. Several of the regular columns offer insight and sound advice. *Contributions*, which predates both *The Chronicle* and *The NonProfit Times*, is also an especially good source of information about useful current books on fundraising. (The editors have had the good taste to feature many of my books over the years.) For more information, contact *Contributions*, P.O. Box 338, Medfield, MA 02052, phone (508) 359-0019, Web site <www.contributionsmagazine.com>.

The NonProfit Times   Published eighteen times per year. Founded by a refugee from an old-style magazine on fundraising, *NPT* regards *The Chronicle of Philanthropy* as an upstart. Some of *NPT*'s columnists—and an occasional news or feature story, sometimes one based on a national poll or survey conducted by the publisher—make excellent reading. *NPT*'s annual surveys of the top 100 U.S. nonprofit organizations and of staff salaries at nonprofits are especially informative. *NPT* is a controlled-circulation periodical and is available free to qualified nonprofit executives. Contact *The NonProfit Times*, 240 Cedar Knolls Road, Suite 318, Cedar Knolls, NJ 07927-1621, phone (973) 734-1700, Web site <www.nptimes.com>.

CASE Currents   Published monthly by the Council for the Advancement and Support of Education (CASE). An excellent source of news and advice on fundraising for colleges, universities, and private schools. A four-color magazine with high production values, its articles are typically solidly researched and well written. Available from CASE Publications Order Department at (800) 554-8536 or (301) 604-2068 or fax (301) 206-9789.

Successful Direct Mail and Telephone Fundraising™   This is a plug for my own newsletter, which (as far as I know) is the only subscription newsletter published in North America that's devoted exclusively to direct-response fundraising (mostly direct mail, telemarketing, and on-line). It's been published under various titles since the mid-1980s. In its current incarnation, launched in 1993, it's bimonthly. Response from readers has been extraordinarily positive (if I do say so myself). For a free copy, contact *Successful Direct Mail and Telephone Fundraising*, Strathmoor Press, 2550 Ninth Street, Suite 103, Berkeley, CA 94710-0142, phone (800) 217-7377 or (510) 843-8888, fax (510) 843-0142, Web site <www.malwarwick.com/successful>.

Books

There are more books on fundraising than you can shake a stick at. To find all the titles in the field that are informative, authoritative, and readable requires skill somewhat greater than shaking a stick—and I don't claim to possess that skill. Hereby, then, with due apologies to my many friends, acquaintances, and colleagues whose truly superb books I'm overlooking (including most of the old favorites), are the few I regard as the most useful for fundraising practitioners intent on mastering a strategic approach to the field.

On-line fundraising   There are two books that will help orient you to the brave new world of on-line fundraising. *Fundraising on the Internet*, edited by Nick Allen, Mal Warwick, and Michael Stein (Berkeley, Calif.: Strathmoor Press, 1996)—yes, it's one of mine—focuses on the use of e-mail and the Internet to acquire, retain, and renew donors. *The Fund Raiser's Guide to the Internet*, by Michael Johnston (New York: Wiley, 1999), is less specialized; it provides a good overview of fundraising in all its aspects on the World Wide Web.

Fundraising Overview   For an annual snapshot of philanthropy in the United States, check out *Giving USA 1999*, edited by Ann E. Kaplan (New York: Helmer N. Ekstrom and the AAFRC Trust for Philanthropy, 1999). (More on AAFRC later). Although econometricians tell me that the mathematical model this book uses to estimate total giving is less than ideal, this slim volume is the closest thing in the field to an authoritative current picture of the state of philanthropy.

Marketing   From one (too limited) perspective, the strategic approach I advocate in *The Five Strategies for Fundraising Success* is marketing writ large. In examining the challenges facing nonprofit fundraisers from a marketing perspective, I've found the most use for the *Marketing Workbook for Nonprofit Organizations* by Gary J. Stern (Saint Paul, Minn.: Amherst H. Wilder Foundation, 1990). Its companion, *Marketing Workbook for Nonprofit Organizations*, Vol. 2: *Mobilize People for Marketing Success* (Saint Paul, Minn.: Amherst H. Wilder Foundation, 1997), is also useful.

Major gifts   Many books, inspirational and otherwise, have been published to give fundraisers insight into the art and science of raising major gifts. The best I've come across is *Mega-Gifts*, by Jerold Panas (Chicago: Bonus Books, 1984). (Panas has written a number of other fine books as well.)

Membership development   One book stands out clearly here: *The Membership Mystique: How to Create Income and Influence with Membership Programs*, by Richard P. Trenbeth (Ambler, Pa.: Fund-Raising Institute, 1986). It's out-of-print but should be available in libraries.

Direct mail   There are two books on direct-mail fundraising that my clients and other readers have consistently found useful and that are widely used as textbooks or training manuals. One is my basic text on the subject, *Raising Money by Mail* (formerly *Revolution in the Mailbox*), by Mal Warwick (Berkeley, Calif.: Strathmoor Press, 1995). The other, a somewhat more detailed treatment of the fundamentals of direct-mail fundraising, is *Dear Friend: Mastering the Art of Direct Mail Fundraising* (2nd ed.), by Kay Partney Lautman and Henry Goldstein (Ambler, Pa.: Fund-Raising Institute, 1991).

Program evaluation   Two books stand out as guides to the process of assessing a nonprofit's development program. Business management guru Peter Drucker—author of many of the most celebrated books on corporate management—teamed up with former Girl Scouts CEO Frances

Hesselbein to create *The Drucker Foundation Self-Assessment Tool: Participant Workbook*, 2nd Revised Edition (San Francisco, Calif.: Jossey-Bass, 1998). This workbook is an excellent point of entry to evaluating a nonprofit organization. Much more detailed and far more specific to the day-to-day challenges facing fundraising practitioners is James Greenfield's big book, *Fund-Raising Cost-Effectiveness: A Self-Assessment Workbook* (New York: Wiley, 1996).

Fundraising fundamentals   Lots of fundraising professionals talk about the importance of developing relationships with donors. The best book I know of that explores this concept in depth is *Relationship Fundraising*, by Ken Burnett (Solon, Ohio: Heights International, 1996). Burnett is an accomplished British fundraiser and a lucid writer.

Monthly giving   Canadian consultant Harvey McKinnon has written the only book I've ever seen on monthly pledge or sustainer programs—and I was privileged to edit the text: *Hidden Gold: How Monthly Giving Will Build Donor Loyalty, Boost Your Organization's Income, and Increase Financial Stability* (Chicago, Ill.: Bonus Books, 1999). It's an indispensable tool for any nonprofit organization that wishes to start or overhaul a monthly giving club.

General   For a general treatment of fundraising, especially for small, community-based organizations, you'll find two of Joan Flanagan's books indispensable. *Successful Fundraising: A Complete Handbook for Volunteers and Professionals* (Lincolnwood, Ill.: Contemporary Books, 1993) and *The Grassroots Fundraising Book* (Lincolnwood, Ill.: Contemporary Books, 1982).

Consultants

There are thousands of people all over North America who have hung out shingles as fundraising consultants (or counsel). It's tough to know who's good and who's not other than by checking references. In any case, relatively few consultants have the breadth and depth of experience to be truly helpful to a nonprofit organization facing the sort of strategic challenges outlined in this book. Most tend to specialize in one or another aspect of fundraising, such as capital campaigns, major gifts, direct mail, donor research, board training, volunteer management, or a couple of dozen other specialties. Many cater to organizations of a particular type (such as environmental, Catholic, international, and so on) or size (often measured by budget).

Many of the best consultants have sought and secured official blessing as Certified Fund Raising Executives (CFREs) by the National Society of Fund Raising Executives or the Association for Healthcare Philanthropy. The popularity of certification, though, is of relatively recent vintage. Some old-timers (yours truly included) and a shrinking number of iconoclastic holdouts among younger folks have resisted the trend and may be the equal of anyone with extra letters after her or his name. The fundraising profession hasn't yet attained the self-regulatory power of the medical or legal fields, where certification can be genuinely exclusionary.

Another rough litmus test to determine who is capable is membership in one of several professional associations. Of course, mere membership rarely means anything. However, every legitimate trade association has its own code of ethics and business practices. If enforced, these codes help ensure straightforward, professional treatment.

Fundraising counsel   The few dozen members of the American Association of Fund-Raising Counsel (AAFRC) are, for the most part, long-established agencies that focus on institutional fundraising issues. Their bread tends to be buttered by capital campaigns and major-donor fundraising efforts for universities, hospitals, museums, and other large nonprofit entities, although some offer other services as well (and some serve organizations with much more modest budgets). For a current directory of members, contact the AAFRC at 25 West 43rd Street, Suite 820, New York, NY 10036, phone (212) 354-5799.

Direct mail   If you're seeking a firm to assist you in direct-mail fundraising, the Association of Direct Response Fundraising Counsel (ADRFCO) is the place to go. Contact them for a free copy of their *Code of Ethics and Business Practices* and for a free list of consulting agencies and other vendors at ADRFCO, 1612 K Street NW, Suite 510, Washington, DC 20006-2801, phone (202) 293-9640, fax (202) 887-9699, e-mail <ADRFCO@aol.com>.

Health care   Hospitals and other health care institutions can turn to the Association for Healthcare Philanthropy (AHP) for information about consultants specializing in advising similar and related nonprofit organizations. Contact AHP at 313 Park Avenue, Suite 400, Falls Church, VA 22046, phone (703) 532-6243, Web site <www.go-ahp.org>.

Education   Colleges, universities, and private schools have a similar resource in the form of the Council for Advancement and Support of Education (CASE), which can be reached at 1307 New York Avenue NW, Suite 1000, Washington DC 20005-4701, phone (202) 328-5900, Web site <www.case.org>.

General   The principal organization of fundraising practitioners in both the United States and Canada is the National Society of Fund Raising Executives (NSFRE). Its local chapters; local, regional, and national conferences; and a growing body of publications and other resources are worth a careful look by every serious fundraiser. NSFRE's Code of Ethics sets the standard for acceptable practices in the field. Most NSFRE members are employed directly by nonprofit organizations, but a good number of consultants have joined as well. (They can be located through NSFRE's national and regional directories.) The main office is located at 1101 King Street, Suite 700, Alexandria, VA 22314-2967, phone (703) 684-0410, Web site <www.nsfre.org>.

Index